MW01225113

An Instinct for Success

Arnold Spohr
and the
Royal Winnipeg Ballet

Michael Crabb

Toronto 2002

An Instinct for Success
Arnold Spohr and the Royal Winnipeg Ballet
© 2002 Michael Crabb

Published by:
DANCE COLLECTION DANSE PRESS/ES
145 George Street
Toronto, Canada M5A 2M6
www.dcd.ca

Editor: Miriam Adams
Reader: Carol Anderson
Copy Editors: Amy Bowring and Kaija Pepper
Proof Reader: Teresa Spanjer
Design and layout: LAMA Labs
Cover photo: Paul Martens

National Library of Canada Cataloguing in Publication Data
Crabb, Michael, 1947-
An instinct for success : Arnold Spohr and the Royal Winnipeg Ballet

Includes bibliographical references.
ISBN 0-929003-45-4

1. Spohr, Arnold. 2. Royal Winnipeg Ballet—History.
3. Ballet dancers—Canada—Biography. 4.
Choreographers—Canada—Biography. I. Title.

GV1785.S68C73 2002   792.8'092   C2001-901607-7

Arts Inter-Media Canada/Dance Collection Danse gratefully acknowledges organizational support from the Canada Council for the Arts, the Ontario Arts Council, and the City of Toronto through the Toronto Arts Council.

Le Conseil des Arts du Canada DEPUIS 1957 | The Canada Council for the Arts SINCE 1957

ISBN 0-929003-45-4   **Manufactured in Canada**

Respectfully dedicated
to the memory of
Gweneth Lloyd and Betty Farrally

Contents

Preface

Evelyn Hart

During my first year as a student of the Royal Winnipeg Ballet's professional division school, my twin sister paid me a visit. It was Elly's first exposure to the ballet world, and to Arnold Spohr. One day, while watching him rehearse the company, no sooner had we edged closer to the window of Studio One than a soloist gusted out of the room, in a torrent of tears. I didn't flinch. This was a commonplace occurrence. My sister, however, was horrified and perplexed. If this "Mr. Spohr" was such a tyrant, why did the dancers not only recover, but also come back for more?

If I think about it, I could not have given her a rational answer then. Now, almost thirty years later, the answer is as enigmatic as tha moment. From the outside looking in it seems a puzzle, but once you enter the world and mind of Arnold Spohr the answer is obvious. You worked for Arnold out of trust, love, hope and respect.

I hope in the pages that follow you will come to know and admire this man as I do. A man who is capable of caring not only for the art but also for the dancers and audiences who trust his "eye" and heart. As a dancer you worked for him because he believes in art and that the impossible is possible. You came back because in proving to him that you were capable (no easy task!), his approval and unfailing standards gave you the confidence and inspiration to excel.

Ultimately, although you were a part of his greater vision, there was an unspoken understanding that there was room for the individual and his or her dreams. As dancers, and as an organization, we set our sights not alone, but under the nurturing guidance of a leader who cherished creativity. He is a man ignited and excited by dance.

To this day, I live in dread of Arnold's honesty (you know you cannot escape the truth and the love behind it), but I welcome his judgement as well. How often has he appeared at my dressing room door, his eyes adrift and misty, and voice mellowed by what he has just allowed himself to feel. After all the years of struggle, pain and criticism, he remains the art's biggest fan.

"Dear heart", "snooky", "honey lamb", "pal", are all endearments that convey the depth of genuine affection, humour, passion and wonder that radiates from him each and every day.

Power and fury remain a vital part of his personality along with a pervading desire for justice and the urge to make things right. Arnold is a warrior. Still to this day, he has an indefatigable desire to learn, teach and share his knowledge and hard-earned wisdom. A wolf in sheep's clothing? Certainly a human being with enough honesty, cunning, courage and love for a thousand lifetimes.

Before each performance as the lights were dimming and "places" were being called, Arnold would call back to us as he left the stage, "Stick together no matter what."

He is a man who lives beyond himself.

Foreword

Kathleen Richardson

Added to the honour and pleasure I feel on being asked to write this foreword is more than a hint of obligation. Apparently, it is what Arnold wants. So …

And why not? Arnold and I have been through a lot together over the years. We have both survived the harrowing crises that regularly confound even the best-regulated performing arts groups and can look back now on undoubted successes.

As it will not generally be known and because it seems suitable for a foreword, I would like to put on record how in 1958 Arnold Spohr became director of the Royal Winnipeg Ballet.

At a board meeting a few months into my first year as president, and three weeks before the season's final set of performances in Winnipeg, the director ended his report by submitting his resignation, effective immediately. He left the room and the city. With him went his incomplete choreography for the forthcoming performances as well as the music director and the principal male dancer.

Disaster and ignominy seemed inevitable until Bob Kipp, a past president, said: "There is only one person who might possibly be able to do the job we need: Arnold Spohr. I'll call him". Arnold accepted the challenge and the results of his three-week marathon were better performances than we had seen for years. The obvious action, then, was immediately to ask him to be director.

We didn't do that because the board was divided. One faction argued that he was only a dancer, just a local boy without experience or training to fit him to be director. The other side took the view that whether he could do the job or not he had earned the opportunity to try. If that can be called reason, reason finally prevailed.

Professor John Graham, head of the production committee, and I called on Arnold. We offered him the position, which he promptly refused on the grounds that he was just a dancer, a local boy without experience or training. Decidedly dashed, we talked on until he agreed at least to consider the idea. He also said he would consult several people whose opinions he valued. He did consult them. They were unanimous in advising him not to accept. However, as all of us who have worked with him know, Mr. Spohr does not accept advice he does not agree with.

How fortunate. How fortunate that he is the sort of person he is. How fortunate the Royal Winnipeg Ballet has been to have had his years as a dancer and choreographer succeeded by so many years of his selfless, dedicated, talented leadership; and then, by his continuing overall interest and enthusiastic assistance.

By incorporating and condensing a lifetime of Arnold's copious notes, recollections, thoughts, philosophy and opinions into this biography, Michael Crabb may well have accomplished what many would consider impossible.

I look forward to reading this book, as I assume you do too. I shall not detain you from it any longer.

Everything has its time and place.

Good fortune does have to do with talent, but you have to be in the right place at the right time.

I guess I was in the right place, for the choice of becoming the director of the RWB gave me my life's work.

Arnold Spohr

An Indelible Impression

I heard him before I saw him.

It was the early spring of 1974. I was sitting in the Green Room, backstage at the Manitoba Centennial Concert Hall in Winnipeg, having a chat with Maggie Morris Smolenski, a former CBC Television personality who was then the Royal Winnipeg Ballet's director of communications. Suddenly I heard this rather high-pitched voice yelling in the distance. It got louder. "What's that?" I asked, with a note of concern. "Don't worry," said Maggie, "it's just Mr. Spohr."

I had only been writing about dance for a couple of years but already the sound of those two words, "Mister Spohr", had a special resonance. Like the sound of his voice, his legend had preceded him. This was the man who during the previous sixteen years had transformed a once struggling little ballet troupe on the prairies into an international success story, into a company with a rich, varied and often innovative repertoire. This was the man who so inspired his dancers that, regardless of what they were performing or whether it was in Moscow or Moose Jaw, it seemed their very lives depended on the outcome. Where the august National Ballet of Canada in Toronto appeared to me immaculate, stately and impressive, Spohr's RWB was joyful, friendly and fervently communicative.

I jumped to my feet and rushed to the hallway in the hope of a direct sighting. All I got was a glimpse of a tall man, wearing what appeared to be some kind of leisure suit, sandals and a large cap, disappearing through the door that leads to the stage – still yelling.

"Is he always yelling?" I asked Maggie. "Not always," she

replied. Then, after a pause, "but fairly often."

I was formally introduced later the same day. The yelling had long stopped. The man I met was almost courtly in his greeting, soft-spoken and outwardly shy. His eyes were penetrating. "So, you're from Toronto," he said, rolling out the name with slightly menacing emphasis. "That's nice." A few more courtesies and he was gone. "I hope you're coming to see the show," he said in parting, more in the tone of an order than an observation. Of course I was. Whatever the yelling had been about, its effect was galvanizing. The dancing was terrific.

It was several months later when I picked up the phone to discover Spohr on the other end. "I'm in Toronto. I'm at the Westbury. We never had time to talk when you were in Winnipeg so I thought it would be nice to meet for breakfast some morning so we can have a little chat."

As I later learned, Spohr likes to do business at breakfast. He's an early riser. He's also sharp as a needle first thing in the day. It gives him a tactical advantage over lesser mortals who are still revving up.

Our "chat" was more in the form of a monologue. Spohr ranged widely and circuitously through a bewildering range of topics, all to do with dance and the RWB. Well, not quite all. Arnold Spohr both worries about and neglects his health. He's always taking some remedy or other. At this time he was seriously exploring the benefits of vitamin supplements. He ceremoniously pulled from his pocket a collection of capsules and tablets of various shapes, sizes and colours, all bundled in cling-wrap. In the process of opening this therapeutic treasure trove he accidentally spilled most of its contents onto the floor. Once we had retrieved all fifteen items, he identified each and explained its benefits.

Occasionally Spohr's voice would become impassioned. The words tumbled out so fast that I wondered how he was able to breathe. Little clumps of saliva foamed in the corners of his mouth. Sometimes they would detach. His mood shifted dramatically, according to the subject at hand. His eyes would at one moment shoot darts. The next, they assumed an almost seraphic calm. Spohr chuckled at his own puns, or waited for a reaction to one of his famous and slightly improper double entendres. He also managed to allude to something I'd written about the RWB and with which he clearly disagreed, but he did it indirectly and without malice.

By the end of it all I was bewildered, entranced, mildly intimidated and very much in awe. This was not a man but a force of Nature. Yes, he seemed more than a little crazy, but it was the craziness of an idealist and, I was fairly sure, a manic genius.

Arnold Spohr has a knack for making you feel like an old friend from first meeting. I was added to his Christmas list that same year and have not failed to receive a card every December since. I would also get occasional postcards from RWB tours abroad and, as the years progressed and I got to know him better, there would be Easter cards, birthday cards, even the odd Valentine. In the fourteen years since his retirement as artistic director of the RWB, Arnold Spohr has often been a guest in my house in Toronto, either for a meal or to stay. He always brings surprising gifts. The gifts, in fact, began as early as September, 1975. The first was a slim, pocket-sized volume of spiritually instructive maxims illustrated with adorable colour photographs of children at play. Several of the sayings bore Spohr's own check marks or underlinings. Among subsequent gifts there have been three brass unicorns, a nestling set of food storage bowls, an enamel saucepan, countless boxes of chocolates, both volumes of Peter Mayle's memoirs of Provence, a photo-biography of Tom Cruise – one of Spohr's favourite movie stars – and an imitation Ming vase. The most important gift, however, has been his friendship. When we first met, I was a young critic. He was old enough to be my father.

Generally, critics and the artistic directors of the companies they write about maintain a respectful professional distance. Communications are formal and functional; not so with Arnold Spohr. He regards critics, however dreadful they may be, as an inevitable, perhaps even essential part of the ecology of dance. Once he is satisfied that you care about the art form and are trying to make some sort of contribution, he will embrace you with a generosity that can be overwhelming. Kindness matters a great deal to Arnold Spohr, not big demonstrative acts but little considerations that show care and understanding.

In 1982, for example, he invited me to give a course of lectures to students in the RWB summer school, the sequel to an earlier course I had given at his bidding at the Banff Centre in 1979. He was an extraordinarily attentive host. One evening he decided to take Galina Yordanova, then in her early years teaching in Winnipeg, to see a movie. He asked me to join them. Yordanova's English was patchy at best. The movie Spohr chose was Walt Disney's Bambi. I am a sucker for classic Disney animated features, sentimental though they may be. So is Spohr. However, the real reason he had chosen Bambi was not for us but for Galina. He knew the images told enough of the story that Galina's lack of English would not be a problem.

I remember, on the way out of the cinema, persuading Spohr to do a childish thing and attempt to run down an ascending escalator. We made it, only to be greeted by a rather disagreeable security guard at the bottom. "You see the trouble you get me into," he said later, giving me one of his celebrated jabs in the chest. It was one of the rare times he has called me a schnook. Usually he reserves that for dancers.

Even when he was still directing the RWB, if I were coming to Winnipeg to see a performance, he'd insist that I be met at the airport by one of his staff. Sometimes he would show up in person to drive me to my hotel. As with almost everything else, his style of operating an automobile is distinctive.

The doors of the RWB would be thrown open – class, rehearsals, the school. He'd take you out to dinner and fight to pick up the check. You were made an honorary member of the RWB family. As far as Spohr was concerned there was nothing to hide, not even his own legendary, madcap way of directing a rehearsal. In his view, the more a critic understands the better he will do his job. He did not begrudge negative criticism if he felt it was fair and informed. "People are entitled to their opinions," he would say. He was immensely trusting but could be easily hurt if one was tempted, as critics occasionally are, to use some supposedly clever but unnecessarily barbed turn of phrase. "People should show respect for each other," he would say. He meant it then and he means it still.

Arnold Spohr has always encouraged me in my writing, always been generous with his knowledge and his compliments. He has enriched my love of dance profoundly.

This book, then, is hardly a biography in the ordinary sense. How could I write a coolly objective account of the life of someone I have come to admire so much as an artist and cherish so much as a friend?

The process of writing this book began when I asked Arnold Spohr if he would like some help in completing the memoirs he had been working on for more than twenty years.

Spohr had laboured away. Pages and pages were professionally typed, annotated, revised and retyped. However, Spohr is always juggling several projects at the same time and somehow this literary endeavour was left suspended in midair.

Lawrence and Miriam Adams, the founders/directors of the Toronto-based Dance Collection Danse, knew that Spohr had been working on a book and decided it was too valuable a project to be allowed to evaporate. However, they were less interested in publishing Spohr's memoirs than in commissioning a biography that would draw on Spohr's writings and papers and also tap into other available sources to produce a rounded portrait.

To this Spohr agreed, not, I suspect, without a measure of trepidation. He correctly understood that I would be talking to people who do not necessarily agree with his interpretation of events or perceptions of his own conduct. He also knew I had my own opinions and, as a journalist, a porcine nose for scandal. Like every arts institution, the RWB has its share of skeletons in the closet and in Spohr's view, not always mine, they are best kept there.

For someone who often appears so volubly larger than life, even flamboyant, Arnold Spohr is actually a shy, humble and intensely private man. He is also neither an angel nor a saint. Not every aspect of the Arnold Spohr legend is inviolable although I think he would like it to be. Spohr possesses an almost childlike idealism. He would prefer the world to be a kind and beautiful place and the people in it to be equally kind and beautiful. It is an ideal that neither Spohr nor anyone else can fully attain.

Age and experience have engendered in him a certain resignation to the frailty of humankind. Once, quite recently, he snapped out this terrifying indictment, occasioned by some naïve remark I'd made. "Eighty per cent of people are vicious, cruel, horrible. They feed off each other like cannibals. They have no heart." It was an uncharacteristic outburst. Spohr, of course, still has a big heart and he has suffered for it along the way.

His self-identification with the RWB, its heritage, its people, is so fundamental to Arnold Spohr's being that he does not even consider his own story to be of any interest beyond its connection to the company. "What do you need to know about that for?" he would ask, whenever I posed a question aimed at his life beyond the RWB.

In a way he is right. I do not subscribe to the voyeuristic fashion in contemporary biography or assume that every public act is rooted in some psychological quirk, which, if revealed, will explain a greater truth. At the same time, it is obvious that there is much about Arnold Spohr, the inner man, that has had a profound effect on the way his outer life has unfolded. How could it be otherwise?

He is a man of principle and ideals. He is tenacious almost to a fault. He's not a quitter. He has a profound sense of duty and loyalty. To this day he loves dance with a consuming passion and wants to share the joy he experiences in it with the whole world. Age has dulled neither Arnold Spohr's basic optimism nor his belief that fate will ultimately decide the outcome. Yet, he has a sense of destiny.

Arnold Spohr and I have had many conversations during the past quarter century. Fortunately, I kept my notes. Naturally, there have been many more conversations since I began this project. I wish I could truthfully say that I know him better as a result but I'm not convinced that I do. This is not because Spohr has been evasive, although he can become frustratingly vague about events he would sooner forget. It is not even because he wants to propagate a sanitized version of his own life story. In the end I believe he remains something of an enigma, even to himself.

The best I can do is offer a portrait, albeit incomplete, of a wonderfully complex and gifted human being whose life is so entwined with the Royal Winnipeg Ballet that it has sometimes been hard to differentiate between a biography of the man and a history of the company.

I have spoken to many of Arnold Spohr's friends and colleagues, to former RWB dancers and board members, critics and other outside observers. Interestingly, quite a few people did not wait to be asked. Once they heard that I was writing a biography, they were eager to contribute. Interviews would inevitably go on much longer than planned. I got used to hearing embellished variations on a number of famous stories about Spohr. I also discovered he had inflicted a few wounds and left some permanent scars. Not all the recalled memories were happy ones.

Spohr was a hard taskmaster. His sarcasm can be withering. In anger, his language becomes corrosive. Much as he genuinely cared for his dancers and staff as individuals, he always put what he saw as the interests of the RWB first. As a leader must, Spohr learned that sometimes people will get hurt and you just have to live with that.

Almost invariably, however, even those who had bitter recollections and critical things to say would end with a version of, "I love the guy despite everything."

I have also worked my way through the relevant RWB archives and whatever personal papers Spohr has chosen to send me. Being a generally frugal person, Spohr often made work notes on the back of things. It explains why he sent along such initially puzzling documents as an ancient laundry receipt, the bill from an auto-body repair shop and a 1980's letter from a plastic surgeon in Toronto reminding Spohr of a forthcoming appointment.

As I have processed all this material I have tried to hold to a principle that Arnold Spohr has always espoused. I have tried to be honest.

Michael Crabb
Toronto, 2002

Hermine and George Spohr

Prairie Grit

In the late spring of 1959 Arnold Spohr, aided by one of many Canada Council grants he was to receive during his career, was in London, England, on a learning and reconnaissance mission. He watched The Royal Ballet rehearse, took private classes with emerging choreographer and director Peter Wright, and even managed to hire a handsome lead male from the Royal Ballet, David Shields.

Spohr wrote a lengthy account of his adventures in a handwritten letter of May 28 to Kathleen Richardson. It was Richardson who, as the Royal Winnipeg Ballet's board president, had been instrumental in securing Spohr's appointment as the company's director a year earlier. Spohr already regarded her as a friend. The letter covered a variety of topics. Its frankness reflects, from Spohr's perspective at least, the close confidence he felt the two enjoyed. It was also prophetic.

Part of the letter concerned what Spohr described as the "matter" of Sonia Taverner, a principal dancer in the RWB who wanted prime billing, ahead of her senior colleague, Marilyn Young. Spohr explained that before leaving he had already offered Taverner same-line joint billing with Young. The two had apparently agreed to this. As Spohr discovered in London, Taverner had subsequently written to Richardson to demand top billing, "or nothing". Spohr was now exasperated by the fact that Taverner, so it seemed to him, had gone behind his back in an attempt to negotiate directly with the board. Difficult ballerinas and meddling boards were two crosses Spohr later learned to bear with considerable fortitude.

In the same letter, Spohr floated an ambitious vision of the RWB as a company that should have a special place in western Canada. He had plans to establish links between the RWB school and similar institutions in Vancouver and Edmonton. The fact that in 1959 there was no RWB school, only the Canadian School of Ballet, which was still the property of company co-founders Gweneth Lloyd and Betty Farrally, did not apparently concern him.

In his grand vision, Spohr also saw Calgary and Edmonton as a potential part of the RWB's natural territory, places to establish closer bonds and raise funds. "The National", Spohr informed Richardson, "has had its own way for <u>too long.</u>" To this day Spohr has a habit of underlining or capitalizing words for emphasis. He triple-underlined "too long".

The "National" in question was, of course, the Toronto-based National Ballet of Canada. The company had made its debut in November, 1951, a full dozen years after the RWB's first performance and two years after the Winnipeg company had become incorporated as a professional troupe. A not always friendly competitiveness marked the RWB's attitude to this soi-disant "National" upstart in Toronto.

Spohr was equally exasperated by the fact that the National Ballet routinely received larger grants from the Canada Council than his own company. Defiantly, he told Richardson: "Even if I have to move Gibraltar, I'm going to try to make <u>us</u> the world's best so everybody will want to give us grants." He was equally galled to find that the National Ballet's founding artistic director, Celia Franca, her resident choreographer and artistic assistant, Grant Strate, and two of her leading dancers, Earl Kraul and Lois Smith, were also in London – "I hear on the National Ballet's expense account."

Spohr told Richardson about Miro Zolan who, he thought, would make an excellent ballet master for the RWB. Like many of Spohr's "discoveries", Zolan had been recommended by Peter Williams, the British writer and founding editor of Dance and Dancers magazine.

Spohr was a master at networking, long before the word had entered common parlance. Conscious of the relative isolation of Winnipeg, he was already displaying a genius for cultivating useful contacts throughout the ballet world. "You have to work connections. That's why I keep notes. Each connection brings a different element." If a new contact proved potentially helpful and interesting, he or she was soon added to Spohr's swelling Christmas card list. At the height of his directorship, it contained more than 900 names. Each card was personally signed, often with an appreciative message. Spohr regularly commandeered students from the school to help. New contacts, whom Spohr deemed particularly sympathetic or helpful, were adopted as friends and treated accordingly. Peter Williams, whom Spohr had met during an earlier visit to London, was one of these.

After an onerous first season as director, Spohr was acutely aware of the need to spread the workload. He told Richardson that he would be ready to sacrifice his request to expand the company to twenty dancers if he could have the Czech-born Zolan as ballet master. Zolan had highly respectable credentials. He showed every promise of being a valuable addition to the company. However, Spohr was canny enough to realise that a so well qualified ballet master might pose a threat to his own position as. Spohr offered Richardson the following bold and politically shrewd statement. "I feel as a safeguard that he knows that I will officially be director for a long time. I feel that I have given my life to the RWB and have constantly worked for its aim, as I am doing now and always will be. Money isn't the object, only a great RWB with the best people surrounding us."

Apart from the fact that Spohr was then only employed on seasonal contracts at the board's pleasure, it was a remarkable declaration, especially for someone who little more than a year before had doubted his own capacity for the job. Although Spohr claims never to have been intimidated by the position, he certainly felt the need to expand his skills and understanding. "I was continuously looking and learning, seeking new knowledge," he explained years later. "That's how you stay with it. You have to be open to new ideas and experiences." This was why he had travelled to London that spring of 1959 to study and observe.

Early on, Spohr had an innate sense that his and the RWB's destinies were essentially the same thing. This belief was buttressed by a steely determination to prove he could do a good job. Despite lingering insecurities, it was this sense of destiny that carried Spohr through what he calls "the long dark tunnel" of his early directorship. It was a survivor instinct that he attributes to his early days, growing up through the Great Depression in a large family in North End Winnipeg – "on the other side of the tracks".

Arnold Theodore Spohr is neither a Winnipegger nor a

Manitoban by birth although, as a Winnipeg Ballet souvenir programme of 1952 described, he was "a completely Western product."
He was born in the small rural community of Rhein, Saskatchewan, to
the northeast of Yorkton, only fifty kilometres from the Manitoba
border. He missed being a Christmas child by minutes; as it was, he
took his first breath very early on December 26, 1923. He was
Hermine and George Spohr's sixth child and fourth son.

Both parents were immigrants. George Ernst Spohr was born
November 3, 1877, and had come to Canada from Kassel, Germany,
in his mid-teens. By age thirty he was a seasoned itinerant
fire-and-brimstone Lutheran minister in search of a wife. In Libau,
Manitoba, his eyes settled favourably on a teenaged immigrant,
Hermine Elsa Schalme. She was born in Latvia on October 6, 1888.
Her family had moved to Canada about a decade later.

Despite the industrious couple's meagre income and peripatetic
existence, Hermine managed to produce and raise a large family
while George spread the fear of God across the prairie. Spohr's
siblings arrived in the following order: Beatrice (1908), Richard
(1912), Waldemar, known as Wally (1914), Agnes (1916) and
George Jr. (1919). The youngest, Erica, Spohr's beloved "little
sister", was born in 1926.

The children grew up speaking both English and German. Their
father also spoke, among several languages, his wife's native tongue.
When the parents did not want their children to understand, they
could conveniently switch to Latvian.

Arnold Spohr remembers nothing of Rhein. By the time he was
two the family had moved to Manitoba, to the hamlet of Waldersee,
about 130 kilometres northwest of Winnipeg. It was here that Spohr
attended his first formal English classes in a tiny one-room
schoolhouse.

He remembers their home; a white farmhouse provided by the
church. There was a shed, painted red, where his mother took the
chickens to chop their heads off. "She was the only one who had the
nerve to do it. She also chopped the wood – Mum did all the dirty
work – and played the organ in church."

In the farmyard, apart from the chickens, there were pigs, ducks,
a couple of cows – and the geese. "I used to love running after them
and watching their wings flap. I think I may have killed a few by
exhaustion. As much as possible I was kept away from the geese."

Young Arnold was, however, allowed to wander in the large garden where his mother would point out the different flowers and vegetables. He also recalls that at Easter the young ones were sent off on a hunt for carefully hidden chocolate eggs, and that his older siblings sometimes took him to a swimming hole on the nearby Grass River. The woods beyond proved less attractive. "We were afraid of them; we'd heard the story of Hansel and Gretel." In later years, Arnold Spohr was to choreograph a ballet for young audiences based on the same fairy tale.

In 1929, the family was on the move again. George Spohr was appointed minister of St. John's Lutheran Church in Winnipeg's North End. Initially, services were conducted in German. English followed some years later. However, to preserve the congregation's cultural heritage, the church offered German-language classes in the evenings for the children. As a high school student, Arnold Spohr taught these classes two or three nights a week, as well as playing the organ on Sunday and occasionally directing the church choir.

Hermine's mother had a house three blocks away at 579 Anderson Avenue. She had moved there from Libau after the tragic death of her husband, who had been cutting wood and accidentally sliced his arm wide open. He bled to death on the way to the hospital in Selkirk. It happened when Spohr was still very young; his maternal grandmother was the only grandparent he ever knew. George Spohr bought his mother-in-law's house and she moved into smaller accommodations in Winnipeg.

Despite his frequent absences, the house on Anderson Avenue was to be Arnold Spohr's home for the next thirty-five years. In winter, there was an outdoor rink across the lane at the back where Spohr and his sister Erica would skate. "She was always better at hockey than I was." There were also outings to the Palace Theatre on Selkirk Avenue where in 1938, Spohr recalls, you could get a ticket for five cents before 1:00 p.m. In the summers, there were often visits to Libau or Waldersee to stay with friends. "We used to go riding and helped with the harvest. I loved stooking the wheat. They were carefree days."

As a school kid, first at Ralph Brown Elementary and then at St. John's Technical, Spohr was an avid sportsman. He was an enthusiastic gymnast. By age ten he was dreaming of becoming a trapeze artist. He played baseball and volleyball, and had a special talent for track and basketball. Yet, he never played on a school team. "I never thought I was good enough." Spohr loved tennis and continued to play into his mid-twenties. He still enjoys watching sports on television, particularly basketball and hockey.

There were the inevitable family squabbles. Spohr's mother delegated a good deal of the supervision of her youngest children to Beatrice, who embraced the responsibility with zeal. "She used to be really strict with us. I remember she used to pull our ears. When I was twelve I'd had enough and slugged her. She slugged me back and I slugged her again. I think she was shocked that I'd defy her like that. It changed our relationship and I learned the importance of standing my ground." Agnes was less fortunate in her relationship with Beatrice. The two could not get along and the conflict finally culminated in an enormous fight after which Agnes essentially became estranged from most of her siblings. She made her own life in Ottawa where she spent her career working for the federal government. Arnold, however, did stay in touch.

Hermine Spohr, quiet, kind and nurturing, had a major influence in shaping her youngest son's character. By general account she was a fine woman, and he adored her. "Everybody loved Mom. She was the healing influence. She kept us together and sane." Hermine made good use of the additional half-lot that went with the house on Anderson Avenue. She built a secluded little arbour. She grew enough vegetables to give some to needy neighbours. "It was the Depression, yet somehow it didn't affect us that much. I think Dad only made about sixty dollars a month to care for all of us. We never expected much and most of the time it didn't feel that we were poor. Mom was a fabulous cook. We ate well. We always got by."

Spohr admits that his German father harboured at least some of the anti-Semitic prejudices that were common in his part of North End Winnipeg in the 1930's. This, however, did not stop Hermine from clearing space on the second floor of the Spohr residence in 1945 to make room for a young Jewish couple and their newborn child. "There was a housing shortage," Spohr explains. "Their new home next door wasn't finished. We all had to double or triple up in the attic for six months until their house was ready. Mom was like that, always helping everybody out."

Hermine also made sure Christmas was a festive occasion for family and friends. "There would be cabbage rolls, pirogies, ham and turkey, carol-singing, and candles on the Christmas tree to honour my father's German background." One guest at a Spohr Christmas gathering has never forgotten the real candles that burned on the tree. "I was terrified that the whole place was about to go up in flames."

George Spohr was a talented man. Apart from his linguistic skills – seven languages in all, among them Latin, Hebrew and Russian – he played the violin and wrote poetry. The house was full of books. "He was very intellectually active. We were in an environment of education, music, literature, with plenty of religion, discipline and tradition." Arnold's father loved opera and classical music. The radio, however, would be tuned to jazz only if his father was out of hearing range.

Interestingly, when Arnold Spohr eventually chose a career in dance, his father did not express disapproval, although it must have been far from what George Spohr had intended for his son. "I think," says Spohr, "for Dad it was okay because it was an art." Even so, as far as Spohr can recall, his father, unlike other members of the family, never saw him dance.

George Spohr died on December 18, 1953. He had been in decline for several years. He suffered from hardening of the arteries, but the symptoms are strongly suggestive of Alzheimer's disease. "At the end he was all skin and bone and his mind was going," says Arnold Spohr. "He didn't know us."

John Hirsch, the celebrated theatre director with whom Spohr worked in later years, believes George Spohr had a strong influence on his youngest son. As Hirsch recounted in 1983: "He inherited from his minister father the ability to inspire and to goad." Spohr may also have inherited a burden of religious guilt that weighed heavily in later years. Frank Bourman, who worked closely with him as his associate director in the mid-1970's, believes it was sometimes a struggle for Spohr to balance what he felt was morally right with the pragmatic needs of running a complex institution. "I think part of Arnold's struggle was that he was always thinking in terms of his upbringing and how good he had to be. He seemed to have a great need to let people know he was an honest person, but sometimes it's hard to go down a path on both sides."

Spohr speaks respectfully of his father but in guarded tones. "He was a fearful father. It wasn't easy to get close to him. Dad was very strict, too strict perhaps. We were brought up as good Lutherans –

baptized, confirmed, the lot – and we were always going to go to hell. We were always taught to fear the temptations of the flesh. Perhaps that's why the religion didn't completely rub off on us." Spohr says that he and most of his siblings, except for George, let religious devotion slip by the wayside in their adult years. Arnold was not alone among the Spohr children to succumb occasionally to what their father would have regarded as the sins of the flesh. He also concedes that the hell and damnation part of their upbringing, an imposed sense of humility verging on unworthiness, imparted by his father's fiery sermons, may have left lasting emotional scars.

His mother's simple religious fervour acted on him differently. "I would watch her in church, the serene look in her eyes, and I could see she was getting spiritual replenishment for the week ahead." Later, in times of crisis, Spohr found himself drawn to church, particularly if there was a choir. Even now the sound of a Bach chorale will bring tears to his eyes. "I still believe a lot in spiritual things, in morality and decency and showing respect for other people." Organized religion ultimately failed to hold him. However, a guiding commitment to the Christian precepts of charity and love – learned more perhaps from his mother than his father – has remained. "I found my religion in giving – being kind to your fellow man; not for personal gain but simply for giving. And in this you find a respect for yourself, because I try to be good and I try to live honestly."

Could the imprint, however, of a strict religious upbringing at his father's hands, the sense of ingrained guilt, have been deep enough to affect the capacity or inclination of the Spohr children to forge stable life partnerships? "Well, who can say? We were all pretty sensitive," is Arnold's laconic, deflective response.

In a family of four boys and three girls, George was the only one to marry. After a career in the RCMP, he took early retirement from the Mounties, settled in Calgary and entered the real estate business. George and his wife Lynda had two children. The daughter, Barbara, was a respected artist and photographer. Sadly, she died at age thirty-two in 1987 of Hodgkin's disease, a form of lymphatic cancer she had contracted in her teens. The Whyte Museum in Banff, Alberta, has thirty-two of her works in its permanent collection, and organized a national touring exhibition of her work in 1993. The Banff Centre presents an award for excellence in photography named in Barbara Spohr's honour.

Arnold Spohr's brother George died in 1989. His son Gregory, who now lives in British Columbia, is Spohr's only known surviving blood relation.

Spohr's brother Wally was well placed to pursue matrimony. He remembers Wally as a great womanizer. "When the war came and he joined the navy I found this pile of letters to Wally from all these different girls he knew. You should have seen what they said. It was like reading Playgirl." The possession of a uniform only enhanced Wally's appeal to the opposite sex. Even after demobilization, when Wally moved to work in the forestry industry in Ontario, his romantic escapades continued, but never all the way to the altar.

Wally, who served in both the Mediterranean and Pacific on HMCS Uganda, was not the only Spohr child to join the war effort. Beatrice signed up with the Canadian Women's Army Corps where her knowledge of German and skills as a translator and interpreter proved useful to the Allies. Richard Spohr served in the army, although he was never posted abroad.

The government required anyone over sixteen years of age to register for war service, and compulsory military service for home defence was introduced. Arnold Spohr remembers going along to "sign up" but was judged unfit on medical grounds, although he cannot recall the specific cause. "The war," he admits, "seemed far away to me."

Winnipeg was as much caught up in the war as the rest of Canada. The Christmas of 1941 was a particularly grim day for those with relatives serving in the Far East. Many Winnipeggers died or were captured when Hong Kong fell to the Japanese. Not long after, as part of an effort to sell more Victory Bonds in support of the war effort, the city was submitted to "If Day". It was a mock Nazi blitzkrieg complete with smoke bombs, explosions and scarily realistic street fighting between the "defenders", making their last stand near the Fort Garry Hotel, and the helmeted "enemy". February 19, 1942, the day of the attack, was bitterly cold. The sirens began to wail at 7:00 a.m. and by noon it was all over. The "Nazis" burned a pile of books outside the public library, fed themselves in the eighth-floor lunch room of the Great West Life Assurance Company and arrested Winnipeg mayor John Queen and Manitoba premier John Bracken. For a moment it brought the reality of war and what was at stake uncomfortably close to home. Winnipeg's "If Day" was reported as widely as Life magazine and The New York Times, yet Spohr somehow missed the excitement. Despite the family's German heritage and name, he does not recall experiencing any anti-German sentiment as he continued his teenage life in Winnipeg. His father still preached without protest in both German and English.

Many people considered Richard to have been the best looking of the Spohr brothers. He was a talented pianist and had a fine singing voice. He also aspired to be an actor and, having left home at age nineteen, sought fame and fortune in New York and Hollywood where he worked as a model. "But he was too nervous," says Spohr. "He was afraid of failure and would miss auditions; so in the end he never achieved his goal. I think that helped make me more determined, despite my own nerves, not to be a quitter but to face up to difficulties. And, you know, when you face them head on they often turn out not to be so bad after all. You just have to make the effort. You don't run away from adversity. You finish what you start."

Spohr maintains a cautious guard over the details of his own personal life. If there are skeletons in the closet, as there invariably are in most people's lives, he prefers to keep them there. "It's nobody else's business," says Spohr. "I don't pry into other people's private lives. Why should they pry into mine?"

In 1964, he decided it was time to move from Anderson Avenue. He located a bachelor flat in the Wolfe Apartments at 427 Cumberland Avenue for $90 a month and agreed to share it with his friend Jerry Shore. Spohr and Shore first met at Winnipeg's summer theatre, Rainbow Stage. Although very different in their family backgrounds, they soon became friends. "They were like real good buddies," remembers Leonard Stone, who also first met Spohr through Rainbow Stage. Stone was a fellow North Ender, who went on to a successful career as general manager of the Winnipeg Symphony Orchestra and later with other orchestras in Canada and the United States. Spohr's connection with Leonard Stone later allowed the RWB to acquire the services of the WSO for its Winnipeg performances.

Jerry Shore was a University of Manitoba graduate. He was three years Spohr's junior and came from a prosperous Jewish family in Winnipeg's fashionable River Heights. His father owned the Shore Candy Company. Jerry Shore trained as a lawyer and became increasingly involved with the entertainment industry until finally switching to the role of full-time producer and impresario in 1964. Unlike the unsophisticated Spohr, Shore was something of a dandy, was a gourmet, and drove a smart car. He was also a great opera lover.

As Shore remembers it, Spohr was babied by his sisters Beatrice and Erica. "They cooked for him, did his laundry – everything. That's where he grew to expect people to do things for him." Shore would phone the Spohr home to speak with Arnold and if Beatrice answered he knew what was coming. "What do you want to talk to him for?" she would demand. "Beatrice really resented me," Shore recalls. "Poor Arnold was hemmed in and hen-pecked."

Spohr says that he had already decided to move out in 1964 and that it was Shore who was anxious for them to share a place. They stayed in the bachelor flat until 1968, then moved next door to the newly completed Regency Towers, and a twelfth-floor, one-bedroom apartment overlooking the pool. The following year, the two agreed that each needed his own space and Shore took an identical apartment on the seventeenth floor, but they continued living in the same building for several years.

The room-mate arrangement worked well in that Spohr and Shore were often away from Winnipeg on business at different times. Spohr, who as a child was assigned his fair of household chores, contends that he has always known how to look after himself. However, from Shore's more fastidious perspective, Spohr was hopelessly undomesticated. "I'd come back from a trip and would have to clear the fridge of opened cans and pots with leftovers caked to them. Then Arnold had this habit of using teabags more than once, but he'd often forget about them and you'd find them around the place all dried out." Spohr still saves his teabags. There was also Spohr's alarming habit of smoking in bed. "I was always afraid the place was going to burn down," says Shore. Spohr eventually gave up the tobacco habit. Spohr also became a favourite of Shore's mother. "I think she grew to love Arnold more than she did me."

It was through Jerry Shore that Spohr met and befriended many of the big-name stars who played Winnipeg, notably Harry Belafonte and Liberace. Belafonte later served as an honorary RWB board member. When he was in Winnipeg, Belafonte would often come to visit Spohr and watch rehearsals. Liberace became a special friend and at least once visited the RWB's studios. He even allowed the women in the office to try on his fur coat and diamond rings.

There is a strong strain of the showman in Spohr. He loves the glitz and glamour of show business. One of his dreams – never fulfilled – was for the RWB to perform in Las Vegas, with Liberace playing the piano part in Paddy Stone's *Variations on Strike Up the Band*. Spohr did however get to tour Liberace's villa in Palm Springs.

When Spohr decided it was time to live alone it was because he felt the need for complete seclusion and privacy. The various subsequent apartments he has occupied have increasingly become sanctuaries that few ever penetrate. The latest, a twenty-second floor one-bedroom beside the Assiniboine River, commands a splendid eastward view towards St. Boniface. On the rare occasions when he proffers personal information, it is often vague and contradictory. Those who consider themselves his close friends are often surprised by how little they really know of the Arnold Spohr that exists beyond the realm of dance.

There has certainly been romance and heartbreak in Spohr's life. In 1977 he told Lawrence O'Toole, then dance critic of The Globe and Mail, that he had loved and lost three times and, as Spohr put it, "like everybody else got depressed about it." Spohr candidly admitted to O'Toole that his salvation was the RWB. "I had the company to keep me bouncing back. When I threw myself into the business of running the ballet, the sun meant something to me again. So there you have it – my career has been one big sublimation."

In more recent years, Spohr has admitted that he deliberately shied away from intense personal attachments after a particularly traumatic romance in his early twenties. He did not fully succeed. His is a trusting, passionate nature. Spohr is a man of sudden enthusiasms, of kindly, nurturing instincts and powerful emotional needs. He may have tried to guard his heart but it has remained susceptible. One former RWB board president goes so far as to suggest that a history of the company in Spohr's reign could be usefully organized around its director's successive and varied "amours" – platonic or otherwise. In Spohr's mind, however, there has only been one true romance in his life, one true partner. And that, of course, is dance.

BY <u>ERIC SKIPSEY</u>

Seduced
by Dance

Dance entered Arnold Spohr's life relatively late. It was his sister Erica who, in January, 1942, persuaded him to escort her to Winnipeg's Civic Auditorium to see the visiting Ballet Russe de Monte Carlo. It took some doing. Initially Spohr refused, so Erica asked their mother to persuade him. Again he resisted, causing Erica to fly to her room in despair. In the end, Spohr relented. "Erica went through a great song and dance to get me there, tears and everything. She literally dragged me there." Like a lot of teenaged boys, Spohr thought ballet was for sissies. For an eighteen-year-old guy from the North End who revelled in manly athletic pursuits, going to see the ballet was not the sort of thing you boasted about to your school chums.

Spohr's seduction, however, was instantaneous. He fell in love with ballet that evening and has never fallen out of it. "I went to keep Erica happy and the next thing you know, I've joined the Magic Kingdom." As his sister recalled years later: "He was in a daze, in a trance." The way the Ballet Russe dancers projected, the vivacity and force of their communication with the audience, was something Spohr would never forget. It was art, it was athleticism, it was entertainment, it was pure theatre. "They had Leonide Massine, Tamara Toumanova, Tatiana Riabouchinska and Frederick Franklin, people who really knew how to project as well as dance. They were all consummate artists. The whole aura hit me like magic. I came out of that performance more enthusiastic than my sister."

The Ballet Russe de Monte Carlo had come to Winnipeg under the banner of the great Russian-American impresario Sol Hurok.

1942 was also the year Agnes de Mille created *Rodeo* for that company. If anyone had suggested to Spohr that twenty-three years later he would be leading the Winnipeg Ballet in a succession of North American Hurok tours, or that *Rodeo* would one day become a mainstay of the RWB's repertoire, he would undoubtedly have said, as he often does: "You've got to be kidding."

In 1942, Spohr had not yet seen the Winnipeg Ballet or thought of taking a dance class. As much as the Ballet Russe thrilled him, it did not immediately occur to Spohr that dance held the key to his future. He was still testing other waters.

Spohr's father had initially hoped that his youngest son might follow him into the ministry but, when that idea met with filial resistance, George Spohr decided Arnold should become a school-teacher. So, off Spohr obediently went for a one-year programme to acquire a teacher's certificate in physical education and music. He helped pay for his tuition by working as a clerk in a local abattoir. For Spohr the prospect of facing a classroom of rambunctious students was even less savoury than counting pigs en route to the meat counter. It set his nerves on edge. He managed to earn his teacher's certificate but, after a week of classroom practice, decided teaching school was not the profession for him. "I didn't like the school system. It was very restrictive and not attuned to the real needs of the students. If I'd become a schoolteacher I'd have been like Robin Williams in that film Dead Poets Society. I was too idealistic."

Then there was Spohr's ongoing love for the piano. His sister Beatrice originally sent him off for piano classes when he was twelve years old. Spohr displayed an aptitude that suggested the real possibility of a performing career. His teacher, John Melnyk, was so confident of his pupil's prospects that at one point he even gave Spohr free classes. Spohr, however, went to pieces before an audience. "If I had to perform in public I'd be sick with nerves. I'd look down at the keyboard and I'd see double. All the white keys would start dancing with the black ones. It was terrible."

Spohr did not give up. He kept studying and climbed his way through the syllabus of the Toronto-based Royal Conservatory of Music until he was finally an associate and by 1946 qualified to put the letters ARCT after his name. Colleagues from Spohr's early days at the Winnipeg Ballet remember him occasionally sitting down at the piano and playing beautifully but, by the time he became the company's director, Spohr had largely abandoned the keyboard. When he left Anderson Avenue, his grand piano stayed behind and was eventually sold. Spohr never acquired another.

Spohr's years of piano study were far from wasted. They gave him a technical understanding of musical composition that fed into his work as a choreographer and ballet director and were his own personal proof that hard work is rewarded. He never forgot John Melnyk. When Melnyk and his wife Irene celebrated their golden wedding anniversary in June, 1998, Spohr sent a warm message of congratulation. "You made music alive for me," he told his former teacher, "taught me the values of hard work, discipline, concentration, and never giving up. You added to my roots and foundation to carry me on life's way, to believe in myself and be successful."

It was more than a year from his fateful visit to the Ballet Russe before Spohr entered a dance studio. In the meantime he had begun attending Winnipeg Ballet performances and enjoyed them, but not sufficiently to tempt him into becoming a dancer. "I was reticent. It was a new world to me. After all, it wasn't the natural thing to do, what with my religious upbringing and so on."

Spohr's own account of what prompted him to sign up for classes at the Canadian School of Ballet has varied over the years. In one version it was his brother Richard who convinced Spohr that he needed to acquire some social dancing skills. At other times Spohr has suggested that it was his own growing enthusiasm that drew him, although he concedes that he needed encouragement from Erica and Richard before he felt confident enough to study dance. In the end, it was Richard who made all the arrangements. Spohr was certainly aware that the Winnipeg Ballet had emerged from the Canadian School of Ballet some five years before and that to become a student was a potential route into the company.

The school's doughty proprietors, Gweneth Lloyd and Betty Farrally, ran it as a commercial enterprise. For the two immigrant Englishwomen, it was a way to support themselves while they pursued their higher but decidedly unprofitable calling, running a ballet company. Lloyd and Farrally hoped to recruit dancers for the Winnipeg Ballet from the school. Anyone with potential was quickly roped in. At the best of times, young men were especially welcome. In wartime they were at a premium.

37

Like all the Spohrs, Arnold was tall – six foot three. With his slender body, long elegant legs, fine features and blond hair it was hardly surprising that Spohr became a target for the ambitious ladies. He was not an unwilling one. "When I started taking dance classes," says Spohr, "it was like the glove fit. It was so athletic, so musical and it had this added artistic thing that made it a real challenge." Although he kept it a secret from most of his friends, Spohr quickly graduated from ballroom to ballet and within three months was dragooned into the corps of the Winnipeg Ballet, making a tentative debut in Lloyd's new work for the 1943 fall season, *The Planets*. He vaguely recalls green tights and the clenched fist he was expected to hold up in a symbolic gesture of warlike strength. Spohr also got to lift a girl for the first time. The ballet was *Zigeuner*, a gypsy-themed work by the talented Winnipeg-born dancer/choreographer Paddy Stone. The girl was Margaret Hample. In comparison with today's emaciated ballerinas, she was a big girl. "I used to rib her about it," says Spohr. "My right shoulder is naturally slightly lower than the left, but I used to tell her it was because of her sitting on it."

As he freely admits, Spohr was not ready to perform but, in typical fashion, was determined to work hard and prove himself, particularly since, so it seemed to him, Lloyd and Farrally showed more interest in another young student in the same class. "It was a challenge to have them notice me, so I had to rise to the occasion." He officially became a member of the company in 1944.

Within two years, Spohr had become a leading dancer and in the course of a decade created roles in more than twenty ballets. Until the early 1950's, Lloyd choreographed almost the entire repertoire. She was very good at working to her dancers' strengths. Farrally was the resourceful ballet mistress who fleshed out and interpreted Lloyd's choreographic intentions. "I got roles because they needed me," says Spohr. "Over the years our leading men, like Paddy Stone left for New York, then David Adams was off to England. So things were just thrown on me. I never really became a good dancer because of my late start, but somehow I looked classical. It fooled other people sometimes, but not me." Many years later, in the midst of a rehearsal in which the dancers were having trouble living up to Spohr's expectations, he began berating them: "When I was on the boards I could do it all." Then, turning to his colleague Frank Bourman, with a wrinkle of a smile, added quietly, "except dance."

Despite his chronic and sometimes strategically deployed habit of self-deprecation, Spohr was by all accounts a better dancer than he allows. His late start did not deter him from getting a solid classical grounding. There were few performances during his early years in the Winnipeg Ballet. Spohr had time to work his way diligently and relentlessly through all the Royal Academy of Dancing examination levels until finally attaining both his Advanced and Solo Seal with honours. He could not find a pianist capable of playing Chopin's Revolutionary Etude, the music for his solo demonstration in the final examination, so he decided to be his own accompanist and made a taped recording of it.

Meanwhile, Spohr was still earning a modest living as a piano teacher. "On Fridays after rehearsal I'd take the bus eighty miles to Winkler to teach until late. Then I'd teach all day Saturday and catch the late bus back to Winnipeg. Sunday I'd be back in rehearsal because that was the day when most of the dancers were free. All of us had jobs or were in school. We were pioneers."

However hard-pressed the Winnipeg Ballet may have been to find capable men, Spohr had real assets, especially his looks – "legs and profile in the Barrymore tradition," as one critic described them. Anatole Chujoy, the influential Latvian-American critic and editor/publisher of the American journal Dance News, first saw Spohr dance in 1949. He told his readers that Spohr "looks like a young god and dances with ease and freedom. He has an excellent elevation and is a very good partner." Brian Macdonald, later to become a renowned choreographer, was writing for the McGill University newspaper in 1950. He remembers Spohr as "this blond semi-Viking presence." Macdonald also noted that the night he saw him dance in Montreal, Spohr was off his pirouettes.

Spohr's technique was indeed limited. Pirouettes were a particular challenge. His feet were questionable – one colleague uncharitably remembers them as "these great flat plates" – but Spohr knew how to make his ballerinas look good. "Mr. Spohr's lifts are something to see," wrote another Montreal critic when the company returned there in 1953. Spohr prided himself on his partnering ability. When the celebrated British ballerina Alicia Markova and her equally famous partner Anton Dolin brought their touring company to Winnipeg in 1949, Spohr took the opportunity to study partnering with Dolin. To his embarrassment, Spohr had to fight off Dolin's unsubtle attempts at seduction. "He invited me to lunch and when I got to the hotel and called up he said he wasn't ready and to come up to the room. When I arrived he was standing there in an open bathrobe and asked me to give him a massage. I was shocked. I was so green."

"Arnold was a wonderful partner," says Marilyn Marshall. As the fifteen-year-old Marilyn Young, she made her official debut with Spohr in *The Nutcracker* pas de deux. "In order for her to gain experience," says Spohr, "they used to put her on in matinees so she soon got the nickname 'matinee Marnie'."

Jean Orr, another of Spohr's partners, concurs. "You always felt secure with Arnold. He was so reliable and attentive and kind." As Jean Stoneham, Canada's first Giselle, she had left the Ottawa Ballet Company in 1951 and opted to join the Winnipeg Ballet rather than the newly formed National Ballet of Canada in Toronto. At the time she arrived, Spohr was mainly paired with Jean McKenzie. He also was required, because of his height, to partner its tallest ballerina, Eva von Gencsy.

Von Gencsy had arrived in Winnipeg as a government-assisted immigrant in 1948. Her ballet training in Budapest had been heavily Russian and von Gencsy had difficulty adapting to what she saw as the Winnipeg company's more precise Royal Academy of Dancing style. "Arnold tamed me. I sometimes took risks and if it worked well it was fantastic. Arnold was not like that. He was the perfectionist. But he was a very wonderful teacher for me and always wanted us to dance the best we could. We used to speak German together but he would bug me about my thick Hungarian accent when I spoke English and get quite annoyed with people who said they liked it. 'Don't tell her that or she'll never get rid of it,' he used to say." Spohr's other complaint was von Gencsy's fluctuating weight. "If I'd gained a few pounds I'd never hear the end of it. Now when he sees how slim I am he asks why I couldn't have been like this when we danced together."

Apart from his prowess as a partner, Spohr also had a marked gift for characterization and comedy in such Lloyd ballets as *An American in Paris* and *Pleasure Cruise*. In his bearded makeup, he left an indelible impression on those who saw him as The Stranger in Lloyd's *The Shooting of Dan McGrew*, her popular 1950 inter-pretation of the famous Robert Service poem. Spohr's dramatic entry in snowshoes through the saloon door, pursued by an ample blast of artificial snow, was routinely a showstopper. "I loved ballets like that," says Spohr. "When you're in pure classical work you're totally exposed, but in dramatic ballets you can escape into the character. I loved being able to become someone else."

By this time Arnold, or "Arnie" as he was familiarly known, had also acquired the nickname "The Gold Dust Boy". It started in 1948 when Spohr created the role of Apollo in Lloyd's self-descriptive ballet, *Allegory*. "Apollo is supposed to be so striking, I decided to put a bit of gold dust in my hair. Apparently it was very effective. Everyone kept saying how stunning I looked, so I kept on doing it."

Spohr was more than a dancer. He exuded an infectious enthusiasm and confidence in the company's prospects. As a company programme of 1952 noted, " ... his intense interest and his loyalty have established him as a mainstay in the institution."

Years later, when Spohr had all but retired from the stage, Frank Morriss of the Winnipeg Free Press offered this assessment: "As a dancer he never has [been], and never will, be great. He started too late, but he had behind him a background of music and a love for what he was doing for the ballet. He was a valuable member of the company because he had presence and taste in whatever he did."

• • •

The Winnipeg Ballet in which Arnold Spohr first danced in 1943 was still an amateur club. It was not until March, 1949, that it reconstituted itself as a professional company. Even then, seasons were short. There were times, especially in those early years, when Spohr wondered if he had made the right choice of career. "I used to debate whether I should stay or not. It was a very insecure job then."

Everyone in the Winnipeg Ballet had to pitch in and lend a hand, whether it was pasting up posters, soliciting donations, selling tickets or washing the studio floor. In 1945 the company began to tour. In February it appeared in Ottawa and in November travelled to Regina, Saskatoon and Edmonton. The atmosphere on tour was jovial and adventurous. The experience of performing in often ill-equipped theatres was constantly eventful. Tour mishaps soon became the stuff of legend. Bad stage floors were commonplace. Animals were another thing. During one memorable performance in Saskatoon, a small dog somehow managed to wander on stage during the show and the dancers quickly adapted the choreography to encourage it back into the wings. The Winnipeg Ballet was a happy family, but that did not mean it was without discipline. David Yeddeau, the company's manager and stage director, made sure of that.

Yeddeau, a multi-talented and stylish young Winnipegger with theatre in his blood, had been introduced to Lloyd and Farrally soon after they launched their Ballet Club in 1938. He was only twenty years old at the time, but Yeddeau was already deeply immersed in the city's lively amateur theatre scene. Although he appeared as an actor, Yeddeau's greatest gifts were behind the scenes. He understood how to put a show on stage, how to make it look good, how to manage a company and how to give the entire enterprise a gloss of true professionalism. "David believed in glamour, theatricality and discipline," says Spohr. "He could do costume and scenic design, write publicity releases and scenarios for ballets, he could both teach and do makeup. He was altogether a thoroughly practised expert in the theatrical arts."

In lending his experience to the two Englishwomen's efforts, Yeddeau was to have a major role in the company's early development. In Spohr's assessment, Yeddeau's participation was crucial. He speaks of Lloyd, Farrally and Yeddeau as a "Holy Trinity" who, by combining their talents, were able to achieve remarkable results. "They gave me a sense of discipline, dedication and integrity. They were working from raw material but they had this genius to make it look good. This was my background."

Yeddeau's influence on Spohr was almost as great as Farrally's. Yeddeau was a showman and even if the Winnipeg Ballet was only a group of high-spirited young people, he expected its members to observe professional standards of discipline and comportment. "David taught me the discipline of theatre. He was very strict with us. He had a particular thing about punctuality. If I was ever five minutes late for a bus or train call he would wipe the proverbial floor with me."

Spohr had been raised to respect authority, but this did not always make it easy for him to accept discipline. "I'd grit my teeth but I'd speak reams with my eyes. There were times I could have killed." In those days nobody had heard of "anger management". There were no self-help books on the subject. Even if there had been, it is unlikely Spohr would have found them effective. Volatility is part of his nature. "When I get upset I can feel the rush of anger. It's like a fluid that fills my body from head to toe. In moments like that I try to turn very quiet, but my being exudes animosity and can permeate a whole room. Even so, it wears off in time and the next day I won't even remember what it was all about."

Lloyd's philosophy of ballet as a popular art and her carefully eclectic approach to programming left an indelible impression on Spohr. Similarly, Spohr never forgot Farrally's practical approach and willingness to put her hand to anything. It was her generous soul, however, that left the strongest mark on Spohr's personality. "Betty was one of the most unselfish people I have met; a generous, thoughtful, loyal friend. She always had time for me. She knew how to cheer me up and taught me how to perform and project. She always rehearsed me diligently, bringing my technique up to strength and developing my understanding of comedy, character and style. She was the power behind the scenes, the one who'd get the show on."

Farrally was a den mother to all the dancers. She would not put up with nonsense from anyone and could have a sharp tongue. Frank Morriss wrote in 1953 that Farrally "behaves like a rather frenzied football coach, alternately cheering and screaming at her dancers." For all the screaming, Farrally's personal warmth endeared her to the dancers. Her cooking alone would have been enough to win the lasting devotion of as dedicated a trencherman as Spohr. "Sunday dinners at Betty's were very special. She fed all the lone and hungry dancers our steak of the week or our roast of the month. We devoured them ravenously. Her joyful, positive spirit kept us all going."

Spohr's time as a dancer with the Winnipeg Ballet straddled most of the important events in its early development. He was part of the increasingly ambitious tours that helped establish the company's national presence, a presence and prestige much enhanced by the advent of the Canadian Ballet Festival Association in 1948.

The festival idea was born of disappointment. In 1947 there had been ambitious plans for the Winnipeg Ballet to travel to a festival of new choreography in Copenhagen, but the company had been unable to raise the necessary funds. Later that summer David Yeddeau was in Toronto and met Boris Volkoff, a Russian émigré teacher who had settled in the city in 1929 and established a thriving ballet studio and, by 1938, his own Volkoff Canadian Ballet. Before this, Volkoff had already taken a group of his students to a dance festival associated with the 1936 Berlin Olympics. It turned out that Volkoff had also hoped to take his troupe to Denmark in 1947. As Volkoff and Yeddeau commiserated, it occurred to them to hold their own

Canadian ballet festival. Despite a devastating Winnipeg flood that threatened to submerge the project, the first festival took place in the city the following spring.

Spohr still recalls his nervousness the night of Saturday, May 1, 1948, when he danced leading roles in two Lloyd ballets, *Chapter 13* and *Etude*, before a capacity crowd that included the Governor General, Viscount Alexander, and his wife. By the end of it all, Spohr was a gasping heap in the wings.

The following year, the Winnipeg Ballet became a major hit at the Second Canadian Ballet Festival in Toronto, inadvertently spurring a group of local ballet patrons to lay plans for a "national" ballet company – before the Winnipeggers ran off with the title.

Since the Canadian Ballet Festival Association had been founded in a spirit of goodwill, it would hardly have been seemly for the Winnipeg Ballet to object to an expansion of the budding dance community. In any case, the board of the newly incorporated Winnipeg Ballet seemed more concerned with fiscal restraint and sticking close to home than with taking a national lead. When Lloyd moved to Toronto in the fall of 1950, it was ostensibly to open another branch of the Canadian School of Ballet, the profits from which would help support the widowed Farrally and her young son. In Spohr's view, however, Lloyd also was eager to know what the Toronto group was hatching and her move was designed to place her close to the action. "She thought she had bigger fish to fry," says Spohr.

Spohr himself was witness, if only peripherally, to the complex chain of events that led to the founding of the National Ballet. During the Second Canadian Ballet Festival of March, 1949, he was billeted with Aileen Woods in Toronto's respectable, old-money Rosedale neighbourhood. Together with two other women, Sydney Mulqueen and Pearl Whitehead, Woods was interested in the prospect of establishing a truly "national" ballet company in Toronto. Spohr remembers Woods sitting him down one afternoon and asking him about the development of the Winnipeg Ballet and what was needed to start a company. "I was encouraging and, although I was only a dancer, I gave her what advice I could."

Both Boris Volkoff and Gweneth Lloyd, however much the latter disavowed any such ambition, were obvious Canadian contenders to head such an ambitious project, but the Toronto group was urged to seek someone from outside the country. On the advice of Ninette de Valois, founder of what became Britain's Royal Ballet, they invited one of her former dancers, Celia Franca, to accept the challenge.

Franca flew from London to Montreal in 1950 to observe the Third Canadian Ballet Festival and saw Spohr dance there. She returned to Canada early the following year with a commission to conduct a feasibility study, but with the clear intention of launching a company. Lloyd, if she had ever seen a role for herself in the new venture, was effectively out of the picture. She continued with her school in Toronto and returned to choreograph two more ballets in Winnipeg including, in 1952, what many consider Lloyd's greatest work, *Shadow on the Prairie*. According to National Ballet records, Franca asked Lloyd to choreograph for the company, but Lloyd said she was too busy. "I think," observes Spohr, "that Gweneth was really put out when Celia arrived on the scene."

Franca's intention was that the Canadian National Ballet, as it was first known, should draw its talent from across the country and so, in the summer of 1951, she conducted an audition tour of Western Canada. According to a number of accounts, Spohr was sent out from Winnipeg on a pre-emptive mission to hire dancers ahead of Franca's tour. He says the story is total nonsense. "Why would I have been auditioning dancers for the Winnipeg Ballet in 1951?"

Spohr does not recall having met Franca during the Montreal Festival of 1950 but certainly spoke with her when she came to the studio of Mara McBirney in Vancouver where Spohr was teaching in the summer of 1951. He did not audition for Franca then or later, when she visited Winnipeg. Although he recalls being told that Franca was interested in him, she never directly asked Spohr to join her Toronto company. In any case, he had already resolved to remain in Winnipeg. "I felt a loyalty to Gweneth and Betty and in the end it was where I felt happy." Also, by this point, Spohr, with two ballets to his credit, had a promising emerging career in Winnipeg as a choreographer.

For some time, Lloyd had been prodding Spohr to create a ballet. He felt no particular urge in that direction, but Lloyd kept pushing. His first work was given its premiere May 2, 1950. Logically enough, Spohr called it *Ballet Premier*. He recounted its genesis in a 1978 interview with Casimir Carter, a charter member of Lloyd's original Winnipeg Ballet Club who had gone on to become dance critic for the

Winnipeg Free Press. "It all began almost by fate. Gweneth said I should do a ballet and so I said 'okay, I'd love to.' But then I had this fear of whether I was going to be good enough. All my life I've had this fear." Spohr kept putting it off until he finally discovered music that inspired him to action. It was Mendelssohn's Piano Concerto No. 1 in G Minor. He rushed to tell Lloyd the good news and began planning his debut work. "It was as simple as that. I'd made a commitment and I'm always as good as my word."

Ballet Premier was a music visualization without plot, for a lead couple and a corps of six women and three men. As a programme note explained, the work "follows the style of The Imperial Russian Ballet and uses the classical technique in modern idiom." At this stage in his career, Spohr's direct exposure to the classics was limited. Although Lloyd had created a few "classical" ballets, they were hardly in the grand Petipa style. It was only after he had created *Ballet Premier* that the company sent Spohr to New York to take a special course in "traditional classic ballet" with Mary Skeaping, then ballet mistress for the Sadler's Wells Ballet in London. Spohr studied excerpts from *Swan Lake* and *The Sleeping Beauty* with Skeaping and returned to stage them in Winnipeg.

Ballet Premier was judged to be an auspicious choreographic debut and earned high praise from an influential balletomane and rising star of the National Film Board of Canada, producer Guy Glover. "He was a great fan," says Spohr. "It was because of him we got to take it to the Canadian Ballet Festival in Montreal." In a report for Canadian Art magazine, Glover declared that Spohr was "the first native Canadian, in fact, to compose a completely realized ballet." Glover went on to express the hope that other Canadian companies would be able to make use of Spohr's talent "before he has been snatched away to London, New York or Paris." When Anatole Chujoy saw *Ballet Premier* in Montreal he declared that Spohr "has the makings of a very gifted choreographer."

Ballet Premier was often revived. The Winnipeg Tribune's S. Roy Maley summarized its appeal as "a ballet to delight the mind and heart." Sonia Taverner, who joined the company as a young dancer from England in 1956, remembers *Ballet Premier* as a great programme opener and as a ballet that all the principal dancers wanted to perform. Thirty-eight years after its premiere, Spohr revived the work for the last time during his final season as director, making only minor changes. The ballet's inherent craft and musicality were clearly evident, even if its attempt to evoke some of the grandeur of ballet classicism in nineteenth-century St. Petersburg appeared quaint. The dancers of 1988, however, did not appear fully committed. They performed well enough on the surface but their hearts were not in it.

The sets and costumes for *Ballet Premier* were by Grant Marshall. His designs picked up on the Imperial Russian resonance of Spohr's choreography. There were asymmetrical, overlapping swags, a couple of candelabra, and short tutus for the ladies. Although *Ballet Premier* turned out to be the most enduringly popular of Spohr's ballets, Marshall remembers the work as "just okay". When the distinguished American critic, Walter Terry, saw Spohr's ballet in 1964 at the Jacob's Pillow Dance Festival in Lee, Massachusetts, he described it as "serviceable" in that the work introduced the company "agreeably on a classical plane". Grant Marshall considers Spohr's second work, *Intermède*, to have been much more sophisticated.

Marshall, who was later to marry ballerina Marilyn Young, was part of a vitally important contingent of hard-working Winnipeg Ballet supporters from the University of Manitoba. The key figure in this valuable alliance was John Russell. He was a New Englander who had come to Winnipeg as a young man to lecture at the university. By the time the Winnipeg Ballet was emerging, Russell was dean of the School of Architecture and later went on to become one of the first board members of the Canada Council. Russell had a fervent interest in the theatre and became deeply involved with a wide range of local theatrical endeavours, including the ballet. "People tend to forget," says John Graham, one of Russell's students, "but it would be impossible to overstate the importance of his contribution right from the beginning." Russell expected his students to become involved in stagecraft and made it more attractive by rewarding their unpaid services as set builders, painters and designers with academic credits.

Graham's first Winnipeg Ballet designs were for *Intermède*, given its premiere in the Winnipeg season of May, 1951. This time Spohr went back to the eighteenth century for his music, to Neapolitan composer Domenico Cimarosa's Oboe Concerto in C Major. Like *Ballet Premier*, the new work was a visual realization of the score, except this time Spohr placed greater emphasis on depicting what he described as "the interplay of musical moods". He thought of it as "a bravura type of ballet and a direct contrast to all that is lyrical and quiet." Although the casting included three principal leads, one man and two women, along with a supporting corps of four women and two men, Spohr tended to deploy the dancers as an ensemble, without obvious distinctions between ranks. The vocabulary was classical but Spohr's objective was to give his ballet a contemporary flavour. Graham costumed the women in tights and leotards with curving patterns that echoed his striking, abstract painted backdrop. The men were similarly costumed. "The ballet," wrote Maley after a later revival, "progressed with a serenity and ebb and flow of pattern that delighted the eye."

Ballet Premier and *Intermède* led some observers, Chujoy among them, to find similarities between Spohr's work and that of the great Russian-American choreographer and founder of New York City Ballet, George Balanchine. Spohr insists that at this point he had never seen Balanchine's work. In fact, he says *Intermède* was partly inspired by British choreographer Frederick Ashton's 1946 abstract masterwork *Symphonic Variations*, which the Sadler's Wells Ballet had included on its North American tour early in 1951. "I think it was Chicago where I saw it," says Spohr. It was, however, the Balanchine comparison that stuck and which Spohr claims was one of the reasons he did not pursue choreography as a career. "I thought to myself, who needs two Balanchines?"

The Winnipeg Ballet, however, was not yet willing to let Spohr discard his choreographic talent. For the fall season of 1953 he created an allegorical ballet called *Children of Men* set to César Franck's 1884 Prelude, Chorale and Fugue for Piano. John Russell's set design allowed the action to unfold on two levels while Spohr's choreography symbolically pitted the goodness of Faith and Light against the Power of Darkness. "It just didn't work the way I'd hoped," says Spohr. It was an opinion with which most concurred. The work was never revived.

Spohr was not to create any further works for the RWB until he became its director, by which time he had also extended his choreographic activities into musical theatre and television.

• • •

Early in 1953 the Winnipeg Ballet embarked on an ambitious cross-Canada tour. By the time it returned home the company had an impressive new title. No one remembers exactly when the idea of adding "Royal" to the company's name first surfaced. The troupe was certainly both conscious and proud of its historic close encounters and brief brushes with the British monarchy.

In 1939, even before it could truly claim to be a company, Lloyd and Farrally's Winnipeg Ballet Club was included in a city pageant at the Playhouse Theatre in honour of the visiting King George VI and Queen Elizabeth. Sadly, Their Majesties missed Lloyd's *Grain* and *Kilowatt Magic*, the two short ballets with which she had humbly hoped to delight them. The company had better luck in 1951 when it gave a Command Performance at the Civic Auditorium for the heir to the throne, Princess Elizabeth, and her husband, the Duke of Edinburgh. Spohr, a sincere and devoted Royalist, was thrilled that his own *Ballet Premier* was part of the gala performance.

There was more than sentiment, however, behind the company's change of name. In the immediate post-war era, becoming the "Royal" Winnipeg Ballet carried enormous cachet, especially if the company hoped to penetrate the United States touring market. Also, it would be a lesson to that "National" upstart company in Toronto. The board of the Winnipeg Ballet, quite understandably, still smarted at what it saw as the Toronto troupe's act of titular hijacking. The pioneering troupe in Winnipeg had plans to correct the situation. When board member John Russell wrote to the Secretary of State in Ottawa in August, 1952, concerning the change of name, he confided that what the company really wanted to be called was "The Royal Canadian Ballet of Winnipeg". That, as Russell was soon advised, would first require the troupe to amend its legal name under the Manitoba Companies Act. This would have entailed a lengthy delay. Since the Winnipeg Ballet was already pondering its touring options south of the border, Russell wrote to Ottawa again in late August saying that the company would be content simply to become "The Royal Winnipeg Ballet."

The young Queen, not yet crowned, approved the application, "on the Governor General's advice", on January 31, 1953. The news was communicated to the board of directors of the freshly dubbed Royal Winnipeg Ballet in a telegram of February 5. This information was relayed to the dancers performing in Montreal. A formal public announcement was made from the stage that evening.

Unlike the charter that transformed the Sadler's Wells Ballet into The Royal Ballet in 1956, the Winnipeg Ballet's name change came with no other privileges. As John Russell acknowledged in a letter of thanks to his contact at the Secretary of State's department in Ottawa, the change did not give the company the right to use the Royal coat of arms or to imply that it operated under Royal patronage. For several years, however, the company was to adopt a logo in which the initials "RWB" were placed within something strongly reminiscent of a coronet, a line drawing of eight ballerinas in romantic tutus arranged in a circle. It appears to have been inspired by a publicity photograph of Lloyd's *Romance.*

A more pressing problem was the RWB's survival. Despite the company's growing artistic reputation and expanding tour schedule, it was chronically short of funds. The RWB was facing a conundrum common to many ballet companies. In order to grow artistically, dancers need to perform and to have choreography that challenges and develops them. Winnipeg is too small a market to sustain lengthy seasons of hometown performances. Therefore the company must tour. Touring, however, is a financially risky venture, with touring revenues rarely covering the costs. The difference can only be made up through private and public fund-raising. For the RWB in 1953, before there were either federal or provincial arts councils, this essentially meant finding private donors. It was not easy.

If the Royal Winnipeg Ballet's chronic financial problems threatened its future, the events of the night of June 7-8, 1954, nearly killed it. A wiring fault ignited a fire at the Time Building on Portage Avenue. Fanned by 110-kilometre-per-hour winds, the blaze defeated the efforts of a small army of firefighters and eventually engulfed several adjacent buildings, including the one that housed the RWB. The company lost almost everything, from the notes of Lloyd's ballets to sets, costumes, orchestra scores, equipment and, of course, a place to work.

The company did rise from the ashes like the mythical phoenix but it required a massive fund-raising drive. The dancers had no choice but to find other work, whatever and wherever they could. When the RWB reassembled fifteen months later, many of the old faces were gone, including Spohr's.

Spohr had not been idle. He found employment at Winnipeg's

McConnell School of Dancing, teaching ballet, modern and jazz. He performed in fashion shows and also began to explore the world of ice-dancing. As a teacher at the Winnipeg Winter Club he learned some of the technical niceties of figure skating and even imagined himself one day choreographing for skaters. It never happened. Early in 1955 he wrote to Bernadette Carpenter, proprietor of a successful dance supplies business in Toronto and publisher of the popular Spotlight Newsletter: "This is like an experimental year, when I can rest as well as create. With the modern and jazz I am creating a whole new idiom for myself." The same year, Spohr choreographed his first television dance number, part of a special programme marking the first anniversary of the Winnipeg station CBWT, and found a new and fruitful outlet for his choreographic talent at Rainbow Stage.

The open-air theatre in Winnipeg's Kildonan Park had been inspired by Vancouver's Theatre Under the Stars. The story goes that during an architectural planning meeting one of the design team, Dennis Carter, looking at a model of the proposed bandshell, noted that if coloured lights were attached to the curved rim of the proscenium it would look like a rainbow.

The 3,000-seat amphitheatre was officially opened on July 7, 1954, with a variety show directed by James Duncan, director of the University of Manitoba's Glee Club. In September, 1955, Duncan went on to direct Brigadoon, the first of many musicals to be presented at Rainbow Stage. Among other objectives, the new facility was intended to provide opportunities "for the development and expansion of local talent". Arnold Spohr was both local and talented and was invited to choreograph Brigadoon. He went on to choreo-graph or, as the credits described it, "stage musical numbers" for Rainbow Stage productions of Annie Get Your Gun and Kiss Me Kate, Can Can, Gentlemen Prefer Blondes and Chu Chin Chow, Brigadoon, again, and The King and I, and Showboat.

There were strong links between Rainbow Stage and the RWB. Pioneering RWB board members such as John Russell and John Graham were active at Rainbow Stage. The summer musicals were also an important source of off-season work for the RWB's poorly paid dancers.

Working at Rainbow Stage was an invaluable learning oppor-tunity for Spohr. Many of the productions he choreographed there were directed by John Hirsch, a man with a fertile creative imagination and burning artistic zeal. Seven years Spohr's junior, Hirsch was already making his mark as a brilliant man of the theatre and he made a forceful impression on Spohr.

In 1947, the Hungarian-born Hirsch had left his war-ravaged European childhood behind and immigrated to Canada. Soon after graduating from the University of Manitoba, he established the Muddiwater Puppets and a children's theatre troupe. In 1957, Hirsch joined forces with Winnipeg-born Tom Hendry to found a semi-professional company called Theatre 77. "The name was a cabalistic thing," Hendry explains. "We were seventy-seven steps from Portage and Main." Hendry was a young writer with CBC Radio and also acted on CBC Television where Hirsch had found employment. Hendry also knew how to organize. In 1958, Theatre 77 merged with the amateur Winnipeg Little Theatre to become English Canada's first regional theatre, the Manitoba Theatre Centre. "We used to call it the only professional theatre between Stratford and Yokohama," says Hendry.

"I used to listen to everything John Hirsch had to say," Spohr recalls. "He could be crazy sometimes, he'd get so excited, so passionate. He'd scream and shout and be all over the place, but the way he worked with actors, the way he motivated them, what he could bring out of them – it was just phenomenal." It was an outwardly improbable relationship, a Jewish Holocaust survivor and this German-speaking son of a Lutheran firebrand. Yet, the two became friends and Hirsch served for several years on the RWB board. "They were both fighters," says actor/director Christopher Newton. "They really saw the potential of the city." Reflecting on his friendship with Spohr years later, Hirsch told an interviewer: "He was an absolute fiend for work and so was I, so we got along well."

"John and Arnold both had this ambition, this need to prove themselves," says Hendry. "For John I really think it came from his past, from his sense of guilt about being the only member of his immediate family to survive the war. He felt this terrific drive to give some point to his physical existence. As far as we knew, Arnold came from this big happy family. I remember him being devoted to Erica, his 'little sister'. But he still seemed very much at home in a theatrical milieu. That was their bond. He and John got along really well together. John liked working with Arnie. He knew he wouldn't let him down."

Hirsch was also helpful in pointing Spohr towards opportunities with CBC Television. Spohr and another former RWB dancer, Kay Bird, created a ballroom act and for a whole season had a feature spot on a weekly show called Cabaret. For television, Bird used her married name so the two could be billed as "Spohr and Scott". Spohr staged all the numbers. Perhaps his most nerve-wracking CBC engagement was a live production of *Slaughter on Tenth Avenue*, the ballet from the popular 1936 Rodgers and Hart musical, On Your Toes. Spohr had not seen the stage show. His choreography drew inspiration from Ray Enright's 1939 movie version, starring Eddie Albert and George Balanchine's then wife, Vera Zorina. Spohr starred in this production, again with Kay Bird as his partner.

In 1958, he choreographed, although did not perform in, a series directed for CBC by Hirsch called Dances of the Nations. It required Spohr to research and then choreograph in a variety of different ethnic styles.

It was Hirsch who urged Spohr to take the opportunity of his break from the RWB to widen his horizons. Spohr had travelled the country and ventured several times into the United States. Hirsch now encouraged him to be more adventurous. Spohr still cannot remember how he managed to save enough money for the trip, but when his work was finished with Rainbow Stage in 1956 he embarked on what was to be his first of many journeys across the Atlantic.

3

Where the Rainbow Ends

In the late summer of 1956, Spohr set sail from Quebec City, bound for Liverpool on the new Canadian Pacific liner Empress of Britain, the third CP vessel to bear the name. His sister Erica was already in England, in Birmingham, studying to be a nurse. Spohr found lodgings in London near Hyde Park Corner and soon made contact with his old friend Paddy Stone and with dancers he had befriended during a 1954 visit to Winnipeg by the Sadler's Wells Ballet. Spohr took ballet classes and went to see a variety of West End shows. He did not expect to dance with the great Alicia Markova.

Lillian Alicia Marks was born in London in December, 1910. She had danced as a teenager with Diaghilev's Ballets Russes and created the title role in George Balanchine's *Le Rossignol*. After the death of Diaghilev in 1929, Markova returned to England and became the centrepiece of its emerging national company, Ninette de Valois' Vic-Wells Ballet, the precursor of the Sadler's Wells Ballet. In 1935, Markova and the Irish-born dancer Anton Dolin, her friend and partner from Diaghilev days, formed their own company in which Markova remained the leading ballerina until joining the Ballet Russe de Monte Carlo in 1938. Markova starred with the recently formed Ballet Theatre, now American Ballet Theatre from 1941 to 1945, and then joined with Dolin again to form what in 1950 evolved to become the London Festival Ballet, now English National Ballet. Although she retired as its prima ballerina in 1952, Markova continued to appear as a guest artist all over the world and did not give her official farewell performances until 1962.

Spohr had met Markova in 1954. In one of its early coups, the

RWB had secured her services as a guest ballerina. "I had heard about the company becoming 'Royal' when I was working at the Met," says Markova. "I was rather impressed. When I arrived in Winnipeg it was bitterly cold and I remember this tall young man, really very tall for that era, being extremely helpful and attentive. Arnold and I didn't dance together, of course. I'd brought in my own partner from the United States, Roman Jasinski. But I do remember Arnold being interested in everything and always paying attention, learning. He seemed to think in the right way and seemed very responsible."

Where the Rainbow Ends was a children's matinee entertainment. In 1954, Markova made her first appearance in the show as the good fairy, The Spirit of the Lake, and went on to dance in three different productions, each of them two years apart. Dolin appeared as St. George. In 1956, Markova decided she wanted three partners for *Where the Rainbow Ends*. An audition was held. "I remember this very tall, handsome man coming in and I said 'I know him.' It was Arnold. He'd come to London to study and he'd run out of money. I told him there really wouldn't be that much dancing for him but he didn't seem to care." Spohr, then thirty-two, was hired. So was a nineteen-year-old Englishman called Ben Stevenson. Years later in Houston, Texas, Stevenson was to provide the same kind of transforming leadership for the city's ballet company that Spohr was soon to offer the RWB.

By the time Spohr got to partner Markova in *Where the Rainbow Ends,* she was forty-seven and past her physical peak, although she retained the ethereal quality that was her ballerina trademark. Even so, Markova was determined to show audiences she could still jump. Near the end of their pas de deux, the climax of the show, she would enter from the wings of the London Coliseum, starting from as far back as she could and gathering momentum as she ran onto the huge stage. The idea was that Markova's partner would sweep her up into an overhead lift, all the time giving the impression that she had executed a soaring jump.

At the best of times, Spohr found it nerve-wracking because Markova wore a long tutu, which made it difficult for him to position his hands accurately for the lift. "We had some pretty close calls, I can tell you." Spohr says he used to check off every performance in his mind: "Another one down."

The performances with Markova were going smoothly – until

Spohr lost his contact lenses. He had the habit of storing them overnight in a glass of water beside his bed. Unfortunately an over-zealous maid, who reputedly had a huge crush on Spohr, had found the glass of water and replaced it with a fresh one. He was horrified. "What did you do with the water?" he demanded. "Down the toilet," came the reply. Spohr was stunned, then saw a glimmer of hope. "Did you flush it?" he asked. "Of course," came the indignant and devastating reply.

Spohr could hardly wear regular eyeglasses on stage and he did not dare tell Markova of his predicament. "I could already see the headlines: 'Dancer drops legendary ballerina to her death'." Spohr remembers seeing this white blur coming at him and getting larger as it hurtled from the wings. He did manage to catch and lift Markova, but she landed in his face. He had to heave her up as best he could. The audience appeared not to notice but Markova certainly did. When the curtain came down she turned on him. "Never," she declared, "put your hand on my crotch in public again." Markova claims not to recall the incident and clearly did not hold it against Spohr. In 1980, she accepted an invitation to return to Winnipeg to stage *Les Sylphides*, the ballet she had danced there in 1954.

As Spohr was to do on all his future travels, he made note of any interesting people he met in England and made efforts to stay in touch. Markova, of course, was one of them. Others included the dance critic and historian Richard Buckle, and Peter Williams, the founding editor of the influential British magazine, Dance and Dancers.

Spohr says he hated London largely because he was freezing to death. "There was no heat." He took off on a European jaunt and by the time he returned found London much improved and basking in spring sunshine. Spohr might have stayed longer if he had not been running low on funds and been needed at home. His mother was ailing. His siblings had largely dispersed and Hermine needed his help. So Spohr set forth on his second Atlantic crossing, this time on a Dutch ship, and arrived to find his mother in a distressing condition and the RWB in turmoil.

Although Betty Farrally was theoretically in charge, her authority was confusingly compromised by the presence of Ruthanna Boris and her husband Frank Hobi. The two had been hired a year earlier, Boris as a dancer and choreographer, Hobi as her partner.

Their relationship with the RWB had begun well. Boris' new ballet for the company, *Pasticcio*, was a success. She and Hobi were impressive performers. They also brought a no-nonsense New Yorkers' brand of professionalism to the RWB. "The kids loved Ruthanna," says Spohr. "She was tough but as I got to know her I liked her a lot."

The board persuaded Boris and Hobi to stay on. Boris was given a degree of control that effectively sidelined Farrally. Nenad Lhotka, the company's ballet master, soon quit in disgust. Most agreed that the RWB was dancing better than ever but the Boris-dominated repertoire had mixed success.

As Spohr was settling back into Winnipeg the situation had reached a crisis point, with Farrally threatening to resign and Boris tossing a gauntlet at the feet of the board. She wanted expansion. The board was set on holding the line and was determined to shrink the company from twenty-two to seventeen dancers. Boris and Hobi left for New York at the end of the 1956/57 season. By early May, Farrally had quit the company too.

Farrally, who objected as much as Boris to the board's policy of retrenchment, always insisted she was fired from the RWB. The board maintained that Farrally had stipulated conditions for remaining as director, which, it decided, could not be met. Therefore, in the board's view, Farrally had resigned. Either way it was an inelegant parting. It was also the end of an epoch. Gweneth Lloyd, who had continued to live in Toronto since her move there in 1950, provided the coup de grâce by symbolically repudiating her title as Founding Director. Lloyd later left Toronto to join Farrally in British Columbia. The two bought a waterside home to the south of Kelowna in the Okanagan Valley and continued their lives as ballet teachers.

The board sent off a letter expressing its "profound regret" and, when a souvenir programme for the 1957/58 season was published, it included photographs of Lloyd and Farrally as well as a gracious tribute. "Wherever and whenever the curtain rises on The Royal Winnipeg Ballet this company acknowledges a debt of affectionate gratitude to its founders." By the 1960/61 season the photos and tribute had vanished from the souvenir book.

Before the board could think of composing such a touching tribute, however, it had to find a new director or there would be no season. It moved with commendable haste and by June 21, 1957, board members were brought up to date on the progress that had been made. Advice had been sought from Ninette de Valois, the woman who had recommended Celia Franca as the most suitable candidate to found a "national" ballet company in Toronto. This time de Valois was more cautious. In a letter to the RWB board she suggested that none of the members of The Royal Ballet would care "to run a company that would be so near the existing National Ballet, which is run by one of their fellow artists." However, de Valois did recommend the thirty-three-year-old British dancer and choreographer, Jack Carter, as being "intelligent and hard-working". Given the way Carter's ballet career blossomed in the 1960's, he might have been a fine choice.

John Russell reported that he had sent a telegram to Robert Joffrey, a respected teacher and the recent founder of his own company in New York. A reply was awaited. There was also talk at the board meeting of a proposal from Nenad Lhotka to return to the RWB as ballet master-director, and of the possibility that Arnold Spohr might be available to serve as ballet master although, as the minutes recorded, "no approach had been made to him". The discussion continued and it was agreed that the previous season's dancers, who were already worrying whether they would have work in the coming year, should be told to "wait another brief period". One board member realistically suggested that a deadline should be set, after which, if a new director had not been secured, the upcoming season should be abandoned.

As the summer of 1957 wore on, dancers began to drift away. The board advertised the vacant director's position and was finally able to interview three promising candidates. They chose Benjamin Harkarvy, an articulate, persuasive and much-recommended teacher and choreographer with his own school in New York. It was to be his first directorship – and a brief one.

The RWB board was still committed to a year of retrenchment. It was to be a Winnipeg-focussed, twenty-six-week season, tentatively budgeted at $42,540. With so little time to spare it was agreed that Harkarvy would fill the RWB's depleted ranks by bringing several dancers with him from New York, as well as a music director.

Harkarvy arrived in September, 1957, in time to attend the company's annual general meeting, which included an unsettling account of the lack of public support during the previous season. More happily, although the company had overspent by almost

$20,000 it still had a credit balance of some $14,000. Harkarvy told the meeting he hoped to preserve "the zest and bounce" that had made the RWB famous but also stressed the need for longer seasons. For the time being, the company's leadership problem appeared to be resolved. One board member went so far as to assure a Winnipeg Tribune reporter that "it is the first time in the ballet's history that it can look forward with such confidence to a successful season and sound future."

Spohr, meanwhile, had his own concerns, most urgently how to make a living. Fortunately, there was his teaching and choreography. That summer of 1957 he returned to Rainbow Stage to work on Chu Chin Chow. It turned out to be a particularly memorable experience for Spohr since he not only choreographed the musical but was unexpectedly required to dance.

Chu Chin Chow proved such a hit that Rainbow Stage management decided to hold it over. The problem was that RWB members in the cast had to leave to begin the new season under Harkarvy. To fill the gap Spohr, John Hirsch, Tom Hendry, Stan Langtry, the designer, and several other reluctant volunteers were required to fill the breach and dance in the corps of Chinese peasants.

Spohr simplified the choreography to suit his largely untrained cast. He had not yet replaced the contact lenses lost down the toilet in London. Spohr rehearsed the volunteers wearing heavily tinted prescription eyeglasses. Given his poor sight and earlier experience with Markova, he decided that in order to avert accidents it would be prudent to wear his glasses during the performance. He hoped his wide-brimmed "coolie's" hat would hide his peculiar eyewear from general view. For added security he taped the glasses to his ears.

All went well the night of his Chu Chin Chow debut until Spohr decided to liven things up. "Here we were lumbering around," remembers Hendry, "when Arnie decides to whip off a couple of spins. He was doing fine until the tape on these glasses of his came unstuck and they went flying off." The result was a near catastrophe. Spohr began floundering around and Hendry saw him edging closer and closer towards the orchestra pit. "Finally, I managed to get close enough to grab his arm, whirl him around and drag him back to safety. I like to think that was the night I saved Arnold Spohr's life."

It was not Spohr's only mishap at Rainbow Stage. In a mid-1950's production of The King and I, directed by Hirsch, Spohr appeared in the "Small House of Uncle Thomas" ballet sequence. He was the sun figure, sent by Buddha to melt the river ice under Simon Legree. Spohr made his entrance at the top of a ramp. It had rained and the ramp was damp and slippery. Spohr lost his footing and slid all the way onto the stage. Everyone laughed, including Hirsch, who joked that perhaps the slide should remain for the rest of the run. Spohr, of course, was mortified.

Although he had not been a member of the RWB since the fire of 1954, Spohr still maintained a keen interest in its activities and in 1957 became ideally placed to do that. With Farrally's dramatic westward retreat, someone was needed to run the Winnipeg branch of the Canadian School of Ballet. Spohr accepted the job enthusiastically and told Lloyd and Farrally that he intended to stay for some time because he wanted to see the school "properly built up". He claims the school was "broke" when he took over and that he had it back in the black within a year.

Spohr was able to watch Harkarvy at work because the school and company shared the same Smith Street studios. However, Spohr kept a respectful distance, watching from the open door. Eventually, Harkarvy invited him in. Later, when two of Spohr's ballets were revived, he was naturally called in to rehearse them.

For Rachel Browne and Richard Rutherford, who were among the six dancers Harkarvy had imported from New York, the first encounter with Spohr was daunting. Rutherford recalls, "My first impression was frankly not very positive. He was eccentric to the point that most of us thought he was crazy." Browne also had misgivings. "He was extremely friendly. You could just feel his warmth. But I was taken aback by his manner. He seemed so unsophisticated. It was as if I'd come across this country bumpkin."

Spohr had a heavy workload running the school. Harkarvy's burden was even greater. He was expected to function as director, ballet master and choreographer – and not spend too much money. The board wanted Harkarvy's first year to be one of reconstitution and consolidation. With a fresh repertoire and reinvigorated dancers, the company, it was thought, would be ready to tour again.

Harkarvy staged two seasons in Winnipeg, in November, 1957, and January, 1958. He revived two of his earlier ballets and created two works. The first was *The Twisted Heart*, a ballet version of the operatic Pagliacci story to an original score by Harkarvy's music director, Richard Wernick. Then came a bravura showcase to Mozart called *Fête Brillante*. Harkarvy's November season was generally considered a success; the second, less distinguished, except for the revival of Spohr's 1951 abstract ballet, *Intermède*. Spohr recalls that it was John Graham and his production committee, not Harkarvy, who decided to present *Intermède*. "I'm sure I didn't programme it," recalled Harkarvy shortly before his death in March, 2002. Still, when he saw the ballet, he was content. "It was very well done in terms of form. It was the decor I didn't like." According to Harkarvy it was also the production committee that selected Spohr's *Ballet Premier* for the final shows of the season in March, 1958.

Harkarvy got on well with most of the dancers. They found him to be an exacting but excellent teacher. His relations with the board, however, soon deteriorated. Harkarvy's shaved head made him look considerably older than his modest twenty-six years. He was still young and ambitious. He wanted a business manager, tour bookings and better costumes. Unlike the board, he did not see the need to bring in guest dancers. The company would be its own headline. Harkarvy considered the board to be intolerably provincial in its lack of ambition for the company. "It seemed they were determined to keep it a small-town company." He clashed dangerously with Kathleen Richardson who, from Harkarvy's viewpoint, seemed to control the board. "Let's say Kathleen and I had a few words." In January, 1958, he even threatened to resign over the issue of a business manager.

Harkarvy continued to work on the March programme but the dancers could sense the tension. He had been scheduled to create a third work for the company but, as the winter wore on, announced that he would not have time. Eventually, Harkarvy's patience was exhausted. The board, he decided, could have their little company to do with as they saw fit. He entered his final meeting on Monday, February 10, with a prepared statement that he also released to the local press. Harkarvy spoke darkly of infringements upon his authority as artistic director and of the "insults and humiliation" to which he had been subjected. He was also armed with an airline ticket out of Winnipeg. Charles Czarny, one of Harkarvy's leading dancers, and music director Richard Wernick had similarly plotted their escape. Harkarvy left little behind except fourteen alarmed dancers and the costumes for *Fête Brillante*. The costumes did not go entirely to waste. Six years later choreographer Brian Macdonald was able to find a use for them in a work he created for the RWB called *Pas d'Action*. The costume credit read "By Chance".

Benjamin Harkarvy's dramatic departure left the RWB board in the direst of predicaments. Unless it could find someone to fill the breach, the company would have to cancel the March performances. Apart from shattering dancer morale, such an action, coming after a fraught and turbulent three years of shifting direction, might well exhaust any remaining public support. Predictably, the media fallout from Harkarvy's flight was not helpful, especially when a majority of the dancers, who at the very least considered Harkarvy to be a brilliant teacher, publicly declared support for their former director. And what would be the reaction of the newly created Canada Council? At the start of Harkarvy's brief regime, it had awarded the RWB a first grant of $20,000.

The board acted swiftly. The day Harkarvy left town, an emergency meeting was called to explain the situation to the dancers. Those involved have slightly varying accounts of the exact sequence of events. Some recall that Spohr was at the meeting and offered to help. Others say it was a few days before the board decided to ask Spohr to step in. In fact, The Winnipeg Tribune of February 11 was able to report not only Harkarvy's resignation but Spohr's commission to finish the job. Spohr vividly recalls the day Harkarvy quit. That evening he was teaching in the school when Kathleen Richardson and the board treasurer, W.A. "Jock" Smith, appeared. After a few pleasantries they explained their predicament and asked Spohr to take over. "Naturally, I said yes. I was brought up to be loyal and co-operative. This was the company on which I was weaned."

Richard Rutherford recalls the transition as being remarkably smooth. "As far as we were concerned the change-over didn't seem so traumatic because Arnold was already there rehearsing his ballet." Whatever the exact sequence of events, it is clear that the board put their money on Spohr because he was available – and prayed they had backed a winner.

The fact that the board turned to Spohr in its moment of need had an ironic twist. In the summer of 1955, as the RWB struggled back to life after the fire, Betty Farrally had been appointed director. Gweneth Lloyd was given the title of founding director. Spohr, still eager to be involved, had applied for the post of ballet master and been rejected. In its official response the board informed Spohr that it was felt unwise for him to rejoin the company in view of his many other interests. What Spohr did not discover until years later was that Lloyd, having heard about his application, had told the board that he was too much of a yes-man and too eager to please to be suitable as ballet master. Perhaps as a consolation, Spohr was offered, and accepted, an invitation to return with his former partner, Jean McKenzie, to dance that November of 1955 in a revival of Lloyd's 1942 ballet *The Wise Virgins*, renamed *Parable*. Now, in February, 1958, he was expected to perform a miracle.

For Spohr, this assignment must have appeared a daunting challenge, but he was not unequipped for the task. He had substantial experience as a dancer and teacher. He had already created three ballets for the company, and had choreographed for television and Rainbow Stage. He had travelled abroad to work and study. On the surface he might have seemed naïve and, as Gweneth Lloyd had observed, too eager to please, but Spohr also had a strong practical side to his nature. Spohr's habit of "looking, listening and learning" meant that he had absorbed a variety of important lessons about how to organize, motivate and rehearse a company.

Many of the dancers were Spohr's friends; they shared a common will to succeed. If Spohr had any misgivings, he did not show them. He just went about the business of doing what he loved best – putting on a good show. He also had little to lose. He had taken on what many considered an impossible challenge. If the shows flopped it would hardly be fair to blame him. Spohr has long had a habit of writing down memorable quotations. In this instance, he probably had in mind one of his favourites: "No man fails who does his best." In any case, he was going to prove he could do the job, even if it "killed" him. For a brief while it looked as if it might.

With only three weeks left before the March performances, Spohr worked with almost manic zeal. In his typical way, Spohr insisted on rehearsing everything within an inch of its life. To some of his dancers, then and later, Spohr's obsession with rehearsal seemed to stem less from real need than from his own anxieties. Spohr has never denied that he has a worrying nature, but his emphasis on long and rigorous rehearsal also stemmed from principle. Sitting at the piano keyboard under John Melnyk's tutelage, Spohr had learned the virtue of constant practice. "If you want to get something right," he says, "you have to keep at it until you do. Talent is nothing without hard work." As a pianist, he had found that with application even the fastest and most complex music had gradually become embedded in his muscles, leaving his imagination free to work on details of interpretation. "That's when you can really start to play." Spohr wanted the same for his dancers. "He didn't want us to count but rather to *feel* the music," says Rutherford. From Spohr's perspective, the more rehearsal, the more preparation, the less the dancers would have to worry about on stage and the more energy they could devote to communicating with the audience.

Rehearsing the company was one thing. Spohr had not planned to perform. As far as he was concerned, dancing with Markova had been his farewell to ballet tights. A few days before the opening night, however, Richard Rutherford was stricken with nephritis, an acute inflammation of the kidneys. He was soon in hospital. As no other dancer was available, Spohr was compelled to step into Rutherford's corps de ballet roles in *Ballet Premier* and *Intermède*.

"I never even got to see the shows," says Rutherford, "but I remember Arnold telling me later how nervous he was. I think it almost killed him." Until then, Spohr had only danced the lead in his own ballets. Now, all six foot three inches of him had to try to merge into the corps. "He was a mess," recalls dancer Ted Patterson. "We were all having major hysterics on stage. Somehow he got through it." Spohr remembers opening night as "a total nightmare". The stress brought him to the verge of collapse. "I remember this cramp, like a gripping feeling on my heart. It just wouldn't stop. I lay down and prayed to God that, seeing he'd got me this far, to please let me finish the performance and then do what he will." God obliged.

Understandably, the performances of March 3 and 4, 1958, were keenly anticipated. The RWB's kernel of diehard supporters kept their fingers crossed. The skeptics wondered if this might be the ballet's last blast. Just a few days after Harkarvy's stormy exit, Frank Morriss told his readers that Winnipeg was at grave risk of losing the RWB and now needed "some unselfish person with the pioneer spirit" to bring it back to what it had been.

In addition to his own ballets, Spohr programmed the Act III pas de deux from *Swan Lake*. Ted Patterson, later to become a valuable teacher in the RWB school, but then still a dancing survivor from the Ruthanna Boris period, had been able to teach the company Boris' 1956 ballet, *Roundelay*. "Ted never forgot a step," says Rutherford.

"Glitter back in ballet as Spohr saves show" was how The Winnipeg Tribune headlined S. Roy Maley's report the next day. "Ballet Premier stirred up the greatest enthusiasm," wrote Maley. "The performance revived memories of the best years of the RWB and hopes that such performances will be common occurrences in the future."

Frank Morriss was equally effusive in the Winnipeg Free Press. "The old spirit of the Royal Winnipeg Ballet returned and the audience in the Playhouse Theatre got the kind of performance that it was accustomed to half a dozen years ago when the company used to fuse dedication and spirit and dance with the kind of inspiration that had heart as well as excitement."

The euphoria engendered by the success of those March, 1958, performances soon evaporated. For the dancers, their main concern was where the next pay cheque would come from. Oddly, Ben Harkarvy had the answer. He had already signed a contract to choreograph a thirteen-part children's TV series called *Toes and Tempo* for CBC. That spring many of the RWB's dancers found themselves once again working with the man who had left them in the lurch only a couple of months before. After that there was Rainbow Stage to look forward to.

The board had a more vexing question. Should it yet again scramble to find a new director as it had in the summer of 1957? Even if a suitable person could be found, how long would he or she last? Recent history was hardly encouraging and the job itself, given the general condition of the company, could not have been described as enticing.

For a portion of the RWB's board of directors the obvious course was to offer the job to Spohr. In their view, he qualified in a variety of ways. He knew the company, he knew the city and he had proved he could function in the studio and put on a sparkling show. He was also, as more than one board member rather unwisely surmised, tractable. Spohr would not be a bother. His appointment would allow those board members who rather enjoyed the experience of running a ballet company to continue to make the really important decisions, with Spohr functioning as an obedient ballet master.

Other board members, looking perhaps for more than a tractable ballet master, dismissed the idea entirely. Spohr, in their view, was largely unqualified. Just because he had choreographed a few ballets and musicals, danced with the illustrious Markova and salvaged the March performances, did not mean he had the capacity to be a leader. Worse still, Spohr was "just a local boy", from the wrong side of the tracks, unsophisticated, unworldly and, perhaps, "skittish". Says Tom Hendry, "There was real prejudice against local boys. John Hirsch had gone through the same thing with Winnipeg Little Theatre. They turned him down as director and he was in tears."

Kathleen Richardson, the board president, felt that Spohr had earned the chance. With the authority of her family name, position on the board and quietly effective diplomacy, she was finally able to convince her undecided board colleagues that the offer should be made. It does not appear to have occurred to anyone that Spohr might not be interested.

Spohr was back at his old job, teaching at the Canadian School of Ballet, when Richardson and fellow board member John Graham, head of the all-important production committee, appeared at the studio door and asked if he could join them for lunch. "I am sure," Graham says, "that Arnold knew what it was about." Graham also says it is important to remember that the board had not turned to Spohr in any sense as a last resort. He and Richardson believed that Spohr was the ideal candidate.

Spohr's initial refusal confounded them. His reasoning sounded uncomfortably familiar since it accorded with many of the objections raised by a portion of the board of directors. "I told them I was only a Canadian and a local full-fledged Winnipegger at that." Richardson and Graham did at least convince Spohr to give the matter due consideration.

Spohr says the idea of becoming the RWB's director had never entered his mind, but it is hard to believe that he could have been as surprised by the offer as he later claimed. "He may have had misgivings," says Graham, "but I rather think he expected to be asked and would have been hurt if he hadn't been."

Even if the hard work of putting on the March performances had exhausted Spohr, it had also been exhilarating. Under his leadership everyone had pulled together as a team and achieved something infinitely better than they thought possible. They had been one happy family. It was the way Spohr remembered the Winnipeg Ballet in its early days and he was the one who had made it happen.

There was more to Spohr's initial refusal than humility and a sense of inadequacy. In later years he confided that he felt fully able to do the job, even if he recognized it would mean acquiring additional skills. In his mind, there would be no point in taking on the RWB unless it were to make the company better and expand its horizons. Says Spohr: "I had this vision of an international company right from the start." To achieve this would entail finding new repertoire, increasing the number of annual performances, and touring more. Would the board support such a course? Spohr had heard enough stories of board timidity to be gravely doubtful. He already had a job. He enjoyed running the Canadian School of Ballet and there was still his career as a choreographer to consider. A number of Spohr's friends thought he would be crazy to accept. "They were very lucky they got him," recalls Hendry, "but the betting was that if Arnold took it he'd only be around long enough to close it down."

Spohr consulted people he trusted. He immediately wrote to his sister Erica, still abroad, explaining his misgivings. Confident of his ability, she urged him to accept. "You'll just find you grow into it," she wrote, reassuringly. Spohr also contacted his mentors, Lloyd and Farrally in Kelowna. In later years, when Spohr had become the company's revered leader, both women liked to take credit for having recommended him to the RWB board. In March, 1958, however, their attitudes seem to have been less clear. Farrally, according to Spohr's recollection, rated his chances to re-establish the troupe as slim at best and was not encouraging. Lloyd merely urged him "to give it a try". Her sincerity, however, is questionable.

According to Brian Macdonald's memory of events, recounted for Dance in Canada magazine during the RWB's fiftieth anniversary year, Lloyd had broached the subject of the company's leadership with him at a lunch meeting in Toronto. Lloyd told Macdonald she had been asked by Kathleen Richardson to scout for someone to help the company out of its predicament. "Are you interested?" asked Lloyd. "Should I be?" Macdonald responded. Lloyd was adamant. "You certainly should." She then, as Macdonald recalls, left the table to phone Richardson.

Macdonald was still uncertain. In November, 1951, he had been one of the athletic warriors stirring up clouds of dust in a staging of Fokine's *Polovtsian Dances from Prince Igor* during the then Canadian National Ballet's debut performance at Toronto's Eaton Auditorium. Macdonald's dance career as a charter member of the company was cut short two years later after he seriously injured his arm performing during the off-season in a Montreal nightclub. After this setback, Macdonald had pieced together a thriving career in Montreal, his hometown. He taught ballet and jazz dance, and choreographed and directed everything from mid-game football spectacles to early dance performances on CBC Television. His star rose dramatically in February, 1957, with the launch of the satirical My Fur Lady as part of McGill University's Red and White Revue. Macdonald and his first wife, Olivia Wyatt, directed and choreographed My Fur Lady. It went on to become a popular hit that summer as it toured across Canada. Despite this, what Macdonald really wanted was a chance to choreograph more reflectively, "anywhere that would have me, but preferably in Canada."

Spohr must already have been offered the RWB directorship and sought Lloyd's advice before her meeting with Macdonald in Toronto. Did she privately harbour misgivings about Spohr's capacity to handle the job? Given her earlier assessment of his character, it is certainly possible. In any case, it was too late. Lloyd returned to the table with the news that the RWB had formally hired Arnold Spohr that very morning. An announcement was made to the media on March 13, 1958.

It does not appear that the board had consulted with any of the dancers before approaching Spohr. In the context of the times this is hardly surprising. The board ran the company. Despite Spohr's success with the March performances, the dancers had given little if any thought to the possibility of him becoming their permanent director. He had been brought in to help the troupe through a crisis and that was that. When they heard the news, however, the dancers were generally content. "I don't think," says Sonia Taverner, "that there was any question in anybody's mind that Arnold was not the right person for the job. We wanted a home, and someone to take the lead and to inspire and guide us. Arnold, to my mind, had just proved that he was more than qualified to do this. We liked him. He loved the dance and so did we."

Until this point, Spohr was known to everyone as "Arnie". With his promotion to the post of director, he decreed that henceforth he should be addressed by the dancers as "Mr. Spohr". Some of the old hands thought this smacked of pomposity, but for Spohr it was important that the dignity of his position should be acknowledged.

"For myself, I didn't really care," says Spohr, "but it's important for dancers to show respect for their director."

Spohr's acceptance of the directorship was very much driven by a sense of loyalty. Some of his happiest times had been spent at the company. He admired what Lloyd had accomplished and was devoted to Farrally. He wholeheartedly shared their belief that ballet was for everyone, and he had a sense of destiny. It had not escaped him that in accepting he would not only be the RWB's first Canadian-born director but the first Canadian to direct any professional dance company.

"Everything has its time and place," Spohr reflected many years later. "Good fortune does have to do with talent, but you have to be in the right place at the right time. I guess I was in the right place, for the choice of becoming the director of the RWB gave me my life's work."

High Ambitions
Harsh Realities

Arnold Spohr signed on as "director" of the Royal Winnipeg Ballet at the princely wage of $100 a week. It was many years before he was accorded the title "artistic director". His initial contract ran for thirty weeks, from late August, 1958, through the following March. Jacquie Darwin, the RWB's business manager, earned more than Spohr. The dancers' pay scale was hardly munificent. Marilyn Young, the company's highest paid ballerina, got a mere $55 a week. Sonia Taverner was close behind at $50. A corps de ballet member made $42. Spohr had his sights set on a company of twenty-four dancers. However, with the 1958/59 operating budget set at an estimated $64,600, Spohr was told he would have to make do with seventeen.

Despite Spohr's claim that Gweneth Lloyd had urged him to give the directorship "a try", she appeared to be most put out by his appointment. According to her, Spohr had promised to take care of the Canadian School of Ballet in Winnipeg, "for a minimum of two years". In recommending Brian Macdonald for the directorship, Lloyd had perhaps hoped to avoid the predicament in which she now found herself. As Lloyd explained in April, 1958, in a rather tart letter to "Miss Richardson" – the two ladies were not on first-name terms – she would now be obliged to hire a qualified RAD teacher from the United Kingdom to replace Spohr. Lloyd expected the RWB to pay the fare. It would be $400, if, as Lloyd suggested, "the girl was willing to come by boat." Spohr admitted to the board that in 1957 he had told Lloyd he would stay with the school for "some time" because he wanted "to see it built up", but pointed out that Lloyd and Farrally had only turned to him for help "because they were stuck." He was foresighted enough to realise that he might want Lloyd's choreography. Spohr told Richardson that it would be wise to pay Lloyd off, "in order to get the ballets". David Evans, the RWB's vice-president, answered Lloyd a few days later to say that the board would cover half the teacher's fare. Evans also stated that the board would like to bring the school and company closer together.

Evans' observation about the school was almost certainly prompted in part by Spohr. From the beginning, Spohr insisted on the need for the RWB to train its own dancers. "It was in my book of plans right there in 1958." Spohr summed it up in words that became a personal mantra: "A splendid school will a splendid company make." In his mind, turning the Winnipeg branch of the Canadian School of Ballet into the School of the Royal Winnipeg Ballet was the logical step. It was four years before the board was able to make that happen and even then, not exactly in accord with Spohr's plan.

For the time being, Spohr had more urgent business. "Everything was in a shambles. It would have been easier to start afresh. There were a couple of sheets of *Sylphides* music, no ballets in the repertoire except the ones performed in March, nothing filmed or on record. I found cleaning up the studios was the easiest task." Spohr did not even have an office, just a desk tucked away in a space off a corridor at the company's Smith Street studios. For several years, Spohr shared it with the costumes for whatever repertoire was currently being performed. "I could dress in whatever ballet was hanging there at the moment."

Soon after Spohr's appointment was announced, the Winnipeg Free Press innocently observed: "It is expected that he will devote his entire time to the Royal Winnipeg Ballet." As Spohr recalls, "it was the understatement of all time." He soon found himself working long hours, seven days a week. "For those first years, constant work became a ritual, with no end in sight. I had to do everything, teach, rehearse, co-ordinate all the departments. But what could I do? Swamped and submerged, I just had to settle down and determine to get through it." His contract may only have been for thirty weeks, but there was scarcely a moment when Spohr was not preoccupied with the company's needs.

Spohr was fortunate that eleven of the previous season's roster agreed to return, because his first call for dancers was not encouraging. "Nobody wanted to audition," he says, "because the RWB's reputation was at such a low ebb." Those returning included Marilyn Young, Sonia Taverner, Beverley Barkley, Kit Copping, Marina Katronis, Erica Mahler, Naomi Kimura and Ted Patterson as well as three of the six dancers Harkarvy had brought with him from New York: Rachel Browne, Frederic Strobel and Richard Rutherford. The newcomers included Olivia Wyatt, Sheila Mackinnon from the Victoria studio of Spohr's friend Wynne Shaw, Michael Hrushowy and David Holmes from Vancouver, and two hirings from New York, Frederic Conrad and the twenty-three-year-old Jim Clouser.

Clouser, who was to remain with the RWB for almost a decade, had auditioned for Spohr during a tour stop in Winnipeg by his former company, American Ballet Theatre. Clouser already knew Rutherford and Strobel as fellow students in New York and was dissatisfied with his teachers and coaches at ABT. Clouser liked Spohr precisely because he was not like other people he had met in the ballet world. "He was exactly what I was looking for," says Clouser. "He was colourful, he was meticulous and he was stubborn, but what he said was often revelatory."

Spohr's next challenge was to give audiences the varied programming that he believed was key to the company's appeal. He always had his own choreography to fall back on but there was a limit to how often his works could be revived. Spohr could stage excerpts from the classics but he still needed real drama, a dash of humour and, if possible, something to make people think. Spohr had travelled to the Banff Centre in Alberta that summer where Lloyd and Farrally headed the dance programme. Lloyd, suitably mollified by the RWB's agreement to help pay to bring a new teacher from England, had agreed to let the company dance two of her works, the lyrical *Romance* and the comic *Finishing School*. Lloyd taught the ballets to Spohr in Banff and also suggested that he ask Brian Macdonald to choreograph for the company.

Spohr had already met Macdonald and was impressed by his drive and intense passion for dance. It was agreed that Macdonald would present a new ballet for the Winnipeg season that October. Spohr was soon to thank himself for heeding Lloyd's advice. Macdonald proved a godsend to the RWB, providing a succession of works that played a major role in developing the company's distinct personality and in winning it international acclaim. "With his versatility and imagination," says Spohr, "Brian was to give us our trademark for this period. He left a strong influence and a distinctive Canadian style – vital, forceful and buoyant."

With the encouragement of John Hirsch, Spohr also com-missioned a ballet from Robert Moulton, an emerging choreographer and teacher from the University of Minnesota's drama department. As Spohr withdrew from Rainbow Stage to focus on the RWB, Moulton, who had connections with people in the Winnipeg theatre community, took over some of Spohr's summertime choreographic duties. Spohr also invited Ruthanna Boris to restage her witty 1956 work, *Pasticcio*, and her light-hearted look at the 1920's, *Le Jazz Hot*. The ingredients were all assembled.

Again, Spohr rehearsed the company with messianic zeal. The previous March, he had been praised for salvaging the season in a moment of crisis. This time he really had to prove himself. The headlines on October 18, 1958, proclaimed his success. "Director Is Unseen Hero of Ballet's Opening Performance", trumpeted the Winnipeg Free Press. Not to be outdone, The Winnipeg Tribune matched the enthusiasm with, "Brilliant Revival Seen For Ballet Under Spohr".

For much of Spohr's reign as director, it was typical for the company to mix and match several works in repertory as a way to induce fans to buy tickets for more than one show. For the opening of three performances that October, Spohr programmed Lloyd's *Romance*, Boris' *Pasticcio*, excerpts from *The Sleeping Beauty* and Macdonald's *The Darkling*. Macdonald had created a smaller version of the ballet for television in Montreal, but the Winnipeg shows were its first full staging. Spohr saved the other premiere, Moulton's evocation of simple prairie pioneer life, *Grasslands*, for the Saturday closing. The ballet's theme strongly appealed to him as a metaphor for the company's own progress. "For years we were pioneers," he says. "We always seemed to be breaking new ground." Classical balance for this programme was provided by a pas de deux from *The Sleeping Beauty* and Spohr's own *Ballet Premier*, with Boris' *Le Jazz Hot* offering a complete change of pace and musical style.

The Winnipeg critics, Frank Morriss and S. Roy Maley, were impressed. Morriss praised the variety of work on view, admired the new ballets, particularly *Grasslands* with its notably modern, expressionistic choreography, and opined that Spohr had managed to bring the RWB back "to the path it trod so successfully until it strayed into devious byways." Maley praised Spohr for having "re-won the admiration and support of balletomanes." According to Maley, the RWB could now "look forward with highest prospects to ultimate international acclaim."

The audience response was just as encouraging. The Harkarvy crisis earlier in the year had taken its toll on attendance. In contrast, with the optimism surrounding Spohr's appointment, the opening in October was almost sold out. The new ballets, each so distinct in appearance and character – Macdonald's with its psychological allegory about love, Moulton's with its prairie theme – won loud ovations. Spohr, who still felt insecure and under-equipped in his new role, was taken aback by the warmth of both the critical and public response. "I guess I was more prepared than I thought," he now reflects. But even then, and in the years that followed, Spohr, the perfectionist whose eye caught every mistake, was often amazed by the good reviews. He grumbled about the bad ones but in his heart conceded that often they were closer to the mark. "We really were not that good at the beginning, but I guess I knew how to produce the shows to look good."

The board executive was so delighted with the results that at a November 6 meeting it was suggested that Spohr should be paid a Christmas bonus of $100. In a moment of brief euphoria the board executive even considered bestowing a $10 bonus on each of the dancers. The latter proposal was rejected on the grounds that such an act of spontaneous generosity might set an unseemly precedent. The board's budgetary conservatism verged at times on the parsimonious, even to the extent of strictly regulating the number of complimentary tickets allocated for each performance. Spohr was allowed four, but the dancers got none. Meanwhile, as the board minutes recorded, "if any members wished to give toward a Christmas bonus for Mr. Spohr for the wonderful job he is doing, they could give their donations to the President." There's no record of how much Kathleen Richardson collected from her fellow board members but she saw to it that Spohr got his $100 anyway.

The cheque came with a congratulatory card expressing the board's sense of good fortune in having found such a fine director. Spohr, who doubtless put the unexpected money to immediate use, composed a warm letter of thanks. "I must say," he wrote, "that I was overwhelmed when I opened the card and saw the content. I <u>really</u> am touched at your kindness to me. I have mentioned many times before, about the truly wonderful board I have; how hard you work, how enthusiastic you are, with such good will and co-operation. I am the lucky one as director to have such a board as you. That is the greatest gift I can have."

Spohr's sentiments were a mix of sincerity and diplomacy, a prelude to the very public and strategic encomiums he periodically lavished on his lords and masters during the ensuing years of his directorship. He had his own coded initials for the board, CCC, meaning courteous, considerate and conservative. The frustration to which he sometimes gave vent in private concerning particular board members was, of course, quite another matter, as was their frustration with him. As Kathleen Richardson, his staunchest supporter, confides, "there were always a few on the board who thought Arnold was totally mad and should be got rid of."

By the time Spohr became director, the RWB had been formally incorporated for little more than eight years. The advent of a board of directors in 1949 had soon become an irritation and burden to Lloyd and Farrally, but Spohr saw things differently. His attitude was shaped by pragmatism and by his own character.

Spohr was determined to stick with the RWB. If board members proved difficult at times, he had to find a way to work with or around them. Spohr also acknowledged that the RWB had developed from community roots. Its early volunteer supporters, many of whom went on to become long-serving board members, felt a parental and proprietorial attachment to the company. The board members of non-profit performing arts organizations today are generally recruited for their fund-raising ability and useful business affiliations. In contrast, the active core of the RWB board during Spohr's directorship was largely made up of well-intentioned citizens with a genuine interest in the company's daily affairs and overall welfare. In times of crisis particularly, the RWB has always been able to count on the personal generosity of a few key board members, but in general its members were not large financial contributors.

"In the early days we didn't always have that terrific a staff," says Spohr. "The board really got in and helped and everything came via the board. Little me had to put his hand up to get heard." Spohr saw value in having a variety of viewpoints and seems genuinely to have welcomed the board's very active interest. The more involved board members became, the more they understood how the company really worked, the more useful and committed they would be. And, as Spohr prudently calculated, if board members were fully involved in decisions it would be harder for them to turn on him if something went wrong. He really had no choice in the matter. For the time being, the board ruled and Spohr, for all his ambition, was obliged to be accommodating. As he wryly puts it: "I was ready for the battle, but I was not a full general yet."

The executive committee was central to the RWB's governance. It maintained its supervision of the company through a variety of sub-committees whose number and special functions grew along with the RWB. The most important of these were the finance and production committees. Spohr's position did not automatically give him a place on either the full board or the executive. Of necessity, Spohr was included in meetings of the production committee since it was there that artistic plans were thrashed out before being taken to the executive and then to the full board for approval.

From one perspective, the production committee might appear to have been an unwarranted restraint on the artistic director's authority and ability to discharge his duties but, again, Spohr insists he was happy to listen to its suggestions. "You can't do it all alone. You succeed by working as a team." As he also quickly learned, if he could win over the production committee to his proposals, they were almost certain to be given a respectful hearing by the executive. At that higher level, he could also count on the confidence of Kathleen Richardson, whose sense of duty and commitment to the RWB's welfare Spohr acknowledged to be as fierce and loyal as his own. "Kathleen," recalls Leonard Stone, "always spoke admiringly of 'our Arnold'. It was as if he could walk on water."

The board understood Richardson's importance to the company. While she often played her hand quietly, she did so with telling effect. If Spohr could win Richardson over it was almost invariably a done deal. If she demurred, Spohr knew it was time to back off – although, as Richardson attests, he developed a masterful ability to keep pushing for what he wanted. Spohr says he had a way of "bulldozing". Their complex relationship – Richardson as the perennially wise counsel, practical helper and "anonymous" fairy godmother, and Spohr as the volatile but brilliant director – constituted an animating dynamic that was crucial to the functioning of the entire organization.

Without Richardson, it seems unlikely that Spohr would have survived as director for thirty years. Without Spohr, it is questionable how long there would have been an RWB, at least one to which Richardson was willing to commit a significant portion of her life and not insignificant part of her private fortune. Although her philanthropy and interests extended well beyond the RWB, it was Spohr who made the company into something Richardson could cherish with almost maternal devotion. The results of their endeavours enriched both their lives and shaped the destiny of the RWB.

Tough as it was, Spohr's first season was almost a honeymoon compared with what lay ahead. Even a mini-influenza epidemic that swept through the company during a gruelling three-week winter tour of Western Canada failed to stop the RWB caravan. Spohr described it as an "acid test" for his well-drilled dancers. The tour had begun in mid-January, 1959. The problems began in Vancouver where Olivia Wyatt fell sick with appendicitis and had to be left behind in hospital. Then the flu bug started, spreading from one dancer to another as they huddled in the tour bus. "The iron lung" was what they called it. It did not help that many of the theatres were cold and damp, and it was not just the dancers who suffered. In Calgary, Nancy Noonan, one of the RWB's pianists, came down with pneumonia. Spohr helped carry a stretcher to take her to her hotel room. Noonan had already got Spohr into trouble earlier in the tour. He had allowed her to stay behind in Vancouver to visit friends while the company travelled on by train. Then Noonan failed to make the plane connection that would have delivered her on time and missed a performance. After that incident, Spohr gave Noonan a dog's collar with a cowbell attached, "so we could keep track of her." From then on, Spohr vowed to have everyone travel together.

There was also the frequent problem of dancing on pitted or slippery stages. "We used to paint white circles around the holes so the dancers would know what to avoid," says Spohr, "and after various experiments, including using Coca Cola on the floor, we came up with a way to deal with waxed stages. We'd mop them with methyl hydrate with Dutch cleanser sprinkled in it." Unfortunately, if the choreography called for floor work, the dancers were liable to end up with white bottoms or spotted white legs. "They had the zebra look or the measled body – very aesthetic." The RWB used this volatile concoction for many years unchallenged, until a school principal –

gymnasiums were a frequent venue – caught them at it. She was afraid the stuff would ignite and burn the place down. When the company started using a portable linoleum floor, it was so thick and heavy that on cold travel days the floor had to be left to warm up and still took a good while to roll out.

Dressing rooms were another hazard. In the old theatres they were usually filthy. Constance "Sindie" Officer, the RWB's long-serving wardrobe mistress, usually went ahead to clean up. "Dear Sindie was a helpmate to all," says Spohr. "She paved the way constantly for a pleasant, congenial company. She looked after all of us. She was our Mom and we loved her dearly." Shirley New, who was later to marry fellow dancer Dick Foose, recalls Spohr's special relationship with Sindie Officer. "I believe she was likely his best friend and confidante. He could trust her and she also gave him good advice. At one point Sindie told me, 'He must follow his heart, but my God he must use his head.' Now that is good advice to anyone, don't you think?"

The company soldiered on. Until it had a touring orchestra, the RWB generally had to work with piano reductions. Spohr would sometimes try to conduct the two pianists, to co-ordinate their tempi with the dancing. "But then he would get so caught up with the dancing," says Richard Rutherford, "that he'd lose his place in the score."

The RWB returned to Winnipeg after attracting some of the largest audiences it had ever seen and winning mostly favourable reviews. When the numbers were finally crunched, the board was gratified to discover that instead of losing almost $5,000 as had been projected, there was only a $2,506 shortfall. Even so, the board vetoed Spohr's request to hire a guest artist for the final Winnipeg performances that March. It was already anticipating a deficit for the 1958/59 season and was in no mood to take risks.

The board's budgetary concerns were exacerbated by the possible financial implications of its first collective agreement with the dancers. A contract was then being negotiated with the Canadian Actors' Equity Association. This meant that Spohr would have to wait longer than he would have wished, until his fourth season, to expand the regular company to twenty dancers. It was another five seasons before the RWB was able to employ twenty-five dancers, the number it has generally maintained ever since. Programming was difficult and touring even more problematic because the small size of the company meant there were no understudies to fall back on.

Despite Spohr's huge workload as director, he still managed to create another ballet, *E Minor*. It was given its premiere on January 15, 1959. As with his two earliest works, Spohr returned to his successful abstract format in which the objective was to produce a visual interpretation of the music. The score was the first Chopin Piano Concerto. *E Minor* featured a lead couple and a corps of six women and five men. The costumes were by Grant Marshall and the decor by John Hirsch. As Ted Patterson remembers it, the set included, "an ugly hanging grand eagle type thing on wires." It was later changed to chandeliers.

E Minor did not enjoy the success of *Ballet Premier* and *Intermède.* Marshall, who designed the costumes, considered it a disaster. "There was a hop for every beat of the music." Spohr readily admits that the ballet did not fulfill his intentions. "I was not happy with it. I was so swamped being the director, I did not give it the time it needed." Rachel Browne, who went on to found Winnipeg's Contemporary Dancers, performed in *E Minor* and has more positive recollections. "I can still remember the extreme musicality the man had. Perhaps some of it was too closely aligned to the music but, for what it was, it was very fine. Arnold doubted his innate talent, but I believe he could have become an outstanding choreographer."

Even if the ballet was not the success Spohr would have wished it to be, *E Minor* was performed frequently in 1959. Spohr had only a limited repertoire from which to programme. He included *E Minor* in the final March performances of the 1958/59 season and it was taken on a tour of Western Canada the following fall. The ballet was presented again on the first night of the RWB's late November performances of 1959, and was then laid to rest.

In total, during his first full season as director, Spohr had staged five revivals and three classical excerpts as well as presenting four new works. The wardrobe department produced 106 new costumes. The seventeen-member company gave forty-two performances, including nineteen school demonstrations, for a total audience of 33,560 people. There were ten Winnipeg performances at the Playhouse Theatre as well as two tours that took the RWB 10,270 kilometres, all the way west to Victoria and as far north as Flin Flon Of the sixteen communities visited that season, four had never seen a professional ballet company before. The year-end operating deficit for Spohr's first season was a modest $3,327.48. It had been a busy, full year and quite an achievement.

In 1969, Spohr wrote encouragingly to Pierre Elliott Trudeau, whom he greatly admired, a year into the latter's first term as Prime Minister. "The first year – the hardest, so they say – is over, and things will begin to level off and go more smoothly. Politics seems to me to be even more taxing and unpredictable at times than trying to get a good show on the road!" The following year, Trudeau was confronted with the biggest challenge of his political career – the FLQ Crisis in Quebec, leading to the declaration of the War Measures Act. Spohr's second year as director was no easy ride either.

Spohr arrived back from his study trip to London on July 3, 1959. The company was called back for a special summer engagement, a July 24 Royal Tour Performance at the huge Winnipeg Arena. The Queen and Prince Phillip arrived too late to see *Finishing School* but were present for *Grasslands* and *The Comedians*. The production committee had decided not to include any of Spohr's ballets. However, if the monarch and her husband found time to glance through the event's well-illustrated souvenir programme, they would have found a large photograph of *Ballet Premier*, the work they had seen during a 1951 visit when Elizabeth was an heir, not a queen.

Another of Spohr's early tasks that summer was to persuade the board to hire Miro Zolan as ballet master. Spohr was told that a $3,500 deficit was already expected for the 1959/60 season. No provision had been made to hire additional artistic staff, although in March the board had already expanded the administration by hiring twenty-eight-year-old Robert Johnson of Toronto with the tentative title of "executive assistant to the president". Jacquie Darwin remained as business manager. Johnson's title was upgraded to general manager the following February. Spohr argued that he needed assistance in the studio in order to spend more time on public relations work and educational, audience-building lecture-demonstrations. By July 6, the board had relented and Zolan was duly engaged for the season at $3,000 plus his travel costs to Canada. It was just as well that Spohr got his ballet master when he did. Had the board known that the Royal Tour Performance was going to be a financial bust, they might have been more resistant.

Zolan only lasted one season. The dancers varied in their

opinions of him, but it was clear that Zolan was qualified, experienced and ambitious. He had all the credentials, in fact, to become much more than a ballet master. Yet, by the end of the season, Spohr wanted the executive to let Zolan go. According to the minutes of the meeting, Spohr told board members that Zolan was undermining his authority. Spohr now says the real issue was competence. "I'd have to go in and clean things up because he didn't have a good enough eye." It was duly decided to buy Zolan a one-way ticket back to London where he was soon re-engaged. In 1958, Ninette de Valois had agreed to help establish a classical ballet company in Tehran. Zolan and his wife, Sandra Vane, were among those de Valois sent to Iran to teach and stage productions. Spohr managed to stay on amicable terms with Zolan and eight years later he returned to the RWB to stage Frederick Ashton's effervescent skating-party ballet, *Les Patineurs* – not, as it turned out, entirely to Spohr's satisfaction. The search for Zolan's replacement continued through the summer. The choice finally settled on Gwynne Ashton, a gifted South African teacher and ballet mistress whom Spohr had met in London. She soon became a valuable support to him.

Spohr fully understood that touring, however onerous, was a necessity for the RWB if it hoped to grow artistically. He knew that Winnipeg was too small a city to sustain the number of performances that professional dancers need. He also understood that by gaining recognition outside its hometown, the RWB would have a better claim to both public and private financial support. Yet, like previous RWB artistic directors, Spohr was faced with a board that seemed reluctant to grapple with so huge a fund-raising challenge.

A 1959 fall tour of sixteen cities in Western Canada had produced dismal results. The dancers were exhausted and the company's coffers depleted. In November, with a projected deficit that had already swollen to more than $15,000, the board contemplated cancelling a tour planned for the following January. It was decided instead to expend extra effort to ensure that the next round of Winnipeg performances was well attended.

Some encouraging news came from Ottawa. On November 7, 1959, the RWB gave a special performance at the Playhouse for visiting members of the Canada Council. The production committee decided to include Spohr's *E Minor* on the programme. The following month Peter Dwyer, then the Council's Supervisor of Arts, wrote approvingly to Richardson: "I was impressed with the company and with the spirit which Arnold Spohr seems to have given it." The board might reasonably have hoped that this endorsement boded a future increase in federal support. Instead, the Council, with three eager yet under-financed professional Canadian ballet companies to feed, was already warning that its resources were stretched thin and that the companies must look elsewhere for funds to expand. Within the Council's close-knit bureaucracy staff members spoke anxiously of "the ballet problem" and were already considering some radical plans to solve it.

At least in the fall of 1959 Spohr had a new hit to offer audiences. The RWB gave the premiere of Macdonald's *Les Whoops-de-Doo* on tour in Flin Flon. *Les Whoops-de-Doo* was to become, in Spohr's words, "our bread and butter ballet" over the course of more than 300 performances, but it had an inauspicious beginning. The set was not finished for Flin Flon and Spohr and Macdonald had to go scouting for chairs that were needed in a particular scene, then paint them, praying that they would dry in time. "If we'd got paint on the brand new costumes," says Spohr, "Sindie in wardrobe would have had our hides." As the tour moved on, there were more mishaps. A corral fence in Macdonald's ballet had not been properly anchored and crashed forward with a terrifying bang. The show had to be stopped so that the fence could be properly secured.

In stark contrast to the symbolism of *The Darkling*, Macdonald's *Les Whoops-de-Doo* was a boisterous, rollicking ballet designed to make audiences laugh, even those who did not fully understand how many choreographers Macdonald was spoofing. One of its six sections was titled "Shooting of You Know Who" and was an affectionate send-up of Lloyd's 1950 Klondike ballet, *The Shooting of Dan McGrew*. In a programme note, Macdonald described his work as: "A whoop-up dedicated to the misalliance of classical ballet and the Western myth." Spohr guided Macdonald to a suitable score, Don Gillis' Portrait of a Frontier Town. Macdonald added clapping and square dance calls. The RWB board had, as was its custom, viewed the new ballet before its premiere. Some members objected to what in their minds were certain salacious elements in the choreography that tended to underline the loose morals of frontier life. Macdonald was required to excise the offending parts.

When *Les Whoops-de-Doo* arrived in Winnipeg in late

November, closing each of the three performances, the critics were thoroughly amused and hailed it as a sure audience winner. Even so, that season the RWB failed to draw the expected crowds. Despite the good reviews, an opening night audience of about 900 had dwindled to 500 by the second performance.

The consequences were dire. By February, 1960, the RWB's financial plight had reached a crisis point. The projected deficit now stood at more than $20,000 and the treasurer grimly recommended that no commitments should be made for the next season. Board member John Condra had already spoken with Alderman Crawford of the Winnipeg City Council and been told that the finance committee, "did not think too highly of the RWB". Several board members stressed the need for a public campaign. John Hirsch said it was important to stress that the RWB was the only true Canadian ballet company. Condra, however, saw little hope. "The public in general," he told the board, "would not care one way or the other if the ballet went out of existence." For Spohr, such a prospect was unthinkable. Whatever it took, the RWB would not just survive but grow and prosper. All he could do was keep working ... and worrying.

Bob Johnson also believed the RWB had a future. He had soon proved himself an effective and imaginative manager. Johnson had varied experience as a production and stage manager and had served as company manager for the national tour of *My Fur Lady* and with another touring theatre group, the American Company of Canadian Players. He was working for a New York agency when the RWB hired him. Spohr liked Johnson immediately. "He was a gentle, kind, intelligent soul and we worked well together. We spent long sessions in our rare spare hours together discussing how to build an audience, how to find something that would engage their interest, something that had never been done before."

Johnson was sympathetic to Spohr's desire to invite guest artists. Johnson, therefore, convinced the board that guests should be hired for the Winnipeg performances of December, 1960, which would also mark the RWB's twenty-first birthday. The spectacular result was the appearance of Olga Moiseeva and Askold Makarov from the Kirov Ballet in Leningrad, the Soviet successor to the former Imperial Russian Ballet. Getting them to Winnipeg was no easy task.

Originally, Johnson had hoped for dancers from Moscow's Bolshoi Ballet. He did not know a great deal about ballet but Johnson did appreciate the magic of the word Bolshoi. The name of the company had effectively become a synonym for the art form after the Bolshoi's triumphant visits to the West in 1956 and 1959. By comparison, except among dedicated ballet fans, in 1960 the Kirov Ballet was still relatively unknown. The Kirov did not breach the Iron Curtain until the spring of 1961, when one of its young stars, Rudolf Nureyev, made his spectacular dash to freedom at Le Bourget airport in Paris. It is understandable, then, why in 1960 Johnson wanted dancers from the more famous Bolshoi. Given the fraught state of Cold War politics it was a long shot. Some board members worried about possible demonstrations by local ethnic groups if the Russians came and Johnson appears to have worked concurrently on an alternative plan.

In May, 1960, Johnson reported to the board that the forty-one-year-old reigning prima of British ballet, Margot Fonteyn, along with her Royal Ballet partner Michael Somes, would be happy to appear with the RWB, but by July it was discovered that she was already committed to dance in Chicago. Everything now depended on negotiations with the Soviets.

After the tour mishaps of his second season, Spohr decided he needed to learn more about the technical aspects of theatre. On the recommendation of Robert Moulton, he registered for a month-long crash course at the University of Minnesota. In Minneapolis, Spohr found himself attending class with students half his age who, as he remembers, had a much easier time learning how to wire plugs and lamps. "I wasn't technically inclined. I was so clumsy at it. I used to practise late into the night." The notebooks Spohr brought back – Spohr is an addicted note-taker – are diligently packed with electrical information, diagrams of circuit boards and drawings of different types of lighting equipment. By the end of the course, through diligent application, Spohr learned how to wire equipment, hang and focus lamps and design simple lighting plots. Given the dubious quality of stage lighting the RWB often endured, Spohr wanted to know enough about the technical aspects not to have to accept lame excuses from stage crews. "Even if I couldn't do it myself, it made me aware of what went into it."

In the summer, Arnold Spohr lost his beloved mother. When her weak heart finally stopped beating on August 10, 1960, Spohr was taking a break in Victoria. It still distresses him to remember the moment. "It was terrible to think I could have been there with her. I'm not even sure who was with her at the end. I cried all the way back on the plane." Five days later Hermine was laid to rest in Elmwood Cemetery, in the same plot as her husband. She was seventy-two.

With the company reassembled and the question of Soviet guests still unsettled, Spohr and his dancers left at the beginning of October for a twenty-eight-stop, 16,000-kilometre tour of Eastern Canada, the company's first in almost seven years. In the course of forty-six days the RWB danced forty-three performances. For some of the smaller centres, such as Woodstock, New Brunswick, it was the first ballet they had seen. Some in the audience had driven more than 160 kilometres for the occasion. In Toronto, Ottawa, Montreal and Quebec City, the RWB played to more discerning but equally enthusiastic crowds. A constant theme of the reviews was the way Spohr had revitalized the RWB. Harold Whitehead of The Montreal Gazette wrote: "Whereas before the Winnipeg Ballet was inclined to over-reach itself on occasion, it now stacks up as a neat, well-disciplined little group that can hold its head up in any company."

In Ottawa, Spohr was mortified when, despite the valiant efforts of conductor Richard Marcus, the pick-up orchestra at the Capitol Theatre massacred both the Benjamin Britten score for Macdonald's *The Darkling* and the Brahms for Michel Conte's *Variations for a Lonely Theme*. Britten fared the worst. The band was not only out of tune, it actually missed cues and skipped whole bars. Says Spohr: "There was a squeak here, a very silent groan there; it was as if the orchestra was in a state of shock. I was traumatized." The dancers, remembering their director's "stick together no matter what" maxim, covered splendidly. "Nerves and utter concentration pulled them through." Afterwards, Spohr went backstage to congratulate Marilyn Young, who by then was a sobbing wreck. To the amazement of both, Kathleen Richardson and the Canada Council's Peter Dwyer soon appeared and declared what a wonderful performance it had been. "We looked at them through glazed eyes," says Spohr, "utterly dumbfounded."

Lauretta Thistle of the Ottawa Citizen justly rebuked the orchestra but was delighted with the style of the company. She observed that the RWB "has lost none of its dynamism, bounce or integrity ... to find such homogeneity and brilliance of ensemble is refreshing and amazing." Spohr's relentless rehearsals were paying off. "The plain fact," wrote John Stockdale of Ottawa's The Journal, "is that this company is getting better and better." In Toronto, Herbert Whittaker of The Globe and Mail noted that the RWB was a company that had developed its own style. "It is energetic, vigorous, even brash; it is cheerful and aware. It is, most of all, good-humoured and capable of wit."

Meanwhile, on the Russian front, Kathleen Richardson's connections in Ottawa helped move along the process of engaging guest stars for December. The official request was made within the context of a recently negotiated cultural exchange agreement. Months passed with no response. Further enquiries were made. Spohr and the board grew anxious. Then, in early November, word came that it would be impossible to send dancers from the Bolshoi. Two artists of the Kirov would come to Winnipeg instead. It was still several weeks before their identities were known, but finally it looked as if there would indeed be Soviet headliners for the anniversary performances.

The board was anxiously hoping that the excitement triggered by the imported guests, even at a cost of $3,000, would allow the anniversary performances to turn a profit because, until this point, the season was shaping up as a financial disaster. At an early December meeting of the full board, the treasurer broke the grim news. Despite the generally excellent reviews for the RWB's Eastern Canadian tour, expenses had exceeded revenue by almost $21,000. Unless something changed, the year-end deficit would be more than $54,000, almost four times greater than originally projected.

Apart from the financial risks and alarmist fears about anti-Soviet demonstrations, some RWB board members, perhaps forgetting that Alicia Markova had danced with the company in 1954, worried that engaging illustrious guests would only serve to highlight the limitations of their own troupe. Spohr had no such qualms. Inviting the Russians had not been his idea, but once Johnson had proposed it Spohr was determined it should happen. He often had to wage a quiet war against the provincial outlook of some of his board, and argued forcefully that it was only by bringing the best to Winnipeg that his dancers would improve. "To be the best you have to learn from the best. I have always had this insatiable desire for growth and learning and perfection." Even if his dancers were compared unfavourably, Spohr believed it would give audiences a clear idea of the kind of standards he one day hoped to establish in Winnipeg.

As it happened, the RWB did not look so outlandishly mismatched. Moiseeva and Makarov proved to be congenial guests, adapting as best they could to the small Playhouse stage, and eager to co-operate with their Canadian hosts rather than upstage them. They called the Winnipeg dancers their "comrades in art". The RWB did its part by treating Moiseeva and Makarov like visiting royalty from the moment they stepped off the plane after a seventy-two-hour journey of multiple delays. The two took to Winnipeg immediately. Moiseeva said the weather reminded her of home and enjoyed daily walks beside the frozen river. Makarov was more interested in seeing Ivan Jackson, Spohr's dentist. "He got all his teeth done. How he managed this every morning and danced in the evening, no one knows. That's fortitude!"

The four sold-out performances of December 27-30 became the talk of the town and the Soviet dancers were given a lively reception. Writing for the Winnipeg Free Press, critic Ken Winters noted that Moiseeva and Makarov could "justly preen themselves over the response they aroused". The big event of each programme was Gwynne Ashton's scaled-down staging of *Swan Lake: Act II* in which the RWB performed alongside the stars. Each programme also featured the Soviet dancers in the bravura *Don Quixote* grand pas de deux. The four evenings were variously complemented with the Winnipeg premiere of Montreal choreographer Conte's *Variations for a Lonely Theme*, Boris' *The Comedians*, Lloyd's *Finishing School* and Moulton's *Grasslands*.

Moiseeva and Makarov were all charm and smiles at the RWB's twenty-first anniversary party on December 29. Tutued ballerinas lined the grand staircase as more than 1,000 guests arrived for the lavish festivities at the Manitoba Legislature. There was a twenty-piece orchestra and an elaborately iced, seven-tier cake decorated with twenty-five ballerina figurines. The one on the highest tier was later presented to the Russians. The RWB knew how to party in style.

In view of the public enthusiasm, the visiting stars also agreed to perform a selection of solos and pas de deux for a special New Year's Eve performance. The RWB danced excerpts from the week's repertoire to allow their guests time to change costumes and rest. Reflecting on the anniversary performances, Winters wrote, "Of course, the imported stars have given it exotic glamour, and some extraordinary dancing, but the company itself is in excellent shape, and director Arnold Spohr and his staff have much to be proud of."

With the new year, Spohr was soon busy creating what proved to be his last work for the company, *Hansel and Gretel*. It was commissioned by the Children's Theatre of Winnipeg and first performed for the general public in February, 1961. The ballet used an entirely adult cast. Spohr says he might have included children if they had been available, but explains that it would probably have taken too long to teach them. Richard Rutherford and Lynette Fry danced the title roles. Ted Patterson was a particularly evil-looking witch.

The two-act *Hansel and Gretel* was set to an arrangement of music from Engelbert Humperdinck's 1893 Hänsel und Gretel opera score. Spohr and his music director, Richard Marcus, laboured hard to extract music that would be suitable for dancing. In the end Marcus composed additional music to suit Spohr's needs. Spohr considered *Hansel and Gretel*, his only strictly narrative work, a moderate success. Although it pleased its target market of children, the ballet did not endure long in the repertory. "This is a grand effort for children," wrote S. Roy Maley, "but certainly does not qualify for production for an adult audience." Spohr remembers Claire Jeffery's sets and costumes as being "lavish in colour and spectacle". There were lots of animal characters – a cat, a mouse, an oriole, goldfinches, three bears, a rabbit and a pair of skunks. Several of the dancers had to play two or even three different roles. *Hansel and Gretel* also included a corps of angels which appeared for a dream sequence. The dancing angels waved wands, but the little lights on the tips kept going out. "It always seemed to me that Arnold was trying to create a Walt Disney ballet," says Rutherford.

The board executive was not pleased when it heard, a few weeks after the *Hansel and Gretel* performances, that Spohr wanted a $20 royalty for evening performances of the work and $15 for the matinees. One board member felt that Spohr had been lax in not settling the matter earlier. And why would he be asking for so much when he surely knew that $10 was the RWB's standard royalty payment to choreographers? A committee was appointed to look into the matter of choreographers' contracts. Certainly, it was argued, Spohr should not be paid an actual fee as were outside choreographers. The RWB board most likely did not know that the National Ballet of Canada's Celia Franca was paid neither fees nor royalties for her original choreography and restagings of the classics. Her salary was expected to cover everything. At the same executive meeting, it was agreed to pay Spohr a salary of $4,500 for the 1961/62 season, as well as $600 for running a company summer school. The dancers' wages did not grow proportionately. Apart from David Shields, who managed to negotiate $75 a week, the remainder of the troupe was then paid $50 to $60, depending on seniority.

By this stage in his career Spohr was more than ready to stop making ballets. "I had never aspired to be a choreographer and in the end it was too stressful and took too much energy. Choreographing is like giving birth. You can't tell if it will end up coming out head or ass first." *Hansel and Gretel* was revived for three holiday season performances in late December, 1963, but from that point on Spohr's concerns were focussed entirely on directing the company, on the development of his dancers and the custodianship of other choreographers' works.

• • •

During the first difficult phase of Spohr's directorship, the RWB was shuffling along rather than forging ahead. Spohr had an intuitive sense of where he wanted to take the company but the board appears to have been either unwilling or unable to formulate a long-range business plan that could support Spohr's artistic aspirations. "Remember," he says, "we were starting from the beginning and the pieces had to be put together. Everyone was riding at this time on the glimmer of what might be." In effect, the company lived from hand to mouth in a state of unstable equilibrium, hoping that somehow everything would work out for the best. As a board member noted, the company survived "because the progress and achievements of Mr. Spohr and his dancers made it simply unthinkable to give up."

In November, 1961, the company returned from a well-received twenty-city tour of the American mid-West. It was hoped that the arrival of a second brace of Soviet guests in December would have the same impact on box office that the first couple had had. Rimma Karelskaya and Boris Hohlov carried with them the illustrious name of the Bolshoi Ballet and, although the overall response was more muted than the year before, the performances sold well. The Russians stayed to join the RWB for January performances in Edmonton, Calgary and Vancouver, drawing critical plaudits but mediocre houses. Spohr was flummoxed. The RWB with Bolshoi stars and still people stayed away? He believed inadequate publicity was to blame. The real excitement of Spohr's fourth season was yet to come.

With suggestions coming from all quarters it is hard to be sure where the original idea to present works by Agnes de Mille and George Balanchine came from, but it was a good one. By then in her mid-fifties, de Mille was known almost as well for her lively writings and public speaking as for her accessible ballets and choreography for Broadway musicals. If the company could persuade her to come to Winnipeg, it would be a major coup. So why not ask? The worst she could do would be to say "no". De Mille said "yes". As she later wrote, "I had learned, in a long and checkered career, that saying 'no' hastily can be nearly as unwise as saying 'yes' hastily." De Mille made further enquiries. "They were Scottish, they said, that is, the ones writing me were, and they did ballet. So I said I would do them a Scottish ballet and it would be a tragedy because that would be easy. Anyone who pays attention can learn tragedy. It's comedy that takes flair and finesse." The end result was de Mille's agreement to stage her 1953 *The Bitter Weird*, with music from Brigadoon, the musical she had choreographed on Broadway in 1947.

The idea for a Balanchine ballet had probably been floating around for some time. Balanchine was already established as one of the greatest choreographers of the twentieth-century, the man who had re-invented his Russian classical ballet heritage for a new age and a new continent. Was the RWB ready to dance his often fast, complex style of neo-classicism? They would only know by trying and Spohr, at least, felt it was a challenge the dancers needed.

It was Sol Kanee who made it happen. Kanee was, in Spohr's apt description, "a powerhouse". He was a wealthy, respected, no-non-sense businessman, a miller and grain exporter, who travelled widely and had impeccable political connections. "He was going to be in New York," says Spohr, "and said he'd go see Balanchine for us to try to get a ballet." The RWB had luckily hit the right moment. Balanchine was in a generous mood and seemed willing to share his ballets widely. At much the same time he agreed to allow the National Ballet to perform *Concerto Barocco*. Balanchine offered the same work to Kanee but, as the story goes, Kanee thought it might be too much of a challenge. He asked for something smaller. Balanchine offered his *Pas de Dix*, to which Kanee replied, "How many dancers does that need?" The ballet, created by Balanchine in 1955 as a showcase for his dancers, had already been broadcast from Montreal by Radio-Canada, the French arm of CBC, in one of several extra-ordinary telecasts of Balanchine's work.

The de Mille and Balanchine works were scheduled for the season-closing Winnipeg performances of March, 1962. Balanchine rarely left his New York City Ballet to stage works elsewhere. The setting of *Pas de Dix* was delegated to one of his former dancers and ballet mistresses, Una Kai. De Mille did come. She arrived with her assistant James Jamieson in mid-February, 1962, to be greeted by what she described as "a committee thick with furs". Spohr had attempted to meet de Mille during a brief visit to New York the previous summer but, when he called her, got a decidedly frosty reception. She first professed to have no idea who he was, which was probably true, then told him she saw no reason for them to meet. "We'll talk when I get to Winnipeg." Spohr was taken aback. "Who did she think she was, the Queen? I wondered what I was in for when she did arrive."

Certainly de Mille could be imperious. Her contacts so far had been with fur-coated board members. As far as she could see, Spohr was merely the ballet master, studiously taking notes of her rehearsals. She ignored him. Spohr admits he found de Mille intimi-dating and discourteous. But as he got to know her better, Spohr understood that her manner stemmed from her own insecurities. De Mille was, however, impressed by the dedication and discipline of Spohr's dancers. After a week she and Jamieson were gone, apprehensively leaving the ballet in Spohr's care. When de Mille returned a few days before the opening, she was astounded to find that Spohr had refined, polished and clarified everything. "Can you believe it? The work had actually improved," de Mille recalled twenty years later. "That's what broke the ice," says Spohr. "We started talking and Agnes soon became one of our best friends." De Mille left Winnipeg filled with admiration for Spohr and the RWB and was happy to sing the praises of both to any who chose to listen.

The opening night audience's response to the two additions was ecstatic. All three performances featured *The Bitter Weird* and *Pas de Dix*, which were variously complemented by familiar revivals of Boris' *The Comedians*, Conte's *Variations For a Lonely Theme*, Macdonald's *The Darkling* and Moulton's *Grasslands*.

The Bitter Weird, with its tragic story of two rival Highland chieftains vying for the same girl, mesmerized the audience. De Mille graciously accepted its enthusiastic ovation. She later told a reporter that the RWB was "a wonderful company with great variety of talent and extremely strong dancers." De Mille brought a number of them to New York that summer, including her particular favourite, Richard Rutherford, to dance in a revival of the musical Brigadoon.

Pas de Dix received an equally warm welcome from the public, although the critical response varied. As Spohr expected, *Pas de Dix*, not considered one of Balanchine's great ballets, had proved a challenge to the dancers. It is set for a lead couple and corps of four women and four men, to music of Alexander Glazounov. Balanchine created it "after Petipa", meaning he had extracted and assembled parts of the great nineteenth-century choreographer's full-length *Raymonda*. There was an overall flavour of Hungarian exoticism and the ballet included a difficult male pas de quatre. It was so difficult that the following October, when the ballet was repeated, Spohr cut the section. "The four boys weren't good enough. They could not get their double tours right," he says. "You don't show the public what isn't ready or good enough."

In his report for Saturday Night magazine, Ralph Hicklin rhapsodized over *The Bitter Weird* and the revival of Macdonald's *The Darkling*, thought the company yet unequal to the challenge of Balanchine's *Pas de Dix* and emphatically hated Michael Conte's *Variations for a Lonely Theme*. However, Hicklin's overall impression was more than favourable. "The Royal Winnipeg Ballet deserves fervent devotion," he wrote. Hicklin singled out Marilyn Young for special praise, declared Richard Rutherford to be "the best male dancer I have seen in Canada" and summarized his feelings about the company in terms that proved prophetic. As the RWB closed its twenty-second season, Hicklin wrote, "… the Royal Winnipeg Ballet is a young, handsome, enthusiastic, intelligent company. Its artistic director, Arnold Spohr, obviously exercises good discipline and has a sense of direction … If those who govern the company's policies – and, of course, raise its funds – take to heart the lesson that it takes greatness to make greatness, I suspect that some great things will come out of Winnipeg in the next few years."

In contrast to Hicklin, S. Roy Maley of The Winnipeg Tribune felt the company acquitted itself well in its first encounter with Balanchine: "The methodical, studied approach at first dissolved later into dazzling technical work towards the end of the ballet." Ken Winters in the Winnipeg Free Press, who had chanced to see Balanchine's own New York City Ballet perform *Pas de Dix* in Vancouver the previous summer, was just as encouraging. In Vancouver, he had found the ballet "heartless as a doll and thin as paper". Now, in the context of the programme Spohr had assembled around it, Winters found *Pas de Dix* much more to his liking and, noting how few purely classical works the RWB had at its disposal, judged it to be "an invaluable repertorial acquisition".

Balanchine's choreography became an important component of the repertory of many North American ballet companies from the 1960's onward. It is interesting, however, that in Spohr's years the RWB acquired relatively few Balanchine works, even as the company's overall technical standards improved. Both Les Grands Ballets Canadiens and the National Ballet of Canada acquired more substantial and representative Balanchine collections. It was fifteen years before Spohr added another Balanchine ballet, and then only his *Glinka Pas de Trois*. *Allegro Brillante* followed five years after that and the spectacular *Tchaikovsky Pas de Deux* arrived in 1982. Apart from their audience appeal, many directors consider Balanchine's work to be ideal for developing speed, precision and musicality. But it was precisely because everyone else was dancing Balanchine that Spohr held off. His goal was to make the RWB distinct and to give the dancers ballets in which they could look their best. If everything could not be tailor-made through original commissions, he at least wanted his acquisitions of existing works to be unusual. It was a shrewd policy because, as it transpired, the RWB's marketability depended not simply on its compact size and ability to travel at relatively little cost, but on the fact that it was different. As de Mille observed of the company: "The repertory is very special and it is their own." The RWB's other great calling card was its unique gusto, its ability to communicate with audiences. That emphatically came from Spohr and from his ability to infuse the company with his own evangelical zeal for dance.

The success of the March, 1962, Winnipeg performances was important in another respect. In Ottawa, the Canada Council had resolved to conduct a survey to decide the future of the country's three professional ballet companies. Peter Dwyer was already reaching the conclusion that, given the companies' chronic financial plights, the best course might be to combine their resources in one organization that would tour the country. The issue was about who should get the jackpot. The National Ballet in Toronto felt it was the logical candidate, but the Council had already grown exasperated with the company's continual pleas for additional help.

In 1961, the Council decided to seek outside advice. It had already asked the National Film Board's Guy Glover for an assessment. After complex negotiation, the Council also secured the additional services of Richard Buckle, the British dance critic and historian, and Lincoln Kirstein, the wealthy, erudite arts patron who had persuaded Balanchine to come to the United States and with him co-founded the New York City Ballet.

As word of the Council's survey spread, the National Ballet and Les Grands Ballets Canadiens made strong arguments for continued support. The RWB seems to have remained oddly unconcerned. At the time, Spohr's impression was that Dwyer was hoping the survey would justify cutting off Council funding to all but the National Ballet. Dwyer, an Englishman and former British MI6 counter-intelligence specialist, might have been thought to favour the Toronto company, but he felt no great affection for Franca. It was, after all, the National Ballet's chronic financial demands that had brought things to a head. All Dwyer and his Council colleagues wanted was a workable solution to their "ballet problem".

A solution was not forthcoming. The results of the survey were never published. Lincoln Kirstein, whose disdain for the National Ballet was already known, had, it transpires, a strong partiality for Ludmilla Chiriaeff's Les Grands Ballets Canadiens and its Russian-style training. Both Kirstein and Buckle were in Winnipeg for the March, 1962, performances and were not about to write the RWB out of existence. The National Ballet fared worst in the survey.

The Council found it impossible to draw a decisive recommendation from the reports. So, after spending some $15,000 on the survey, the Council was left to manage its "ballet problem" as best it could, which meant no change. Independently, another British critic, A.V. Coton of The Daily Telegraph, had taken his own look at Canadian ballet early in 1962 and, in an article widely republished in Canada, declared he found it odd that some Canadians thought three companies amounted to too much ballet. As is usually the case in Canada, regional diversity triumphed over national homogenization.

In late August, 1962, Spohr started the season by providing his dancers with the stimulus of a renowned guest teacher, from London, Audrey de Vos. She stayed for six weeks and was the first of many distinguished teachers whom Spohr was able to persuade to come to Winnipeg. De Vos' approach had great appeal for Spohr and became a lifelong influence. "She really knew how to place a body, how to coordinate all its parts to move and jump. She was like dynamite with a positive energy and knowledge that would electrify the students. She could change bodies in a week, releasing them and setting them free to dance." De Vos was impressed by the dedication of the Winnipeg dancers whom she found adaptable to new ideas and styles.

While de Vos was at work, the RWB finally did what Spohr had been wanting from the start. It officially launched its own school in new rented premises on Smith Street that brought the administrative and artistic sides of the company under one roof.

Gweneth Lloyd no longer had any official role in the affairs of the RWB but she was still the long-distance proprietor of the Canadian School of Ballet in Winnipeg. The school and company had long shared the same rented premises. The school was an independent commercial operation and provided Lloyd with a modest but significant source of income. It also served as a useful source of intelligence concerning RWB goings-on, and Lloyd was not shy about using it. For example, in the summer of 1959, when she learned that Spohr had chosen not to hire a number of girls from the school who had been studying on scholarship, Lloyd complained to Kathleen Richardson. Her letter compared Spohr's chosen dancers un-favourably with her own scholarship students. "I had always hoped that the policy of the RWB would be to encourage our native dancers and not to go abroad for them unless absolutely necessary." In a courteous but firm reply Richardson pointed out that the company engaged by Spohr included ten Canadians, four Americans, two English and one South African. Reassuringly she informed Lloyd: "There is a general instruction to Arnold (with which he fully concurs) to take Canadian dancers in preference to any others of like ability." Beyond this requirement, Richardson explained, the choice was Spohr's alone. The exchange served to underscore the ambiguous relationship of Lloyd's Canadian School of Ballet with the RWB.

Spohr had continued to emphasize the importance of founding a company school. For him it was fundamental. All great companies, he argued, were built on the foundation of a school, pointing to Britain's Royal Ballet and Balanchine's New York City Ballet as prominent examples. It was, of course, exactly the way the RWB itself had emerged almost twenty years earlier, except Spohr was now aiming for was a school with two distinct divisions. The general school would serve for amateur and recreational dance fans, attracting wider local interest in the art form, building potential audiences and, he trusted, turning a profit. A separate division would train those with the talent and potential to become professional dancers. To develop the RWB otherwise was, as Spohr would fondly repeat, "to put the cart before the horse". In Spohr's mind, the RWB's post-fire crisis years were a watershed. Although he intended to build on the traditions established by Lloyd and Farrally, Spohr saw his own advent as director as a fresh beginning.

From June 26 to August 6, 1961, the RWB had held its first summer school under Spohr's direction. David Shields, who had now taken on additional duties as a company ballet master, and soloist Lynette Fry made up the rest of the faculty. Almost sixty students from Canada and the United States were enrolled and the summer school managed to show a small profit. The following year, the RWB formally acquired the Canadian School of Ballet. The way it was accomplished did little to improve the RWB's already cool relationship with Lloyd. In December, 1960, at its own cost, the company had invited Lloyd and Farrally to the twenty-first anniversary celebrations, but they had politely declined.

It was the company's decision to move into rented premises of its own that finally resolved the issue of the school. Lloyd realized it would be impractical to try to operate her school without the RWB as a co-tenant, particularly if the company intended, as it clearly did, to launch its own school in new premises. In a series of exchanges with the RWB board, Lloyd tried to negotiate the best deal she could. With little leverage at her disposal, Lloyd was ultimately compelled to accept the modest payoff of a five-year appointment as curriculum advisor to the new company school at $1,000 per annum.

The prospect of an official school excited Spohr and he had assumed that ultimate authority and responsibility for its operation would rest with him as the company's artistic director. He was deeply hurt when the board decided to put the new school under the separate direction of his former dance partner, Jean McKenzie. Although it remained part of the RWB, the school was placed under the supervision of a separate board of directors. Spohr was asked to head the school's curriculum committee.

Spohr was later to discover that Lloyd had intervened in his plans. He came across a letter she had written to Richardson. "... entre-nous, much as he appears to be making a success of the directorship of the RWB I feel very strongly that Arnold would not be the right person. His academic background does not give him the authority." Spohr maintains that his academic credentials as a ballet teacher in fact outranked both Lloyd's and Farrally's. "Imagine Gweneth's gall," says Spohr.

For Spohr, the future success of the company depended on the school. Although he knew it would take years before the full benefits were felt, Spohr expected the school to become the major provider of new dancers for the company. From a practical standpoint this would reduce the RWB's dependence on outside recruits. More importantly, it would allow the company to groom students to fit its specific artistic needs. Spohr therefore felt strongly that, as artistic director, he should be in a position to decide how the students would be trained, particularly given his own professional teaching qualifications and experience. From the immediate perspective of the RWB board, it was more important for the school to produce sufficient revenue not only to underwrite its own activities but also to generate a modest surplus for the company.

Without full authority over the school, Spohr was compelled to use a combination of wile, badgering and diplomacy to shape its development according to his master plan. This vision included creating a professional stream that would be distinct from the larger commercially-based recreational school. In 1962, a first step in this direction was taken when, at Spohr's urging, a special roster of advanced classes was arranged for students with obvious professional potential. This special training stream was the precursor of a professional division within the school that was established eight years later. Meanwhile, Spohr, through his annual study trips abroad, took it upon himself to search out a training system that would produce strong, versatile dancers.

• • •

Even in his senior years, Arnold Spohr loves to travel. Bus, train, ship, plane, camel; the mode of transportation hardly matters. His mind still hungers for new experiences and for understanding. In his formative years as the RWB's director the hunger was intense. "My travelling was part of my educational programme," says Spohr. Although he never felt himself to be truly off the job, the short seasons in Spohr's early directing career provided him with ideal opportunities to see the world and he did not hesitate to grasp them. Several of his journeys were specifically to study dance, often with the assistance of Canada Council grants.

In 1962, he observed classes in Moscow and Leningrad. He also visited the schools of Britain's Royal Ballet and the Royal Danish Ballet in Copenhagen and watched performances and classes in Oslo, Stockholm, Paris and Vienna. Spohr took copious notes. What he wanted to understand most were the fundamental principles, the foundation stones, on which the different systems were based. It was in Stockholm that he first met the great Russian-born teacher Vera Volkova. At this point she was long settled in the West and was considered its leading authority on the Vaganova system of ballet training. Spohr became an instant disciple. "I saw her teach just one class and said to myself, 'This is it'." For six summers in a row Spohr travelled to study with Volkova in Copenhagen and was finally able to bring her to teach in Canada. As a result, Volkova was to have an important influence on the RWB and its school.

Spohr also visited New York to see Balanchine's School of American Ballet and even ventured to the temple of American modern dance, the Martha Graham studio. Wherever Spohr went, doors opened for him. His direct, friendly manner and obvious enthusiasm were hard to ignore. "You see," he explains, "I've never been not me. People befriended me and I stayed friends with them from then on."

In 1963, Spohr circled the globe in a three-month trip that included stops in ten countries. On April 3 he headed west to Honolulu, then on to Japan, Hong Kong, Thailand and India. From there he travelled to Israel and Egypt. Along the way Spohr saw a dizzying variety of performances. In Japan he watched a Geisha ceremony and the Grand Kabuki Theatre, as well as a Western-style review. According to Spohr, the show, with its 300 girls, put the Rockettes at New York's Radio City Music Hall to shame. In India, he was taken to a wedding. "The groom," he recalls, "was seven, the bride six, and the sword used in the ceremony was bigger than the groom." In Thailand he saw ceremonial folk dancing and in Egypt, inevitably, belly dancing. "It must be the origin of the bumps and grinds," Spohr told a reporter on his return to Winnipeg. His guided tour also took in the Valley of the Kings, the Sphinx and the pyramids. In Israel, Spohr visited many of the biblical sites he had read about as a child under his father's instruction. And, of course, there was more folk dancing. The serious study part of Spohr's 1963 tour included another stay with the Royal Danish Ballet to learn about its crisp, light-footed Bournonville style of dancing. Then he continued to London to take advanced classes in the Cecchetti method.

As far as Spohr was concerned, everything fed into his work as a director. "I feel all dance is related in some form or style," he told critic S. Roy Maley. "Ballet does not begin and end with the five positions. Ballet has to do with people, emotions, colour, attack, styles, rhythm, etc." For Spohr, watching people carry a load of rags down a street in Calcutta or a geisha pouring tea in Kyoto could be as instructive for his understanding of human movement as the most refined pirouette. Even the movement of animals fed his imagination and stocked his motivational arsenal as a coach in the studio.

In the spring of 1964, Spohr made a month-long tour of South America where, among other memorable experiences, he almost got caught up in a crowd of stampeding soccer fans in Peru and witnessed a nighttime voodoo ritual in Brazil. "They were sacrificing animals which were strewn on the ground. The grass was covered with blood. The hearts of the animals were hung on the trees."

There was more blood two years later when Spohr set off on one of his greatest adventures, to Africa. He still recalls vividly the blood dripping from the fangs of a lion as it ripped into the flesh of its freshly killed prey; and the towering Masai warrior he met in Kenya. Then, there were the snakes. "Someone told me they liked to crawl in and curl up under the bed. I didn't want to wake up and find some cobra in my face." Spohr made sure to check under the bed but still had restless nights. Although he claims to have stuck to bottled drinks in Africa, he managed to contract an agonizing intestinal ailment. Jerry Shore remembers getting a distress call from London as Spohr made his way back home. "I met him at the airport and took him straight to St. Boniface Hospital." It was several months before Spohr felt thoroughly cured.

• • •

In Spohr's fifth season, 1962/63, the company danced only five public performances in Winnipeg. "We still have to overcome the Winnipeg block to ballet and get decent houses," Spohr explained to the Winnipeg Free Press. That did not stop local complaints that the RWB was preoccupied with touring and was offering its home audiences too many revivals. Spohr was becoming dejected. "Slowly we were putting things together. I was chipping away constantly. But where was the breakthrough going to be? It all seemed so dark."

That fall Spohr had been driven to distraction as dancer after dancer was felled by injury during a tour of the north-central United States and Ontario. "Thank heavens we rehearsed everything thoroughly before we left and had understudies prepared to cover if needed," says Spohr. By now, he also made sure the company went on the road with its own small orchestra, as an insurance against the kind of musical disaster that had occurred in Ottawa during the company's previous visit.

Spohr did introduce a new ballet to Winnipeg in December, but for children not adults. There were six Christmas performances of Toronto choreographer Don Gillies' *The Golden Phoenix*, which was, like Spohr's *Hansel and Gretel*, a commission from the Children's Theatre of Winnipeg. As Spohr saw it, these were ideal opportunities to instill a love of ballet among young Winnipeggers and therefore were an investment in the company's future. Programming ballets specifically for family audiences became a continuing theme in his directorship.

Spohr took the RWB on its first overseas tour in 1963. The company danced in Jamaica from January 5 to 11 at the celebrations marking the island's independence from Britain. The RWB proved so popular that during the visit it was asked to give three extra performances. One was in the capital, Kingston, for almost 20,000 children, all smartly dressed in their school uniforms. "The uniforms were different colours," says Spohr, "so they looked like a tulip field or a multi-coloured blanket." The company danced on a platform stage in the blazing sun, in the middle of a huge sports stadium. The dignitaries, including the governor general, Sir Clifford Campbell, sat close to the stage. The children were seated at a respectful distance. Many of them had been bussed in from outlying communities and were seeing ballet for the first time. Within twenty-four hours of flying home, the sun-tanned dancers found themselves in sub-zero temperatures. They were back on the tour bus heading for Saskatoon. When they moved on to Regina they found the stage so pitted with holes it had to be covered with masonite.

The tour to Jamaica cost the RWB more than $7,500 but by year end the overall season deficit was not much greater than that. This was the result of stringent cost controls and a fund-raising campaign that brought in $40,000. Nevertheless, Spohr worried that, without a major breakthrough that would in some way inspire the company's supporters, the RWB was likely to remain stuck where it was – on a plateau.

Spohr was convinced the RWB now had the potential to achieve greater heights. He was slowly building his artistic team. The multi-talented Jim Clouser – dancer, composer and choreographer – had by now contributed several works to the repertory and became Spohr's assistant. A school was in place which, given time, would allow the company to generate its own supply of dancers. Already the company roster included several seasoned artists with more than enough talent and personality to light up a stage. Even if the RWB's home audience was unpredictable, the company was steadily establishing a presence and reputation across Canada and in the United States. Audrey de Vos, who had returned to teach in December, 1963, appeared to share Spohr's optimistic ambition. "The remarkable development of the Royal Winnipeg Ballet since my last visit a year ago," she told a reporter, "strengthens my belief that this is a company with a bright future. Its exceptionally fine spirit of vitality is a tribute to Mr. Spohr who has achieved a balance of discipline and individual development rare in the ballet world today."

The 1963/64 season turned out to be the breakthrough Spohr had been praying for. It might not have been, but for the presence in January, 1964, during the company's Winnipeg season, of an influential American with the key to the RWB's future. His name was Ted Shawn.

The Sky
is the Limit

Jacob's Pillow, in the Berkshires near Lee, Massachusetts, is a magical place. It started as a hilltop farm. The locals thought the switchback road up to the property looked like the rungs of a ladder, Jacob's Ladder. Then someone decided one of the rocks that dotted the property resembled a pillow. So the farm, modifying the biblical allusion, became Jacob's Pillow. In the days of slavery it was a safe haven on the Underground Railroad. Dance did not come to Jacob's Pillow until 1930, when American dance pioneers Ruth St. Denis and her husband Ted Shawn bought the farm. In 1933, after the two had separated, Shawn remained, making Jacob's Pillow the summer home of his company of eight male dancers. The "tea-lecture" demonstrations Shawn's company gave were the beginnings of what, after World War II, became a thriving annual summer international festival that featured every imaginable kind of dance. By the 1960's, "The Pillow", its short-form name, was a mecca of dance. Since critics and producers from all over came to see what was going on, it was a place where everyone was eager to appear.

Arnold Spohr had been trying for three years to get Ted Shawn to invite the RWB. He knew that Les Grands Ballets Canadiens and the National Ballet had already danced at The Pillow and that rankled him. Spohr's chance finally came when Shawn agreed to come to Winnipeg in 1964 to see what all the fuss was about. Shawn already had a one-week opening tentatively marked off for the RWB. Whether they would get it depended on what he saw. Shawn was duly impressed. "He loved our dancers," says Spohr, "the way they projected and their joie de vivre." As Shawn put it to a reporter: "The dancers all appear to be having a wonderful time and this quality infects the audience." Shawn was particularly impressed by the company's men and also admired a recent addition to the repertory, *Aimez-vous Bach?*, a restaging by Brian Macdonald of his clever choreographic trip through ballet classicism and beyond. Spohr, Shawn declared, must bring both it and his company to the festival that very summer. He told Spohr he was going to try to open up a two-week spot for the company. "I almost danced for joy when I heard that," recalls Spohr. "Our rises from plateau to plateau had been minor compared with this. It was going to be our big chance, the moment I'd worked so hard for, when I finally could see the light."

The light seemed to be pouring in from all directions. The Peruvian ambassador to Canada, Max de la Fuente, had seen the RWB and in March, 1964, told the board that he believed the company would be a perfect cultural ambassador to South America, particularly since Winnipeg was to host the 1967 Pan-American Games. Fuente was going to speak to some of his other South American ambassador colleagues in Ottawa about it. Almost exactly two years later, the RWB embarked on the first of several visits to South America.

Also in March, 1964, Macdonald created another light-spirited work. With his genius for satire, Macdonald produced a wickedly hilarious send-up of Russian nineteenth-century story ballets, complete with a convoluted plot and a diva ballerina. He called it *Pas d'Action*, a compact little ballet for one woman and four men. "We were in terrible financial problems," says Spohr. "The costumes were old ones pulled from the wardrobe. We were being creative on very little money. Brian really saved us with his imagination and un-believable drive, breaking new ground and giving us our character, a mix of serious and fun. No one can live without humour or some fun, otherwise you have a slow death." In recognition of his contribution, the board named Macdonald official choreographer to the Royal Winnipeg Ballet. "Another first," says Spohr. "Brian deserved it."

As much as Spohr acknowledged the RWB's debt to Macdonald, he felt it worked both ways. Years later, when the RWB was riding high, Spohr would describe Macdonald as one of his many choreo-graphic "discoveries". In a letter to William Como, editor of Dance Magazine, Spohr wrote: "He [Macdonald] was just busy doing a lot of TV and getting nowhere, so we gave him his start." It was while working with the RWB in 1963, Spohr went on to explain, that Una Kai, ballet mistress for the Joffrey Ballet, first saw Macdonald's work and took word of it back to New York. The result was a commission from Joffrey. *Time Out of Mind*, the work Macdonald created in New York, was, as Spohr puts it, "Brian's passport to international success."

The dancers were already in high spirits when they arrived at Jacob's Pillow in July, 1964. The company had used Shawn's invitation as the anchor for a northeastern United States tour, opening with a three-day appearance at the Boston Arts Festival early in the month. The tour included a swing into Atlantic Canada so that the RWB could become the first ballet company to dance in the theatre of the new $5.6-million Confederation Centre in Charlottetown. Six provincial premiers were there to see the company dance and a Royal Message from Buckingham Palace, congratulating the RWB on its twenty-fifth season, was read from the stage. The company ended the tour, its first in summertime, under a tent, dancing for a near-capacity audience at the Long Island Arts Festival. As the tour progressed there was the now familiar catalogue of illness and injury. "It was like an injury corps," quipped Spohr to The Winnipeg Tribune. Richard Rutherford danced with a high fever. Fred Strobel put a hip out. Worst of all, leading ballerina Sonia Taverner injured her foot early on and Marilyn Young was called out of retirement to replace her. "I've never had so many emergency rehearsals in my life," says Spohr.

On opening night at Boston's Public Garden stage, lightning began to flash ominously during de Mille's *The Bitter Weird* and drops began to fall. As the rain came down the musicians, fearing for their instruments, dropped out one by one. Someone held an umbrella over the pianist, Sylvia Hunter, and the company danced on. The audience stayed too.

"Dance theater is their forte, in a relaxed and relaxing manner," wrote The Boston Globe's Margo Miller. "Purists may shiver, but ballet is fun", headlined the Boston Herald. "A raw company, bold, brash and full of sass," rhapsodized Alta Maloney of The Boston Traveler, "without the polish of its European counterparts and totally lacking in the sly sensuality of some more effete groups, they brought a new kind of cool Canadian air here." Kathleen Cannell of The Christian Science Monitor noted the RWB's ability to win people over. "They danced with a joy, vitality, and mastery that conquered the capacity audience with the first steps."

The first week's reviews from Jacob's Pillow were equally positive. The company had been billed as Shawn's star attraction of the summer, the "crown jewel" he called it, and the RWB did not let him down. Spohr's *Ballet Premier* was politely received as an effective vehicle for introducing the dancers and displaying their classical abilities. The hits were *Aimez-vous Bach?* and *The Bitter Weird.* Marilyn Young and Richard Rutherford were often singled out for special praise. So were Jim Clouser and the young Bill Martin-Viscount, one of Spohr's special protégés. As Shawn himself had noted in Winnipeg, the RWB had unusually gifted men.

It was at The Pillow that Walter Terry became one of the company's most ardent admirers. "The company, directed by Arnold Spohr," Terry wrote in the New York Herald Tribune, "is composed of youthful, exuberant, personable and excellently trained dancers, equally at home in classical measures, in jazzy comedy, or in intensely dramatic dance. Here, indeed, is one of the most engaging ballet groups functioning this side of the Atlantic." Allen Hughes of The New York Times, while slightly more reserved than Terry, admired Spohr's "adventurous programming" and the dancers' impressive versatility. According to Hughes, the RWB demonstrated that "a ballet company need not have great size or dazzling dance technicians to ensure its artistic success".

"Jacob's Pillow," says Spohr, "was proof that there is nothing like rehearsal and hard work; some of our dancers were yet deficient in technique but knew the roles and the technique submerged into the role." Spohr did not miss a line, thrown almost as an afterthought, into Richard V. Happel's glowing review in the Berkshire Eagle: "Ballet director is Arnold Spohr whose high artistic standards are evident throughout." Lillian Moore, covering the second week's completely different programme for the New York Herald Tribune, picked up on the theme: "Arnold Spohr, the director, has every reason to be proud of his fresh and appealing company, and Ted Shawn must be congratulated for bringing it to Jacob's Pillow."

In 1964,William Littler, today one of Canada's most seasoned and respected dance critics, was a young writer for The Vancouver Sun. Late that August, he interviewed Spohr, who had come to Vancouver to teach at Mara McBirney's school. Spohr was forceful and direct in explaining his ideas, particularly his concept of the art form and his goals for the company. What he said was in effect his credo: "I believe ballet should be entertainment. People shouldn't be afraid of it. I want to make sure our company always has something vital, interesting and alive to give to its public, so ballet can gain its rightful place here as it has in Europe; so people will go to ballet as they would a football game, because it is part of their lives and heritage.

"That's why every year I have got to bring forth ballets that are alive and meaningful and of the spirit of our country. This is a lifetime job – to keep the art alive, to train dancers who can pass it on to the next generation. I never want our company to get too big so the dancers will feel like numbers. Everyone is important and everyone belongs.

"The newest member of the company should feel he is essential to the company – and he is. With this sense of belonging and achieving, you get results, you build a tradition."

• • •

In notes for the personal memoir Arnold Spohr may yet write, he greets the advent of the company's twenty-fifth season, 1964/65, thus: "THE DAWN BREAKS – DAYLIGHT APPEARS – RESURRECTION AND THE LIGHT – THE CAVE DOORS SEPARATE AND WE CAN NOW SEE THE SKY AND STARS. HEARKEN TO THE AIR AND SUN – THE SKY IS THE LIMIT."

The summer of 1964 totally revitalized Spohr and bolstered his sometimes-wavering confidence. In six years as director he had learned a great deal, surmounted many hurdles, honed his dancers into an effective ensemble and proved the company had a place in the wider world of dance. Spohr's belief that the RWB could aspire to international stature was clearly now achievable. More importantly, others began to believe it too. Within little more than a year Spohr would be leading his company to London, three years after that to Paris, Moscow and Leningrad, then to Central and South America and as far away as Australia. "The world," says Spohr, "was opening up for us and fortune was beginning to smile." However, it took more than Spohr's artistic abilities and energetic leadership to make it happen. It needed street smarts. Enter J. Sergei Sawchyn.

Sawchyn joined the RWB as general manager that summer. During the next eight years he was to play a central role in transforming the RWB into Canada's pre-eminent international touring attraction. Sawchyn and Spohr were an odd pairing. It took Sawchyn a while to get used to what he calls Spohr's "campy showiness" and "spittle-producing effusiveness", but a respect developed and Sawchyn even found himself adopting a few theatrical affectations of his own. He and Spohr negotiated a not always easy yet effective relationship. The results were astonishing in both scope and pace. Seasons grew longer. Tours became more frequent and extensive. The whole organization became intensely focussed and driven. When Agnes de Mille staged *The Golden Age* for the RWB in 1967 everyone was too busy to see that its title summed up what they were living through.

Like Spohr, Sawchyn was born in Saskatchewan. Unlike Spohr, it took him longer to leave. He grew up in a large working class Ukrainian family in Regina. His parents were members of the Communist Party of Canada until the organization was officially banned early in World War II. From childhood, circuses and carnivals fascinated Sawchyn. As a scrawny kid, one of his favourite haunts was the carnival midway where he would sometimes shill for the ball-throwing concession. As a teenager, he once had a job setting up folding chairs at the Armories in Regina for a visit by the Minneapolis Symphony. Sawchyn was intrigued by the whole idea of a travelling orchestra. After the concert he approached a musician and asked where he was going next. "Saskatoon," was the answer. Sawchyn was mightily impressed. The musician, tugging off his bow tie, added, "Buses and small towns are no fun, kid. Never take up the fiddle!"

Sawchyn began buying the trade paper, Billboard. In the 1950's it covered everything from musical theatre to the recording industry. "It is surely in those pages that I first fell under the spell of the exaggerated quotation and the superlative adjective. Other friends wanted to perform when they were young. Me, I just wanted to produce it, put it on the road, make it happen."

Sawchyn moved to Winnipeg in 1959 as area manager for a direct-sales sterling silver company. He built a home, married, had a son and launched a side business with three ice cream trucks under the name Tommy Tipper's Freezer Fresh. For a while Sawchyn even operated a trampoline centre called Jolly Jump. His lawyer, Colin Crawford, was president of Rainbow Stage. In 1963, the general manager's position became vacant and Crawford offered the job to

Sawchyn. He accepted and promptly had his new Chevy painted in rainbow colours.

It was while making a public plea on Rainbow Stage's behalf to the council of suburban St. Vital in 1964 that Sawchyn ran into Vaughan Baird. Baird was part of an RWB search committee for a new general manager. Baird was impressed by Sawchyn's pitch to the burghers of St. Vital and told him he should apply for the ballet job.

Sawchyn had seen the RWB perform. He remembers the special ambiance of the old Pantages Playhouse – also the small audience. He recalls Fred Strobel dancing the lead in Peter Darrell's *Chiaroscuro*. He had to look up the word in the dictionary when he got home. Sawchyn was also impressed by the music, the colour and especially the lighting. However, this was scant qualification to be the company's general manager, so he called Baird and declined the invitation to apply. Sawchyn admits his own insecurities and mis-conceptions may have influenced the decision. Unlike the Soviet Union where ballet had been opened up to the masses, in capitalist societies, it seemed to Sawchyn, ballet was still the domain of a privileged elite. Then there was the homosexual issue. Sawchyn insists he was not what would now be called a homophobe, but he did have sensitivities. "In a time," says Sawchyn, "when we didn't talk openly about such things the rumoured 'gayness' of dancers and ice skaters could be shameful."

By the time news of the RWB's success at Jacob's Pillow filtered through to the Winnipeg newspapers, Sawchyn was reconsidering the prospect of working for the company. "By some instinct I felt the civic danger of failing to capitalize on it. Those years of reading Billboard perhaps prepared me intuitively to recognize what was needed. 'Stunning', 'Magnificent', 'Unequalled', 'As seen in New York'. I knew what I would do given the chance."

Sawchyn now asked to be a candidate for the job. Baird gave him an icy response, but Sawchyn got his interview. "I remember Kathleen Richardson's smile and her eyes widening as I went on and on." He was signed to a one-year contract at $600 a month. Sawchyn quit Rainbow Stage immediately and worked at the RWB without pay for several weeks before his contract was activated.

As far as Sawchyn knew, Spohr had not been consulted. He remembers Kathleen Richardson explaining to him early on that he must understand that Spohr was only the "director" of the company.

"Artistic direction", Richardson explained, came from the board, from the production committee. Sawchyn's response was that Spohr was still going to get top billing – "Arnold Spohr: Director". That was show business. As general manager, Sawchyn wanted to create a strong public image for Spohr. His name was profiled in almost everything the company published. Oddly, Spohr's actual billing fluctuated. As early as 1967, the season souvenir book carried bilingual billings and Spohr became "Director/Directeur artistique". In the early 1970's, the souvenir books began listing him as "Artistic Director", then switched back to "Director". Whatever the title, it was increasingly clear that Spohr was the man at the top and the centre.

Sawchyn and Spohr already shared something in common. Like Spohr, Sawchyn had come to embrace the notion that ballet is an inherently popular art, as Gweneth Lloyd had asserted years earlier, "beer and skittles for the people". The art itself did not have to change. What it needed was high-powered marketing, based on Sawchyn's belief that there was a large potential audience to be tapped. Spohr was delivering high quality goods. They just needed selling.

In this regard, Sawchyn had the full agreement of another newcomer to the RWB, James R. Cameron, an employee of the advertising agency Cockfield-Brown. Jim Cameron knew a bit more about ballet than Sawchyn. While still a student at the University of Manitoba, he had even seen Spohr dance in a Winnipeg Ballet performance of 1947.

By 1964 Cameron had drifted far from ballet and was a busy family man when his boss, a former RWB board member, told him he had received a visit from Kathleen Richardson. The RWB needed someone to write a brief that would convince Lester Pearson's Liberal government to send the company to the 1965 Commonwealth Arts Festival in London as the Canadian exponent of Terpsichore's art. Richardson and the board were determined that the honour should not fall to that self-proclaimed "National" troupe in Toronto. Kathleen Richardson and Sol Kanee, soon to become president of the RWB, both had excellent connections with the Liberals in Ottawa, which they put to effective use. But there still had to be a formal proposal.

Cameron was aware that Pearson, in the midst of a battle over a new Canadian flag, had more important things on his mind than tutus. So, Cameron decided to take his commission to write a brief quite literally. If it was to get Pearson's attention, the "brief" better live up to its name and have all the hallmarks of an official document. The brief contained just three points. The RWB was provably portable. It already had a good reputation abroad. The company was distinctly Canadian. Cameron supported this succinct summary with impressive and voluminous addenda.

"If Pearson laughs," an Ottawa official told Cameron, "you're in." Pearson laughed. The RWB got the nod for London. Cameron was taken onto the board with responsibility for publicity and ticket sales. It was a responsibility that jibed well with Sawchyn's ambitions for the company. In many ways, both men felt like outsiders, to the extent that they were not part of the well-connected social elite that made up much of the board. Cameron and Sawchyn forged a friendship that has lasted until this day. They thought it was ridiculous that the RWB hardly had enough season subscribers to fill two rows in Winnipeg's almost 1,500-seat Playhouse Theatre. Sawchyn still recalls the exact number of subscribers when he arrived, 137. He and Cameron were determined to remedy the situation.

When Sawchyn joined the RWB, arts marketing was in its infancy. The concepts of branding, high-powered promotion and mass marketing were scarcely understood. Sawchyn launched a broad offensive on several fronts. The "Winnipeg" in the company name did not mean much to foreign audiences, so Sawchyn had "Canada's Royal Winnipeg Ballet" painted in big, bold letters on company trucks and tour buses. At home he launched major subscription campaigns. Appealing brochures went out in mass mailings. Telemarketers went to work, enticing customers with tales of the enchantments awaiting them at the ballet, and urging them to sign up before it was too late. By the 1970/71 season, subscription sales had risen to 6,509.

Once the Commonwealth Festival engagement in London was confirmed, Spohr began to worry. "Everything was happening for us so fast." In August, 1965, Spohr delivered a formal "Director's Report" to the company's board of directors. He says it was his first such report because in the past he always seemed to have been away, "studying, learning, shopping for new talent and ballets". Having reviewed the previous season's successes and the bright prospects of the new one, Spohr sounded a note of warning: "From these giddy heights a good fall could occur. With much more hard work, concentration, discipline, dedication, another Mount Everest must be achieved; ever onward and upward."

Dick Foose, then a dancer with the RWB, remembers getting off the plane after the overnight flight from London. The dancers stopped by the hotel to drop off luggage and then were bussed straight to Sadler's Wells Theatre, which had been assigned for rehearsals. "All we wanted to do was sleep, but Arnold was so anxious. He wanted everything to be perfect. He thought we needed to 'get our feet under us' and so we had to warm up and run through a few things."

The tour to London was another important milestone for the RWB. It was the first Canadian ballet company to dance in the British capital. Attendance at the Piccadilly Theatre was initially disappointing. On opening night, September 16, Commonwealth Arts Festival organizers had also programmed a huge, multi-cultural dance gala at the colossal Royal Albert Hall. However, by the RWB's third and last evening the theatre was almost packed. Those who came were immediately charmed. Macdonald's ballets – *Pas d'Action*, *Aimez-vous Bach?* and especially *Les Whoops-de-Doo* – worked their usual magic with audiences. Compared with the cool reserve and understatement of British ballet, the Canadians were extroverted, funny and even a little impudent. It was a breath of fresh air. On closing night the cheering and rhythmic clapping for *Les Whoops* went on so long that Spohr finally ordered an encore of the "Jingles" section. David Pulver, reporting for the Winnipeg Free Press, wrote that Spohr was beside himself with joy. He kept exclaiming, "I can't believe it – to have this kind of reception in London! It's marvellous, marvellous, marvellous!" According to Sawchyn, it was the first time ever that the company had been cheered on to an encore. Rudolf Nureyev was in the audience and insisted on meeting the dancers afterwards. When Spohr finally got to the stage door an enthusiastic crowd was waiting for his autograph. "Imagine, in London they wanted my autograph. Little me from Winnipeg."

The London critics were careful to distinguish between the dancing and the repertoire. The former they generally admired. About the latter they had mixed feelings. Writing in the Sunday Times, Richard Buckle thought the classical duets on the programme were offered "as a kind of affidavit". He continued, "but what we don't see so often, and are consequently bowled over by, are such high-spirited and irresistible personalities as Richard Rutherford, Jim Clouser and Bill Martin-Viscount." Commenting broadly on the repertoire, The

Observer's Alexander Bland – a collaborative pseudonym for Nigel Gosling and his wife Maude Lloyd – was guarded. "In fact it aims at a simple appeal; the loftily poetic, the far-out, the profound are not its line. To elevate this area, which lies dangerously near to musical comedy, to the level of art is not easy. This lively troupe often achieves it." Picking up this theme in the magazine Dance and Dancers, John Percival suggested the nature of the repertoire reflected the RWB's need to cater to the tastes of Canadian audiences, which, Percival wrote, "on this showing were not, on the whole, notably sophisticated or subtle."

Still, by the time the RWB had completed its tour with performances in Cardiff, Glasgow and Liverpool, Sawchyn and Cameron had plenty of glowing press extracts to add to the RWB's promotional kit. Sawchyn had moved quickly on his original instinct to capitalize on the company's success at Jacob's Pillow. The glowing reviews had been copied and packaged in impressive informational kits that went out to dance critics, ballet companies, impresarios, theatre managers, cultural mandarins and Canadian ambassadors. Says Cameron: "I could write press kits, but it was Sergei who imagined them."

Like many RWB board members of the time, Cameron found himself spending many evenings away from his family, working for the company. In 1966, he quit his ad agency job and went to work in the president's office at the University of Manitoba. "It was the time of the student rebellions," he explains. "The university needed someone to connect it with the media." By 1969, the student movement had gone flat as a pancake. That autumn, Cameron was planning to head for Toronto, where, as he puts it, "all good ad men go". Then the RWB's board president persuaded him to stay as Sawchyn's associate. Cameron agreed. "Sergei made an art of management and we got on well."

Sawchyn used Jacob's Pillow as the leverage to secure major engagements abroad in cities the RWB had scarcely dreamed of visiting. The bread-and-butter tours across North America continued, but with more panache and efficiency. Sawchyn's dream was to make the RWB Canada's best known touring attraction, at home and abroad, and he wanted its Canadian identity to be at the forefront. Sawchyn proudly told a reporter in July, 1971: "We don't see ourselves as a Royal Winnipeg Ballet. We see ourselves as Canada's oldest ballet, as a national ballet and one of the nation's treasures."

Sawchyn quickly branded the RWB as accessible, dynamic, youthful and exciting. It had been all these things before he arrived – now everyone knew. Sawchyn also believed in brand affinity and since New York's Hurok organization was identified in the public mind as the classiest presenter of international performing arts attractions in North America, he decided the RWB should be on the Hurok roster. The RWB embarked on the first of eight marathon Hurok tours of the United States in the fall of 1965.

The tour brought the RWB to New York for the first time. It danced at Hunter College Playhouse, and then crossed the East River to perform at Brooklyn College's Walt Whitman Auditorium. In advance of the company's arrival, the New York Herald Tribune had printed a glowing account of Spohr and the RWB by Walter Terry. "If Winnipeg's ballet company dances as well for us in Manhattan as it did at Jacob's Pillow or last month in its own home town, we are in for a truly royal treat." Terry kept up the good work once the company opened on October 29, but Clive Barnes, only recently arrived from London to be dance critic of The New York Times, was soon begging to differ. In a review filed after both New York City performances, Barnes wrote: "This is a lively troupe, going nowhere in particular, but going there with a charming zest. The albatross it wears round its neck is the absence, or so it seems, of any creative choreography." Then came the real sting. "The company's qualities of vitality and freshness are evident. But if this company intends to make its mark in anything other than a purely local fashion, it will require a far firmer sense of artistic purpose." Spohr can still get upset about that review.

Barnes' judgement can partly be explained by his general antipathy for Agnes de Mille's choreography. Spohr had shown *The Bitter Weird* and de Mille's 1964 work, *The Rehearsal*, a theatricalized account of how dancers prepare, which de Mille herself narrated. But, without articulating it, Barnes had also hit on a dilemma that even Spohr could acknowledge. Within its limited resources the RWB needed to build a repertory that would appeal to the many small centres it visited and to its Winnipeg audience, yet also please more sophisticated tastes. Finding the right balance was a constant challenge.

Touring had undoubtedly earned the RWB considerable prominence in Canada and a growing reputation south of the border. The

Hurok tours turned the RWB into a household name among ballet lovers in the United States. The human cost was rarely talked about, the sheer relentlessness of life on the road. Spohr's dancers may have been one happy family in his mind, but after a month of forced companionship in buses, dressing rooms and hotels, even the happiest family can get snippy. The dancers used to joke that the people who planned the tours used a big map and a set of darts. Wherever the dart hit was where the company would play the next night.

Writing in March, 1969, Frank Morriss recalled his own experience on tour with the company and the way Spohr kept everyone going. "He was always the first up in the morning and the last to bed at night. When the dancers were in low spirits, which was often, he spurred them on. If they deserved a verbal spanking, they got that, too. But I think they always realized, in the end, that they deserved it."

A sampling of the statistical record is numbing. During that first sixty-day Hurok tour in the late fall of 1965, the RWB travelled almost 17,700 kilometres, coast to coast, dancing in thirty-seven cities. A winter tour in 1968 covered forty-two cities in fifty-five days. In October, 1971 the company left on a forty-seven-day tour, during which it gave a total of thirty-nine performances in everything from high school gymnasiums to elegant opera houses, in thirty-five cities. All but three of these engagements – Spokane, Tucson and Urbana – were one-night-stands. Dancer Bonnie Wyckoff wrote to an absent Spohr from a winter tour in 1976: "On our way to Kalamazoo today – honestly, I feel like sending the Hurok office a map of the U.S.A. the way this tour is zig-zagging back and forth!"

Spohr was more than aware of the problem and was constantly urging Sawchyn to attempt to negotiate less exhausting tours. However, Hurok's attraction to the RWB was the fact that as a touring operation it filled a gap that larger, costlier, less intrepid companies could not. The RWB was compact and efficient, had an accessible, portable repertoire and was ideally marketable to smaller com-munities. Unless the company was willing to change its whole character and scale of operation, lengthy bus-and-truck tours were its inevitable lot.

When he toured with the company, Spohr would find whatever way he could to maintain the dancers' spirits. His presence alone had its own invigorating effect. Spohr's regular seat on the bus was right at the front and he tried to make a point of occupying it well ahead of the scheduled departure time. It positioned him ideally to glare through narrowed eyes at any late arrivals. Chronic latecomers were in any case traditionally greeted with a chorus of hissing to which even Spohr was not immune. Sometimes on tour, if there had been a reception after the performance, Spohr would be inclined to tarry with the local grandees while the dancers waited impatiently to return to their hotel for a good night's rest. In one such instance, having been met with a particularly hearty round of hissing, Spohr snarled: "Well, all you have to do is dance."

Sawchyn turned the RWB into an amazingly efficient touring machine. During its constant travelling, the RWB learned a great deal about how to move sets, costumes and equipment quickly and economically, but Sawchyn saw plenty of room for improvement. He sketched the first drawings of aluminum ladders to which stage lamps would be permanently attached. In the past, the company had carried cast iron stands and iron pipes and then fixed loose lamps to them. The new ladders could be positioned on stage straight out of the crate. In preparation for the 1968 tour to France, the USSR and Czecho-slovakia, Sawchyn designed wardrobe containers made of aluminum with zippered vinyl sides to replace the old 200-pound crates. There were huge savings in freight costs. The job of turning Sawchyn's bright ideas into reality fell to Hungarian-born Tibor Feheregyhazi. He was then the RWB's production manager and many years later became artistic director of Saskatoon's Persephone Theatre.

The ingenuity of the RWB's packing system earned the company many compliments and, as the word spread, its production staff would routinely be asked where such serviceable containers could be acquired. It soon dawned on Sawchyn that there was money to be made. In 1969, the RWB started a modestly profitable sale and rental side-business called Tour Lite. Sawchyn's money-making schemes were many and various. Having made "RWB" a known brand why not franchise it to selected ballet schools across Canada? The scheme might even turn up some fresh talent for the company. By 1971, he was even mulling over the idea of selling specially packaged "RWB" tea.

Spohr did not let Sawchyn's inventive marketing tactics lull the company into a sense of false security. "You're only as good as your last show," was another of Spohr's constantly quoted mottos. As he told a reporter: "The public is not gullible and stupid. You can induce them in, but once they're there you have to produce for them. There has to be something happening."

Sawchyn brought a new energy to the RWB, one that matched that of its artistic director. Spohr, however, was sometimes wary of his new manager. There was an inscrutable, mysterious dimension to Sawchyn's character that made Spohr uneasy. He did not completely trust Sawchyn's motives. There was a volatile chemistry between the two that could flare up into heated arguments.

By this point, Spohr had begun to take Valium to calm his nerves. "There were times he got so overwrought," admits one of the dancers, "that we would drop one in his coffee before an opening just to quiet him down." When Spohr needed to snap into high gear he would take a stimulant. "He became increasingly irritable and unstable and resorted to placing blame, as stressed-out people most often do," remembers Sawchyn. "In meanness, I denounced him as a 'pill-popper' in several of these set-to's. My temper had worn even shorter, and it was a bad combination." As Jim Cameron recalls: "They used to fight a lot. In the end, I really don't think they liked each other."

"Arnold always seemed to be on the point of resigning," says his friend and sometime room-mate Jerry Shore. He even remembers times when Spohr would return to their apartment so demoralized and despondent that he would talk dramatically of "putting an end to it all". Histrionic and hypochondriacal Spohr could be, and frequently was, but suicide was simply not his style. That would have been equivalent to quitting. Some way or another, he would do his best to get along with Sawchyn.

Kathleen Richardson, meanwhile, liked them both. "Sergei was young and ambitious and he came to us after a string of mediocre managers. While Arnold developed the company, Sergei found the stages. He was absolutely brilliant at that. The two locked horns frequently but that's not so bad. The creative sparks that came off were to everyone's advantage."

Many of the dancers were also wary of Sawchyn. To them it seemed as if he viewed them as dispensable pawns, marketable commodities in a larger game. Spohr steps cautiously around the issue. "The constant touring, always breaking new ground, sapped their energy. I sometimes felt that the dancers were not always looked after honestly and properly or paid due heed. The result was unrest."

It is not uncommon for dancers in ballet companies to distrust management. Sawchyn's responsibility was to sell the company, boost revenue, control costs and run an efficient administration. This set of priorities inevitably put Sawchyn on a collision course with the dancers who, not unreasonably, considered themselves woefully underpaid. Spohr generally tried to keep out of any disagreements, but occasionally he felt impelled to intervene. In one instance, during the company's visit to Leningrad in 1968, three male dancers stormed into Spohr's room backstage shortly before a performance. Their pay envelopes were short. As Spohr understood it, money that the dancers were said to owe the company had been deducted. They were so incensed that Spohr was worried it might affect the quality of the performance. He promised there and then to make up the amount from his own pocket. However, not knowing the details of the situation, Spohr was diplomatic enough to give the money to the men's girlfriends rather than to them directly.

If Spohr harboured any fear that the locus of power within the company was shifting, he could always count on the loyalty of the dancers. Although he drove them hard, they knew that Spohr ultimately had their interests at heart. "They make or break the company. Give them true support, love, care, harmony, honesty and trust. My philosophy is that happiness breeds success, so never hurt anyone."

The Taking of Paris

The Winnipeg Tribune of November 21, 1968, ran a large editorial cartoon. Two gendarmes are observing a clamorous crowd gathered outside the Théâtre des Champs-Elysées in Paris. With recent student demonstrations in mind, one of the officers has a worried expression. The other comforts him with the caption: "No, it's not another riot, just that Winnipeg Ballet."

The RWB's appearance at Jacob's Pillow in 1964 was a major breakthrough, reinforced by its 1965 appearance at the Commonwealth Arts Festival in Britain. The company's visit to France, the USSR and Czechoslovakia three years later firmly sealed the RWB's international reputation and was a turning point in Spohr's career as artistic director. However much the company's success was the result of a team effort, Spohr's ability to inspire the RWB was ultimately decisive. It was from the heady events of 1968 that the image of Arnold Spohr as a miracle-worker took firm shape.

The 1968/69 season had begun with a July engagement in Stratford, Ontario. It was followed by an intense rehearsal period leading to the company's inauguration of the new Manitoba Centennial Concert Hall. The new theatre, with a huge stage to fill and almost 800 more seats than the Playhouse to sell, represented a fresh challenge to the company. In an act of unprecedented bravado, Spohr and Sawchyn conspired to capture international critical attention by unveiling four additions to the company repertoire on the same programme. All were by noted American choreographers and two were commissioned works. New productions of Todd Bolender's *Donizettiana*, in its North American premiere, and Anna Sokolow's

Opus 65, kept company with creations by John Butler and by the twenty-six-year-old maverick, Eliot Feld.

Donizettiana, the programme opener, was an abstract music visualization in classical style. Butler's erotically charged and allegorical *Labyrinth*, to Canadian composer Harry Somers' Five Concepts for Orchestra, featured David Moroni as a man torn between two women – Christine Hennessy and Dianne Bell. Butler's programme note described it thus: "A man enters the labyrinth of the world today, a landscape of unreasoned terror and violence." His choreography, angular and sculptural, had more in common with modern dance than classical ballet. After the intermission, the mood lifted with Feld's new ballet, *Meadow Lark*. It was only his third ballet, but Feld's earlier works – *Harbinger* and *At Midnight* – had marked him as a choreographer to watch. Feld was already notorious for the appalling way in which he treated dancers. Spohr's attempts to mollify what he described as Feld's "cruelty" had little effect. Yet *Meadow Lark*, set to a Haydn flute quartet, was all joy and sunshine, a warm-spirited ballet that both challenged the dancers with its technical subtleties and admirably suited their effervescent person-alities. The evening closed on an arresting note with Sokolow's part humorous, part sinister observations on the dance rites of alienated contemporary youth. *Opus 65*, set to a jazzy score by the American composer, arranger, occasional performer and producer, Teo Macero, was decidedly avant-garde by Winnipeg standards. Even so, as the dancers ended the ballet, sitting on the edge of the stage and glowering at the audience, the house erupted in enthusiastic applause.

The programme was a bold exercise in repertoire building and Spohr made sure that Clive Barnes, now established as the most influential dance critic in North America, was there to see the results. Barnes was duly impressed. Apart from filing a generally favourable review, he followed up with a more reflective article under what at the time became a much-quoted headline: "How can the Royal Winnipeg Ballet be that good?"

"Perhaps Winnipeg's very isolation," Barnes suggested, "makes it look more closely and lovingly at its own arts." Again Barnes reminded his readers that the RWB had been more notable for the freshness of its dancing than for its repertoire but praised Spohr for giving the company "a strong personality of its own". Much to Spohr's delight, Barnes noted the unusual vigour of the male dancing and ended on a high note. "It looks as though a new wind is blowing across the prairie."

Barnes was only one of several leading critics enticed to Winnipeg by Spohr's adventurous new programming. Among others were, from New York, Walter Terry, writing for The Saturday Review; Doris Herring from Dance Magazine and an exceptional gathering of Canadian critics – the Ottawa Citizen's Lauretta Thistle, Ralph Hicklin of the Toronto Telegram and Nathan Cohen of The Toronto Daily Star. Opinions varied on what Hicklin called "an extravaganza of new riches", but the dancers, despite Barnes' reservations about their competence in pure classical work, emerged with their collective reputation burnished to a high gloss. "The Royal Winnipeg Ballet," declared Cohen, "is one of the few companies in North America with a truly distinctive style."

The performances should have boosted the company's confidence as the countdown for the Paris International Dance Festival began, but the pressure of preparing so many ballets soon took its toll. Spohr had already vowed never again to present so much new work on a single programme. In an unusual move, the RWB had scheduled a second autumn appearance in Winnipeg. The programme was to include works destined for Paris and de Mille had returned to Winnipeg to revive *The Golden Age*. Then Hennessy sprained an ankle in rehearsal and Shirley New injured a foot. Spohr saw disaster looming. "I was having a fit." He was forced to replace Macdonald's *Pas d'Action* with Gloria Contreras' *Moncayo 1* and drop the de Mille ballet. The disgruntled lady, before decamping for New York, made public her opinion that too much strain was being placed on the dancers and that the RWB needed four additional lead performers. Spohr was, conveniently, "unavailable to comment".

When the RWB left Winnipeg for Paris on November 15, 1968, it was still unclear whether its prima ballerina would be able to dance at all. A report in The Winnipeg Tribune suggested that Hennessy might be able to appear by the time the RWB arrived at its second stop, Leningrad. Nobody, least of all Spohr, imagined that Hennessy was about to become the toast of Paris.

The RWB's Paris engagement had great symbolic significance. The art of ballet may have had its beginnings in Italy but its full flowering had occurred in France. Even if the Paris of 1968 was of far less consequence as a ballet capital than either London or New York, the city still enjoyed an image of sophistication and high-brow culture. The venue itself had great historical significance. In 1913, the first performance of Vaslav Nijinsky's ground-breaking choreography for Stravinsky's *Sacre du printemps* had provoked a riotous reaction at the 2,000-seat Théâtre des Champs-Elysées. How, Spohr wondered, would its chic audience respond to what Clive Barnes described as the RWB's "prairie freshness"?

Spohr took scant comfort from the fact that another Canadian dance troupe, Les Feux Follets, had appeared at the same Paris theatre earlier in the fall. The critics had been guarded in their response to the Quebec company's folkloric brand of cheerful Canadiana, but the audiences responded warmly. There was, however, as Spohr knew well, a difference. The RWB would be measured by the precise and well-established standards of classical ballet. Prairie freshness alone would not be sufficient. Only the most die-hard Parisian balletomanes had heard of the RWB. To their later regret, some of the local critics regarded the company's appearance as inconsequential enough to justify skipping the opening performance. Few had a clue where Winnipeg was.

Spohr was worried that his company, with minimal decor and simple costumes, would look like a poor cousin to such other festival participants as the Vienna State Opera Ballet, the Ballet of the Teatro Colón from Buenos Aires, New York's Alwin Nikolais Dance Theater and the well-upholstered Ballet de Strasbourg. In a last-minute bid to add a touch of opulence to Macdonald's *Pas d'Action*, the RWB's production manager, Tibor Feheregyhazi, was sent off with the equivalent of $400 in his pocket to buy richer-looking coloured velvet to replace the simple black curtains that had been brought from Winnipeg. About an hour before the show, Feheregyhazi returned with suitable fabric only to find the French stagehands were taking a supper break. "Arnold was in an absolute frenzy," says Feheregyhazi. "I tried to calm him down." Finally the stagehands appeared and, with only minutes to spare, did an expert job of attaching tie lines.

Spohr's programme was cleverly designed to offer a mix of styles and themes and to create an emphatically distinct image for the company. The German critic, Jochen Schmidt, described Spohr's programming as "a supreme stroke of theatrical genius". The company opener, *Aimez-vous Bach?*, had already proved its popularity with Paris audiences. At the 1964 Paris festival, the ballet had won Macdonald a gold medal when it was performed by the company he then directed, the Royal Swedish Ballet. The mood shifted from the lucid classicism and jazzy dance riffs of *Aimez-vous Bach?* to the darker tones of Todd Bolender's psychologically probing dance for three couples, *The Still Point*. Next came Macdonald's hilarious "story ballet to end all story ballets", *Pas d'Action*, with its savage spoof on classical ballet conventions. The evening closed with Sokolow's disturbing commentary on disaffected youth, *Opus 65*. In this instance, rather than sitting on the edge of the stage, the cast ended the ballet by jumping into the orchestra pit.

The dancers approached their opening performance with trepidation. Beautiful costumes and decor had not spared the Ballet de Strasbourg from being booed off the stage. Spohr watched Macdonald's rehearsals of *Aimez-vous Bach?* with particular concern. "Brian was so nervous he'd made all these changes to the tempi. I told the kids to do it just the way we'd rehearsed it in Winnipeg." The dancers protested. The choreographer was telling them how he wanted it danced. Now their director was ordering them to disobey. "You do it the way I say," retorted Spohr. "If there is a problem with Brian I'll take the responsibility. I'm still the director here." They did it the way Spohr wanted and it went off perfectly. "I don't think Brian even noticed. If he did, he never mentioned it to me. How could he? We'd made it such a success."

The reviews for the November 19 opening performance stunned everyone. The dancers knew they had connected with the audience. Despite the sporadic boos that greeted *Opus 65*, the RWB received multiple standing ovations. Critics are rarely swayed by the crowd, but in this case they were equally charmed.

One of France's most respected critics, Claude Baignères of Le Figaro, led the pack. "This classically trained company refuses to cling to academism as a scholastic ideal. It freely takes liberties with traditional vocabulary, but only after having demonstrated that it is unbeatable in the more orthodox technique." Like the majority of his colleagues, Baignères favoured the Macdonald ballets over their American companions. René Sirvin of the right-wing morning daily L'Aurore was equally fulsome. "This sincere company takes such tremendous pleasure in dancing that it is visible to all who watch; a company which puts its heart into doing its best, and through this shows itself to be far superior to the other companies at the festival."

Olivier Merlin of Le Monde went so far as to describe the RWB as the best classical company ever to have appeared at the Paris festival, but regretted the inclusion of a parody ballet, Macdonald's *Pas d'Action*. Thomas Quinn Curtiss' review in the International Herald Tribune read: "The performance of this gifted, youthful Canadian company is a sheer theatrical delight, fresh, crisp and overflowing with an exhilarating spontaneity." Curtiss boldly predicted that the RWB was "certainly destined for high honors".

Christine Hennessy was quickly being singled out as a veritable star. Her brilliant portrayal of Princess Naissa in *Pas d'Action* was especially favoured. Sirvin proclaimed Richard Rutherford "the great revelation of the whole evening." Baignères and Schmidt were equally attentive to the corps. Unusually for a critic, Baignères named ballet mistress Gwynne Ashton and ballet master Eugene Slavin. "They know well how to get from their pupils a total individual mastery and a collective discipline." Reporting for Frankfurter Allgemeine, Schmidt compared the RWB corps de ballet's "fresh, athletic prowess and their immaculately clean performing" with that of the Stuttgart Ballet and Royal Danish Ballet. Youra Bousquet of Combat, another French daily, was astounded that dancing of such high calibre could come from a country better known for its "wheat and meat". A week later Leo Ryan filed a special report for the Winnipeg Free Press, crisply summarizing the critical reaction in Paris: "They came, they were seen, and they conquered". Now for Russia.

Sawchyn had worked hard to engineer an invitation to the Paris International Dance Festival. He had worked even harder to penetrate the Iron Curtain. Sawchyn flew to Moscow "on the coat tails" of the Montreal impresario, Nicolas Koudriavtzeff. Sawchyn went with one sheet of paper, a contract written in Cyrillic. On the way back to Winnipeg, Sawchyn stopped in Ottawa with the signed contract to see Jean Gignac, then head of the Cultural Section at the Ministry of External Affairs. Gignac was not pleased. The ministry, he said, had no money in the current year's budget to support the RWB's visit to Russia. Sawchyn waved the contract in front of Gignac. The RWB would be going anyway. "Eventually," says Sawchyn, "we got a paltry twenty-five thousand dollars." The federal government got a lot of mileage out of its investment. "Our embassy in Moscow had never been as proud of Canada as it was during that tour."

When Spohr heard the news that Sawchyn had booked Russia, he was aghast. "He just collapsed into his chair, boom, like a sack of onions," says Sawchyn. "He went white. He hadn't expected it, I suppose, and he was tired. We'd been going at this increasing speed for three years. He was very negative. What would we take? Were the dancers good enough? How were we going to find the time?" Sawchyn repeated what he had told Gignac. "We have a contract. I've committed us to Russia. We can't not go." It did not take long before Spohr was his ebullient self again. "My Gawd! I don't believe it!"

Spohr and his dancers hardly felt like conquering heroes by the time they reached Leningrad. The journey was an ordeal in itself. Their flight was delayed in Warsaw and, when news came that Leningrad airport was snowed in, the company was diverted to Moscow and travelled the rest of the way by train. Leningrad offered little encouragement. It was cold, damp and dark. The hotel accommodations were dismal. "My hotel room was small, bleak, the bare necessities," says Spohr. "Our ballet mistress Gwynne Ashton's was similar, only she had the good fortune of having a broken window stuffed with newspaper." Food was in short supply and the city itself, once the glory of the Romanoff empire, was sadly dilapidated. At least the theatre, the almost 4,000-seat October Hall, was new.

Then, as the dancers rehearsed for their Leningrad opening, the news arrived from Paris. The RWB had been awarded the festival's gold medal for best company and Hennessy the same honour as best female performer. "I was totally flabbergasted," says Spohr. "Here we were this little company from Winnipeg, Canada, and we'd just been judged the best out of all these companies. It was almost unbelievable."

The RWB celebrated with a champagne reception and official approbation from the highest level arrived in the form of a telegram from Prime Minister Pierre Elliott Trudeau. He congratulated the company on its "blistering performance" and described its medal-winning achievements as a "grand jeté" for Canada.

Hennessy's triumph in Paris inevitably sparked rumours that she would soon be lured by more lucrative offers elsewhere. Hennessy was by then in her third season with the RWB and might understandably have been attracted by a big-city company that promised less bus-and-truck touring and a more glamorous home than

Winnipeg. But, as Hennessy told Frank Morriss, who was on tour with the RWB, she was inclined to stay. "I feel I am in good hands. Arnold Spohr, the artistic director, is very kind and Miss Ashton works very hard with me ... They know me very well and they try to bring out the best in me." Hennessy remained with the company until 1971, long enough to enjoy a second round of accolades in Paris. She was not the first company ballerina to discover that a humane and artistically nurturing environment can be its own reward.

The Leningrad engagement was the toughest part of the tour. Instead of applause the company was greeted with virtual silence. "I guess they didn't understand what we were about," says Spohr. For once the RWB's prairie freshness failed to enliven audiences. There was also sickness to contend with.

"In Russia," says Shirley New, "most of us had bouts of the trots, but we had been warned by the embassy and had lots of Kaopectate with us." It got so bad that a doctor would sometimes come to the theatre before a performance to give injections for nausea and diarrhea. The shots did not work for Shirley New. "Good old Arnold. He had two buckets put in every wing where needed. Wardrobe changed my costumes so I could use the Arnold buckets quickly and make the next entrance. I refused going into a Russian hospital and chose to perform sick instead." New was hospitalized on the company's return to Winnipeg and was off work for almost four months.

Spohr had worried whether he had suitable repertoire for Soviet audiences, particularly for Leningrad with its refined taste for pure classicism. In this case he had good cause for concern. Not just in Leningrad but elsewhere, critics were puzzled by programmes consisting of what they described as "divertissements". "Our ballets with their sometimes complicated plots and mimic scenes," wrote one Soviet critic, "are not familiar to Canadians."

In the city where Marius Petipa had created his classical masterpieces, Macdonald's *Pas d'Action*, with its fun-poking at the more ludicrous conventions of nineteenth-century story ballets, got a cool reception. One critic lamented the absence in the repertoire of ballets that tackled "problems of social significance". Natalia Dudinskaya, a celebrated former ballerina and wife of Konstantin Sergeyev, artistic director of Leningrad's Kirov Ballet, recorded her impressions for Pravda and was diplomatically generous in her assessment. Clearly she did not fully understand the intent of *Pas d'Action* but did appreciate the company's "mastery of classical movement, pure and chaste in content and dramatically clear in plot".

Both the weather and the audiences improved once the company reached Odessa and the Black Sea. The audiences clapped and a critic for Znamya Kommunizma (The Communist Banner), wrote that the RWB ensemble "shows an excellent command of the classical school of dance, and is innovative as well." The critic, I. Lisakovsky, went so far as to describe the company as "Canada's Bolshoi Ballet". Indeed, the RWB could have been forgiven for believing it was, after the reception that greeted it in the Bolshoi's home town, Moscow.

People thronged to the city's 2,000-seat Operetta Theatre. "There was such a demand for tickets," says Spohr, "the police had to keep control." One report said police had forcibly to eject some young enthusiasts from the lobby when it was discovered they did not have tickets. Everyone who mattered already had theirs, including Maya Plisetskaya, the Bolshoi's prima ballerina. "She got right up there in the aisle and cheered us," says Spohr. The RWB's last night in Moscow, Sunday, December 15, was, as a Canadian Press dispatch related, "marked by wild emotion inside the theatre and turbulent scenes outside". At the conclusion of the performance the audience thundered its approval through an estimated twenty curtain calls, throwing bouquets and personal notes for the dancers.

Buoyed by this happy tumult, the company promptly packed up and headed for Czechoslovakia. It was a less than auspicious time to visit the country. Early in 1968, a political upheaval had placed a reforming Slovak, Alexander Dubcek, in power. The easing of Soviet-style totalitarianism under Dubcek, in what came to be known as The Prague Spring, so alarmed the Kremlin that in August Soviet tanks rolled into the Czechoslovakian capital. Dubcek and his cohorts were shipped off to Moscow for intensive scolding. By the time the RWB arrived, most of Dubcek's reforms had been repealed under Soviet pressure, and the atmosphere in Prague remained tense. The Soviets were not at all happy that a ballet troupe from the West would be touring Czechoslovakia, but somehow the RWB managed to wangle it. Spohr says the journey was grim. "There were Russian soldiers everywhere."

The company performed in Kosice, Bratislava, Brno and finally in Prague. Again, this time in Kosice, police had to be called in to control the crowds. The previous February, the Canadian Olympic hockey team had beaten Czechoslovakia at the Winter Games in Grenoble, but then gone on to suffer a humiliating defeat at the hands of the Russians in the final game. Reviewing the RWB's Prague performances, Dana Pascova of the Czech daily, Svobodne Slova, could not resist making sporting allusions. "Even though it is not possible to measure these two performances on the scoreboard as it is in hockey, any comparison was unequivocally a success for our guests, although the tradition in this case was ours, not as in hockey, where the tradition belongs to the Canadians." As a big hockey fan, Spohr was delighted. "You see our hockey team lost but we went and we won!"

Spohr and his dancers, drained by their adventures, returned to Winnipeg on December 22 and promptly went on strike. Somewhere during the tour Spohr had needed extra rehearsal time. Sawchyn had, as the dancers understood it, agreed to pay the overtime when the company returned home. Once back in Winnipeg, however, Sawchyn told them the company simply could not afford it. The dancers went to their union. The union told Sawchyn to set a deadline and pay up. The dancers arrived the morning of the deadline, changed into their practice clothes, but just sat in the lounge waiting to see what would happen. "Our mini-strike," says Shirley New, "was a culmination of frustration and I believe we had the roar of success in our heads to stand up for ourselves for a moment." To the dancers' delight, Spohr came into the lounge and told them to "stick to their guns". They had been afraid he was going to tell them they were all fired. "Arnold wasn't pro-union," says Dick Foose, "just anti-Sergei. Sergei had screwed up and was costing Arnold rehearsal time." Hours passed. Phone calls were made. "It was the most horrific few hours we could ever imagine at that time," says New. Finally Sawchyn told Foose, then the union representative, that cheques were being cut and that the dancers could go to work.

The RWB's success in Europe caused a surge of civic pride in Winnipeg. Spohr, as team captain, was the justly acknowledged hero. As Frank Morriss reminded his readers, had it not been for Spohr the RWB might easily have perished a decade earlier. For Morriss, it was Spohr's unusual combination of skills and personality traits that had made him a great director. "To be the father of a ballet company," wrote Morriss, "you need to be as sensitive as [a] barometer, as tough as a pine plank, as imaginative as a poet and as resourceful as a politician. And these qualities are not to be found gift-wrapped in any corner store. Furthermore, you must be unselfish as a saint, because you'll never get rich and you'll never have a moment's rest."

The board of directors' satisfaction with the RWB's success could not but reinforce its confidence in Spohr's artistic leadership. However much work everyone else had put in, Spohr had delivered the goods where it really mattered, on stage. There were a number of consequences. One of them was almost immediate and of great significance to Spohr. Eight days after his return from Europe, he was made director of the company school, the position Spohr believed he should have had when the school was launched in 1962.

The following spring, almost exactly eleven years from his appointment as artistic director, the board organized a testimonial dinner in Spohr's honour. On Sunday, March 30, 1969, an assortment of city dignitaries and RWB supporters gathered at Winnipeg's Fort Garry Hotel for a hearty six-course dinner which, according to the printed menu, featured "Roast Prim [sic] Ribs of Beef au Jus". Naturally, the meal was peppered with an assortment of speeches.

Whoever was responsible for soliciting congratulatory messages did a good job. Among a thick sheaf of telegrams and letters were those from the ballerinas Alicia Markova and Beryl Grey in London, impresario Sol Hurok in New York, Canadian Secretary of State Gérard Pelletier in Ottawa, and the National Ballet's Celia Franca in Toronto. In the circumstances, Franca could have been forgiven for eyeing Spohr's moment of glory with a degree of wistful envy. Only a few months earlier, Franca had survived a nasty showdown with her board of directors, during which she had tendered, then later withdrawn, her resignation.

Any lingering misgivings about Spohr's leadership on the part of a few RWB board members were, for the time being, firmly quieted. As a printed tribute in the evening's programme summed it up: "A company achieves world recognition through the combined energies of many uniquely talented individuals, but the most vital ingredient is the catalyzing force that orchestrates these diverse resources. Such a force is the dynamic, vibrant Arnold Spohr."

In June 1969, Sawchyn and Cameron cleverly exploited the company's success overseas by launching the thirtieth anniversary season subscription campaign with what, at first glance, looked like an eight-page English-language edition of the Soviet daily, Pravda. "Powerful Western Force Invades Kremlin", read a front-page headline in red. There was even a bogus story filed by the Soviet news agency, TASS. "Instead of attacking in accordance with the rules set down by the Geneva agreement, the imperialists danced right into the hearts of the glorious Russian people before any resistance could be organized." Inside there was a translation of a genuine Pravda review of the RWB's performances, as well as an official letter from Winnipeg mayor Stephen Juba. He exhorted his fellow citizens to support a ballet company that won their city international recognition as a true centre of culture. This was a big change from the days when city councillors held their noses when ballet was mentioned.

• • •

After the medal-winning triumph of the RWB's 1968 visit to Paris, Spohr was certainly hoping for a return visit but could hardly have foreseen how soon it would occur. On March 31, 1970, the six-year-old Harkness Ballet, founded and financed by the American heiress Rebekah Harkness, dropped a bombshell on the management of the Théâtre de la Ville in Paris. The company was cancelling its previously contracted engagement for the month of June. Officially the Harkness Ballet's withdrawal was owing to an "urgent reorganization of the company". In fact, the troupe was being disbanded.

Companies around the world soon began to compete for the now vacant spot on the theatre's summer schedule, but it was the RWB that the Paris impresario, Ouly Algaroff, was anxious to book. The RWB was busy with its final Winnipeg shows of the 1969/70 season when Algaroff contacted Sawchyn. Within little more than a week a deal was struck for the RWB to dance in Paris that summer, June 2-28. After that, it would remain in Europe for a five-city tour of Italy, including performances at the Nervi Festival, near Genoa.

"Winnipeg is a company of great merit," Algaroff explained to Tim Creery of Southam News. "A month in Paris is a long time but the company is striking for its very extensive repertoire and its range from classic to modern." The RWB's accessibility also appealed to Algaroff. Three years earlier, the Théâtre de la Ville, formerly the famous Sarah Bernhardt Theatre, had been renovated with substantial financial support from the city government, and reopened with the goal of appealing to a socially diverse audience. In a note to subscribers, Jean Mercure, the theatre's director, reminded them that the RWB had made it a "point of honour" to maintain the standards of classical ballet, but also to pursue the creative freedom and exploration necessary to keep the art of dance alive.

Paris was welcome news for the RWB. The company had originally hoped to appear that summer at the Stratford Festival in Ontario, but the plan fell through. As Sawchyn told Creery: "We were facing unemployment for our dancers, low morale and a draining off of talent." Now, with Paris in place, the RWB was facing one of its busiest seasons ever. From Europe the RWB would go straight to Ottawa and Toronto, then south for a three-week tour of Central America and the Caribbean. Another forty-city Hurok tour of the United States was already booked for the winter of 1971. Altogether the full season offered the dancers the exceptional prospect of forty-eight weeks paid employment.

The April performances in Winnipeg marked the end of the 1969/70 season. The company reassembled on May 4, leaving less than a month to prepare for Paris. The roster of dancers was largely unchanged except for the conspicuous absence of principal dancer Sheila Mackinnon, one of the few survivors from among Spohr's first hirings in 1958. Mackinnon had injured her right knee during rehearsals for the April 2-4 performances in Winnipeg. She had still appeared in Brian Macdonald's new ballet *Five Over Thirteen* but, by the time the Paris deal was signed, Mackinnon was in a full leg cast and, at age thirty-two, facing the very real prospect of a premature end to her career. "I'm sorry we've lost Sheila Mackinnon for this engagement," Macdonald told Frank Morriss. "She was very important to us and a fine dancer." Fortunately, Mackinnon was able to return to the stage a year later, but her absence left a gap in the company's top ranks. "It seems," noted Spohr, "every time before a big tour comes up we are tested by calamity and have to overcome adversity."

The last things Spohr needed at such a time were distractions, even of a pleasant kind. However, having already accepted the offer of an honorary Doctor of Laws degree from the University of Manitoba, he dutifully suited up for the May 21 convocation. The next day's papers carried photographs of Spohr resplendently robed in silk gown and tassled velvet cap. It was a proud moment and Spohr relished it. Nor did he seem averse to the fact that many of his dancers and colleagues now began to address him as "Dr. Spohr". Many still do.

By the time the Paris invitation arrived, the RWB had already accepted proposals from Brian Macdonald for a brace of new and very Canadian ballets. One was to be a setting of Leonard Cohen poems with a sound montage by Harry Freedman. The other would propel the RWB into motion to the live music of the innovative Toronto rock band, Lighthouse. Paris would get the Cohen ballet. The Lighthouse collaboration was scheduled to receive its premiere at the National Arts Centre in Ottawa when the RWB returned from Europe. This meant that Macdonald would be actively creating throughout the tour.

As Algaroff had earlier observed, four weeks is a long run for a visiting company in a foreign city. Only the first two weeks were covered by subscription sales. Algaroff worried that the remaining two weeks would be slow to sell. Instead, box office returns were strong and the closing night was a total sellout.

Spohr had assembled an ambitious repertory of a dozen works, including five by Macdonald, to be presented in three different programmes. Had there been more time to plan, Spohr and his company could have been spared a good deal of work. Everything had been rehearsed and the requisite costumes, sets and properties transported to Paris when Algaroff and Mercure intervened to rearrange the programming. Several ballets were scratched. Spohr was not pleased but accepted the decision. "I listen to local impresarios because they know the taste of their cities and theatres." Spohr did not always defer to impresarios. If his instincts gave him strong barometric readings on the prevailing audience climate, he would do his utmost to present the ballets he earnestly believed would work. Almost invariably in such instances, they did.

The highlight of the 1970 Paris engagement, the premiere of Macdonald's *The Shining People of Leonard Cohen*, was scheduled in the middle of the run to allow enough rehearsal time. It was a wise decision because problems developed with Ted Bieler's mobile set design and it had to be modified in Paris. However, as Claude Sarraute of Le Monde noted disapprovingly, the delay meant that the RWB opened in Paris with an all-Macdonald programme that included two humorous works, *Aimez-Vous Bach?* and *Pas d'Action*.

They were already familiar to Paris balletomanes from the company's 1968 appearance. Only the more sombre *Five Over Thirteen* was a local novelty. It featured a Harry Freedman score, ominous fibreglass shells designed by Canadian sculptor Walter Redinger, and a choreographic exploration of group dynamics and human inhibitions. The audience did not seem to care about the ubiquity of Macdonald ballets. He was a known and popular choreographer in Paris. Another new Macdonald work, *Jeux Dangereux*, had recently been presented in the same theatre by France's Ballet-Théâtre Contemporain. As Sarraute rather disdainfully recorded, the RWB's opening-night audience exploded with enthusiasm and applauded everything indiscriminately.

Christine Hennessy, the company's reigning ballerina, was again especially praised. Le Figaro's Claude Baignères marvelled at Hennessy's ability to balance for so long on one toe in *Pas d'Action* and at the power of her jumps. "The acrobatic leaps which let her fall back into the arms of her four partners one after another relegate even the performances of the specialists of the Bolshoi to the order of timid flutterings."

As the Paris performances continued, reaction to Macdonald's extended pas de deux, *The Shining People of Leonard Cohen*, was very positive. Sarraute was enraptured. Macdonald's response to Cohen's love poems, wrote Sarraute, "radiates ardent grace and supple sensuality". Macdonald's wife Annette av Paul and her partner David Moroni also received high praise. "The dancers", wrote Sarraute, "are luminously beautiful, and their feelings of wonder find admirable plastic expression on the stage." Baignères praised the way Macdonald had built a modern idiom on a foundation of classical dance and wrote of the ballet's "very pure sensuality and a dynamic which identifies itself with the happiness of existence."

Reflecting on the season as whole, David Stevens' assessment in The International Herald Tribune was just what Spohr wanted to read. Stevens noted that the RWB, "Canada's leading ballet troupe", was one of a select group of dance companies as important for what it had created as for the quality of its dancing. "A number of ballets it has brought into being have enriched the repertories of other companies on both sides of the Atlantic and contributed, quietly but effectively, to the artistic vigor and variety of contemporary dance as a whole."

The heavy workload in Paris took its typical toll on dancers and late in the run Spohr had to send to Winnipeg for a replacement for one of his injured women. Eighteen-year-old Madeleine Bouchard did not even have a passport when she received the call. On June 22, she had to stop off in Ottawa to collect one. By the next evening, Bouchard was on stage in Paris.

The RWB had good reason to feel satisfied as it headed south towards Italy. Its collective efforts had symbolically been crowned by Spohr's appointment on June 26 as an Officer of the three-year-old Order of Canada. Altogether, 1970 was proving to be a year of honours for Dr. Spohr. In March he had become the first member of the dance community to receive a Canada Council Molson Prize, then worth a handsome $15,000. Now he had been decorated by the nation "for his contribution to the growth of ballet in Canada". The diplomas and citations were successively added to those already decorating the walls of Spohr's Winnipeg office.

It would be another three years before Kathleen Richardson, whose continuing philanthropy helped sustain the RWB, received the Order of Canada. However, in the spring of 1970, Richardson's efforts did receive high-profile recognition when Agnes de Mille spoke before a United States Congressional committee. In describing the prerequisites for a great ballet company, de Mille cited the example of philanthropists, such as Richardson in Winnipeg, willing to support an organization through its painful growing stages and beyond. Justice R. J. Matas, then RWB president, sent Richardson a transcript of de Mille's testimony and penned a tribute to Richardson with which Spohr would have heartily concurred. "Every time our Royal Winnipeg Ballet dancers take curtain calls before those wildly cheering, packed houses in Paris," wrote Matas that June of 1970, "we know that they are in part bowing for you."

Spohr had little time to bask in the glow of cheering, packed houses and the latest in a string of public honours. He had to contend with a company wracked by internal tensions. Added to the day-to-day stress of foreign touring, the RWB was confronting the issue of what to do about Brian Macdonald.

Today Spohr and Macdonald have patched up past differences and maintain a warmly cordial relationship. In 1970, however, the RWB's two most celebrated figures were heading for a major split. The tour to Paris and Italy had brought matters to a head. The stress of finishing a new work in the midst of the Paris engagement had brought out the temperamental worst in Macdonald. Only days before the premiere of his Leonard Cohen ballet, Macdonald threatened to walk out on the company. Sawchyn and Spohr believed that Macdonald's demands in the studio were responsible for the high injury rate. "Brian was destroying my dancers," says Spohr, "so I had to get rid of him."

As far as demanding choreographers are concerned, Macdonald is in good company – Antony Tudor, Jerome Robbins, Agnes de Mille, Eliot Feld, to name only a few. In retrospect, Spohr is inclined to attribute what he calls Macdonald's "ruthless" treatment of dancers to nervous anxiety and the insecurity typical of many creative artists. As it was, while some of the dancers disliked Macdonald, others responded well to his unrelenting intensity. In 1970, however, there were other factors at play.

Everyone acknowledged that Macdonald had provided a stream of works that gave the RWB a notably hip, progressive and creatively Canadian image. In praising the RWB during its Paris visit, critic David Stevens had deemed Macdonald "the man most responsible for the company's current artistic profile." The only problem was that, from Spohr and Sawchyn's perspective, Macdonald had become impossible to work with.

On July 6, when the RWB moved on from Paris to Verona, Sawchyn found time to write to Roy Matas. It is not clear whether the letter was ever sent, but the draft that survives in the archives reveals Sawchyn's grave concerns about Macdonald.

Despite Macdonald's important contribution to the RWB, Sawchyn concluded that the cost in terms of internal wrangling and the wear and tear on dancers was too great. Sawchyn also wondered if Macdonald might be planning to supplant Spohr. Sawchyn certainly concedes that he and Sol Kanee, who continued on the RWB board beyond his presidency, sometimes wondered whether Spohr had already done his best work and that it was time to seek new artistic leadership. In 1970, however, even if Sawchyn had reservations about Spohr, he had greater ones about Macdonald. Sawchyn warned that even to entertain the thought of handing the RWB to Macdonald would be a disaster.

One thing both he and Spohr had learned from the tour, Sawchyn wrote, was that it was a big mistake to produce new choreography on the road. "We must assure that choreographers are not again on tour with us." Spohr denies that he saw Macdonald as a threat to his leadership but, after the premiere of *A Ballet High* later that summer of 1970, it was sixteen years before Macdonald returned to create a work for the RWB.

The break with Canada's most internationally renowned choreographer had significant implications. Although, among Canada's three oldest ballet companies, Montreal's Les Grands Ballets Canadiens then held the numerical record for staging works of original Canadian choreography, the RWB also liked to be regarded as a crucible of Canadian creativity.

The ballets added to the RWB's repertoire by Spohr during his thirty-year directorship make an impressive record. More than a third of the almost 130 ballets he presented could be considered "Canadian". This includes works commissioned or acquired both from Canadian-born choreographers and from choreographers within the RWB itself, such as the Americans James Clouser and Salvatore Aiello. However, a majority of these Canadian works – twenty-nine ballets to be precise – joined the repertoire in the twelve-year period between 1958 and 1970. These were the years when Macdonald was most closely associated with the company. Indeed, almost half of the Canadian works in that period were Macdonald's handiwork. During the remaining eighteen years of Spohr's reign as director, there was not only a sizeable reduction in the overall flow of commissioned ballets but also a marked decline in new Canadian content – only twenty-one works. Despite the later success of Norbert Vesak's *The Ecstasy of Rita Joe* and *What to do Till the Messiah Comes*, Spohr was never again to find a Canadian choreographer as prolific or as finely attuned to the character of the RWB and the mood of the times as Macdonald.

Just as the flow of Canadian choreography into the RWB repertoire began to slow after the break with Macdonald, the National Ballet, with admittedly greater resources, presented almost forty new works by Canadian choreographers in the period 1971-1988. Many of the choreographers – Ann Ditchburn, James Kudelka, Timothy Spain, Constantin Patsalas, David Allan – were company members who emerged through the National Ballet's annual choreographic workshops. Under the artistic directorship of Erik Bruhn, 1983-1986, outsiders, such as modern dance choreographers Robert Desrosiers, Danny Grossman and David Earle, were invited to work with the

National Ballet in order to remind the company's audiences of the scope of Canadian creative talent. During the same period, Les Grands Ballets Canadiens was even more aggressive in championing Canadian creativity.

Unless one subscribes to a strictly nationalistic evaluation of Spohr's programming record, these facts are not in themselves of major import. However, they are a reflection of the realities that Spohr had to confront and also, perhaps, a reflection of his own fundamental attitudes. The RWB was a touring company. In some respects it was the victim of its own success. Spohr had no way of predicting the future, but his timing had been impeccable. The early years of preparation had positioned the RWB perfectly to take advantage of what later came to be called the "Ballet Boom". The 1960's saw the beginning of an unprecedented explosion of interest in ballet that continued for almost twenty years. The image of ballet as stuffy and elitist gave way to something altogether more sexy and liberating. In response, regional troupes began to appear in major cities across the United States. Within this emerging ecology, the RWB had established a particular niche. "I think the RWB had the secret," says Macdonald, "appearing in the same cities every year with new repertoire and then dancing their asses off."

In order to satisfy presenters and audiences, the RWB continually had to refresh its repertoire, if not with original ballets then at least with works that were unfamiliar to its audiences. In such a busy schedule and with a relatively small roster of dancers, there were enormous pressures on available rehearsal time. Creating new work is time-consuming. New work is also hard to budget accurately and cost overruns are commonplace. It is often more practical and affordable to buy ready-made.

The high incidence of Canadian ballets introduced during the earlier part of Spohr's directorship, in retrospect, seems to owe as much to pragmatism as to policy. Until his appointment, the company had largely relied on in-house choreographers, including Spohr. In 1958, the RWB's reputation was such that it was hard to recruit dancers, let alone find a fresh repertoire. Macdonald was available, ambitious and full of ideas. So was James Clouser, who contributed eight ballets between 1961 and 1966. It was logical to use them both.

Beyond this, there seems to have been no systematic plan to foster choreographic creativity from within the company. As the

RWB prospered and its international reputation as a dancing ensemble grew under Spohr's leadership, it became a viable contender for works by such established choreographers as George Balanchine, Frederick Ashton, Todd Bolender, John Butler and Agnes de Mille. Meanwhile, Spohr was continually on the lookout for less well-known choreographers whom he believed could lend distinctive variety and excitement to the repertoire. Spohr was open to suggestion and often used his formidable network of contacts to solicit ideas. Despite his preference for "known quantities" he was often willing to take programming risks.

Spohr's genius was an almost uncanny ability to assemble programmes that would stimulate his dancers and entertain audiences. Putting on a good show, creating moments of theatrical magic and sending people home happy were his paramount concerns. To ensure this happened, he had to be an excellent ballet master, an incomparable ballet master. To direct a company, in Spohr's view, means being in the studio.

A Great
Theatre Director

The 1950 fall edition of Impression, a small Winnipeg quarterly arts magazine, included an article under the title "Choreography and Its Approaches". The author was Arnold Spohr. At this point in his career he had but one choreographic credit to his name, *Ballet Premier*.

As Spohr confidently launched into his theme, he asserted that a successful ballet is achieved through a harmony of theme, music, steps and decor. As an accomplished pianist, it was not surprising that he identified music as a crucial starting point. "The choreographer," wrote Spohr, "must have inspiration from the music or the creative senses will not function freely."

Spohr then proceeded to analyze the approach of three different choreographers: Gweneth Lloyd, George Balanchine and himself. Lloyd, he explained, would sit with a record player and visualize the whole ballet. She would then commit the choreography to paper in the form of notes and diagrams before teaching it to the dancers in the studio.

Balanchine, wrote Spohr, would also come to the studio with his music chosen and general ideas framed, but allowed the steps and structure to emerge as he worked with the dancers.

Spohr described his own approach as falling somewhere between these extremes. With his clear understanding of musical form, he found himself guided towards certain steps and patterns, but would also improvise if necessary until he found the appropriate movement. Spohr would write down the basic structure as a reference, but carried most of the choreography to the studio in his head. In a handwritten text, which may well have been part of a longer draft of his finished article, Spohr also wrote: "I can close my eyes and see 18 or 20 dancers all in different positions, doing different steps and actually see the pictures it will make. Thus I can work very quickly for I don't spend time experimenting on a dancer."

The recollections of those who worked with Spohr corroborate this description of his working process. Some even thought it odd that Spohr did not work more collaboratively with the dancers in the creation of movement. Richard Rutherford remembers his surprise in 1958 when Spohr began rehearsing his new Chopin ballet, *E Minor*. "He didn't work with you as a dancer. He had it all mapped out on paper. You just had to learn the steps. He agonized over everything. I found that strange. It was so different from Brian Macdonald who used to have me rolling across the floor and doing all kinds of crazy things to develop the movement."

The most significant and revealing part of Spohr's article is its conclusion. Credit, he writes, must be given to the dancers for they are the choreographer's instruments. He extends the analogy by extolling the crucial role of the ballet mistress. "She is the conductor and the dancers the orchestra, bringing to life what has been a latent or restless force within the choreographer's being."

At this early stage of his career, Spohr already had a clearly articulated and particular theory about the essential function of the ballet mistress/master. Like a conductor with a musical score, the ballet master, explained Spohr, must have the ability and prerogative to interpret the choreography. Without that additional input, the choreography will lack the vital force necessary to bring it to life for an audience. In later years this special directorial approach came to be known as "the Spohr touch".

Spohr still holds firmly to the belief that movement has its own inherent logic and drama. Every measure of music carries its own subtle message. He works endlessly to bring clarity, musicality, dramatic nuance and dynamic texture to every step.

In February, 1958, when Spohr was summoned at short notice to rescue the RWB's season-closing performances, he scheduled Sonia Taverner and her partner Fred Strobel for a rehearsal of the Black Swan pas de deux, a toe-shoes-and-tutu classical showstopper from Act III of *Swan Lake*. Prince Siegfried believes the woman before him is none other than Odette, the baleful swan maiden to whom he has sworn eternal devotion in Act II. In fact, it is Odile, tantalizingly offered as a potential bride by the evil magician Von Rothbart, with the intention of deceiving Siegfried into breaking his earlier vow.

As it was lunchtime, Spohr had brought his sandwiches to the rehearsal. He proceeded to eat them in front of Taverner and Strobel. Working lunches soon became a pattern in his life. Dancers grew accustomed to seeing Spohr surging around the studio, one hand directing, the other grasping a slice of pizza or a fried chicken leg. He never quite mastered the art of simultaneous yelling and masticating.

Taverner and Strobel worked their way through the slow, adagio section of the pas de deux. "Technically, you're not bad," Spohr reassured Taverner, "but you've got to become the Black Swan. You have got to seduce this young prince." And then he set to work. Every step, every musical phrase had to have a motivation. Spohr poured out ideas and images, a seemingly bizarre catalogue, goading his dancers to draw from their own imagination. Instead of shaping a phrase of movement mechanically from the outside he wanted it to be an expression of something that had emotional meaning for the dancer. "Arnold had brought the story to life through simple ideas drawn from day-to-day living," says Taverner. "It made such sense to me that I never forgot it. I was able to build on these ideas and make the Black Swan my own creation."

Sometimes Spohr would demonstrate, not to impose an exact idea but to give a general sense of what he wanted. Taverner remembers him becoming Odile, running across the stage, then looking back to check on Prince Siegfried before launching into a couple of pirouettes, hoping that Strobel would be there to catch him as Odile dived into a swooping arabesque.

Rachel Browne would later watch Spohr rehearsing Taverner. "His approach was down and dirty but it brought forth phenomenal results. It was amazing to see what he got out of her, the fire and the guts. Arnold's eye was so sharp. He had this gift for pinpointing exactly what was lacking in a dancer and also this extraordinary perception, this ability of seeing the potential of what a dancer has."

Spohr is not unaware of his own special genius. For him it has always been distinct from the regular function of a régisseur, the person entrusted with teaching and maintaining works in the repertoire. "I love to extend the imagination and find the intangibles that make the emotional lifeblood of a character. I love to find the exact core of what a dancer is to feel, or the true essence of how and why to move." As Spohr wrote in a 1976 letter to de Mille, in reference to a member of his own staff whom he described as "a very fine régisseur", "he really can't coach or bring out hidden talent. I FEEL FEW PEOPLE CAN." Spohr's use of capitals suggests the vehemence of his opinion.

Most of those who have watched Spohr at work in the studio, or had the direct benefit of what David Moroni calls "Arnold's eagle eye", would agree. "He was an absolute master in the studio, simply one of the greatest ballet coaches in the world," says Moroni. "With his wild energy he could seem totally off the wall but he knew how to motivate you. You could never fool Arnold Spohr in a rehearsal. He made you understand the truth of what you were doing. And he had the audience in mind all the time. He was the bridge. It gave the RWB an identity that was unique." As Jean McKenzie once put it: "He shames you into doing it." Says William Starrett, who danced with the RWB in the mid-1970's, "He'll haunt you. He's relentless. He makes you have to do it. He's also very honest. That's why people listened to him. When he did pay you a compliment, it really meant something."

Walter Terry, the respected American dance critic and historian, was so delighted by what he saw of the RWB during its 1964 appearance at Jacob's Pillow that he was determined to find out more. In the fall of 1965 he spent a whole week in Winnipeg observing Spohr at work. "No one person," Terry wrote, "no matter how talented, makes a ballet company. But one can spark it into action." Such a man, Terry continued, was Arnold Spohr. After watching Spohr in the rehearsal studio, Terry summed up his impressions with the subsequently much quoted statement: "Arnold Spohr is one of the greatest ballet directors I have ever watched at work. Furthermore, he is a great director, and I mean theater director." Terry continued by providing a vivid and perceptive analysis, explaining how Spohr's eye for nuance is balanced by a broad understanding of what each ballet requires. "Mr. Spohr does not rechoreograph someone else's work. He does no violation to the choreographer's intent, content or concept. He honors these elements by bringing them out again in new rehearsals."

In 1973, Agnes de Mille wrote a witty, if not entirely accurate, potted history of the RWB. In it she paid tribute to Spohr's remarkable gifts as a ballet master. "Spohr is a conscientious, not to say finicky, rehearser. He attends all the choreographer's rehearsals and keeps notes on the creator's demands and explanations. The work is later analyzed, taken apart, reassembled and polished and explained often to the point of exhaustion."

Brian Macdonald says there were occasions when he had to plead with Spohr to stop. "They were about the only times we'd disagree. He'd clean the soul out of a ballet so that it had become automatic. I'd tell him I didn't want it to be all neat and clean." Spohr pushed hard for what he wanted and would not give up until he got it. The dancers became used to hearing: "Okay kids, once again full out with enthusiasm."

The company's dancers, several of whom already held Canadian Actors' Equity cards through their work with Rainbow Stage, had become fully unionized by 1960. It was often frustrating to Spohr to have to abide by a prescribed work schedule in the studio. "His idea of working hours was out of the Stone Age," says Sheila Mackinnon. "It came from the way he'd worked with Lloyd and Farrally." When Ted Patterson served as the company union steward he would often have to play tough with Spohr. "Arnold was a real bugger about giving breaks. He'd say 'We'll break when I say so' and I'd say 'No, we won't. I'm the union rep' and I'd call the break. Arnold didn't like it, but he learned."

"He could be a pussycat and a tyrant," says Moroni. Spohr does not deny it. "My religious background has not made me an angel. I can be a tyrant when it comes to people not being serious with their work. Every second wasted I never get back. Remember that I am an artist, so I am supposed to be temperamental, and I am. But I get over it and then everything's fine again." Fine perhaps for Spohr, but not necessarily for everyone else. "Arnold," says Frank Bourman, "did not always appreciate that it is easier to attract with honey than with lemon."

Bill Lark, an American who had served two years in the airforce before returning to dance, remembers how scary Spohr could be. "I think everybody was a little bit afraid of him. He would get in your space, just like a drill sergeant. I remember one time he had the whole company watching me repeat this variation for half an hour. It was trial by fire." Today it is hard to imagine professional dancers accepting the kind of treatment Spohr could mete out. "He could cut you down to nothing in front of everybody," says Gordon Wright, a dancer during the early 1980's. "There were times he made me feel about half an inch tall." Spohr also poked and punched his dancers to get a point across. "He'd hit you, and I mean hit you," says Starrett. "I'd be bruised all over." Spohr still pokes and prods.

"He appreciated those who worked hard," says Evelyn Hart. "He made you earn his respect. He would not give you a role unless you earned it. But if he trusted you, it was all the confidence you needed."

For his part, Spohr insists that he always tried to remain sensitive and responsive to the individual needs of his dancers, striving to find whatever key would unlock their full potential and particular talent. Yet, for some of his dancers, Spohr's outbursts were frightening and intimidating. "Arnold is unaware of the effect he has on people," concedes Kathleen Richardson. "There were those who found him very difficult to deal with and who did not respond to his approach." Even Bonnie Wyckoff, one of Spohr's staunchest champions, admitted to Maclean's magazine in 1978 that his uncompromising approach could have negative consequences. "He challenges our resourcefulness, but he is also capable of inhibiting dancers, destroying their self-confidence, even driving them out of the company." More than twenty years later, after working with other directors, Wyckoff was able to add a further perspective. "I would beg Bob Joffrey to *direct* me, but he was incapable and mostly absent. It was the same story with Oscar Araiz. 'What do you want from me?' we would mutually plead, time and again, to no avail. Mr. Spohr knows how to direct a dancer, to find that particular dancer's unique point of motivation and how to work it up to an astonishing level of creating."

Marina Eglevsky joined the RWB in 1971 and immediately found Spohr hard to work with. "I was scared of him. He was loud, crazy and intimidating. I didn't feel he really liked me." Eglevsky and her husband, Salvatore Aiello, had been hired by Spohr in New York. He had spotted them in a class at the studios of American Ballet Theatre. Eglevsky and Aiello were among several very talented dancers rudely jettisoned into the job market when their former company, the Harkness Ballet, was unexpectedly disbanded. "Sal and I were looking very specifically for a company that was small and which had a diverse repertoire because Sal was more contemporary and I was more classical." Aiello had an easier time dealing with Spohr. For Eglevsky it was a difficult adjustment.

"I think my fear actually attracted him to pick on me," says Eglevsky, "yet, I knew that if I could somehow get beyond this fear that there was something to gain." Eventually Eglevsky mustered the courage to tell Spohr that she did not respond well to being shouted at and things began to improve. "He took me into the studio alone and somehow pulled it out of me. What I learned from him was that you could always go beyond." Even so, when John Neumeier invited Eglevsky and Aiello to join the Hamburg Staatsoper Ballet in 1973 they both welcomed the opportunity. In Neumeier, Eglevsky felt she had found someone who truly understood and supported her as an artist. "It was with John that I really gained my grounding. It enabled me, when I returned to Winnipeg, to get out of Arnold what I needed. He could take one little tiny segment and he would work and work on it. In the end it was an essence he gave, like a key, and I could take it and use it for the whole thing."

When British-born teacher Hilary Cartwright began working with the RWB school in 1976 and had a chance to see the already legendary Spohr in action she was taken aback. "I found him very forceful and opinionated in a big friendly-dog kind of way. One felt all the way through that his heart was in the right place but that his methods were not so constructive." As Cartwright saw it, Spohr's approach was old-fashioned and unsound. "His way was to shout and scream in order to break their spirits. Then, he would encourage and coach them and say he'd made them what they were. But he had most of them in fear. He could be vicious. It made my blood curdle." Cartwright later agreed to work with the company in the 1977/78 season only because Spohr seemed willing to let her take over the rehearsals. "I believe in developing people by encouraging their strengths. You don't say 'it must be like this.'"

There were times when Spohr's tyrannical side pushed his dancers too hard. Richard Rutherford remembers a particular confrontation during a rehearsal of *Hansel and Gretel*. Rutherford, then still a corps member, was getting tired of the stopping and starting, the constant working over details. "I argued with him about the counts of a movement at a point in the choreography where we had left off the day before." Spohr got in a huff and retorted angrily, "Listen, I'm the director, I'm the choreographer and we'll start where I say so. Do I make myself clear?" Rutherford, who was notoriously temperamental, snapped. "As far as I'm concerned," he told Spohr, "you can take the whole thing and stuff it up your ass. Do I make myself clear?" Rutherford says he had reached a point where he was beginning to wonder what he was doing in Winnipeg. "I may even have wanted to get myself fired so I could go back to New York." If so, Rutherford misjudged Spohr. "Instead of firing me, Arnold loved me more and made me a soloist, so I stayed for another fourteen years."

Not all dancers fared as well. In 1981, Spohr was in the main Portage Avenue studio rehearsing Paddy Stone's latest work for the company, *Bolero*, set to the popular Maurice Ravel score. It involved much whirling of capes. Spohr was known at times to focus his attention on a particular dancer whose work he did not consider up to standard. That day it was a corps member named Ted Marshall. Spohr would not let up. Finally Marshall had had enough. He threw down his cape, stomped all over it, glared at Spohr and shouted "Fuck you!" He then turned, walked up the stairs and in a dramatic exit, slammed the door behind him.

The music stopped. The dancers stood silent and motionless, wondering what terrible vengeance would descend upon the head of their unfortunate and intemperate colleague. Spohr sat staring into space with the blank expression that years before Betty Farrally had dubbed "Arnold's camel look". David Moroni called it "The Great Pan Face". Finally, after what seemed an age, Marshall reappeared at the studio door, quietly returned to his place, picked up the cape and looked sheepishly towards Spohr. "Okay everyone," ordered the hard-driving director, "let's pick up where Ted told me to fuck myself." And that was that. The rehearsal continued without further incident. Marshall was not asked back the following season.

"Nothing is ever quite good enough for Mr. Spohr, so there's always a push," explained régisseur Cathy Taylor to a reporter in 1982. "It takes a lot of self-confidence and character to match wits with the man, and those who can't take the heat get weeded out early. It's great for the company. Believe me, there are no wimps in the Royal Winnipeg Ballet." Once, as Spohr worked relentlessly to correct a variety of details carefully listed in his notebook, he actually expressed complete satisfaction with at least a handful of the dancers. "You were just excellent," he told them. Then after a pause added self-mockingly: "Imagine that! I actually thought something was excellent."

Spohr had an instinctive sense of how to keep the corps together in ensemble work. "Arnold was a master at putting in the finishing touches," says Gordon Wright. "He had this amazing way of spacing the corps that would keep a ballet tight on stage. On tour, where every night was a different theatre, he became adept at adjusting the spacing to fit. He was truly excellent at that." Marilyn Lewis danced with the company from 1965 to 1968 and years later became one of its régisseurs. "Arnold's peripheral vision was so incredibly acute," says Lewis. "It gave him this amazing spatial sense." Spohr's ability to communicate this sense of space to his dancers, as well as endless rehearsing, saved the company countless times. In 1982, for example, the RWB was performing Vicente Nebrada's *Our Waltzes* in Germany. Earl Stafford was at the piano. At a very busy section in the finale the lights suddenly went out. Stafford kept playing and when the lights came back on after what seemed like an eternity, the company was still dancing, perfectly spaced.

Spohr's spacing sense proved particularly useful during the 1974 South American tour, when the company was obliged to dance in Brasilia on an open platform stage in an enormous arena. Spohr discovered that the President of Brazil and his entourage would be seated directly to the left of the stage. It would be almost equivalent to watching from the wings. Since he could not shift Brazil's head of state, Spohr decided to shift the dancers instead. "We incorporated a theatre-in-the-round aspect," Spohr explains, "and restaged the ballets to angle them in favour of the president."

Spohr's genius was as a coach and rehearsal director rather than as a conventional classroom teacher. Daily class is crucial to the working dancer. In classical ballet it follows a time-honoured progression of exercises that develop sequentially to stretch and warm the whole body in preparation for the rehearsals and performances that follow. Although it provides an opportunity for the teacher to monitor and correct any technical problems, the overall flow and pace of daily class and the effectiveness of the combinations of movement are important to dancers.

In the early years Spohr, of necessity, taught daily class, but as he began to assemble a support team he generally left the task to others. When Spohr did teach class in later years, the dancers would often find excuses not to attend. "He had good things to say but he'd talk forever," says Bill Lark. "We dreaded it." No one questioned Spohr's knowledge or his enthusiasm. The problem was that Spohr had too much of both. In his quest for perfection, he would sometimes get obsessed with detail and stop the class to explain a movement while the dancers stood around getting cold. "He'd get lost and was easily sidetracked," says Marina Eglevsky. "He often seemed disorganized, and then there were the times when he got carried away by his enthusiasm," says William Starrett. "I remember the day we almost died with hysterics. There was Mr. Spohr wearing sandals and purple bellbottoms that were too short and done up with a rawhide draw-string and he's trying to demonstrate an arabesque penché. The next thing we knew, he'd fallen behind the piano and when he popped up his hair was on end and his glasses all askew."

Spohr was always concerned with exposing his dancers to a variety of influences and styles. He placed great importance on inviting guest teachers from different backgrounds – Audrey de Vos, Vera Volkova, Maria Fay, Kirsten Ralov, Jorge Garcia and many more – in order to expand his dancers' versatility. He could not take the dancers on his frequent study trips abroad, but he could bring the world to their doorstep.

Spohr's work in the studio, the way he goaded, bullied, cajoled, shamed, incited and encouraged dancers to push beyond their limits, had one ultimate goal. Spohr wanted audiences to experience the same exhilaration, the same emotional thrill he remembered from so many years before, watching the Ballet Russe. "Dancers, choreo-graphers, directors and teachers", Spohr once wrote, "are all constantly striving for that magic moment when the spirit, the soul, call it what you will, reaches that private world we can move into for an evening to be remembered." Spohr was convinced that those magic moments could only result from hard work and meticulous attention to detail, particularly to musical phrasing.

After working so hard to make the dancers look special, Spohr also wanted to be sure audiences could see them. He had little tolerance for gloomy lighting. Subtle, atmospheric lighting plots might work effectively in opera or theatre, but in ballet the steps are the dancer's language and they must be seen. This sometimes put his own technical crew in a difficult position. In October, 1971, as soon as choreographer John Butler and his lighting designer, Gil Wechsler, had left town after the company premiere of *Sebastian*, Spohr began demanding more light. In proper loyalty to his profession, John

Stammers, the company's lighting man, protested but Spohr would not brook objection. In the end, Spohr won. As Jim Cameron later observed, "Arnold had this strange thought that the people who paid for tickets actually wanted to be able to see the dancers on stage." In Spohr's later years it got to be something of a joke among the dancers that the older their director became, the more lumens he demanded. The dancers may have laughed, but Spohr understood audience needs better than anyone.

• • •

Spohr has never restricted his interests as a teacher and coach exclusively to the RWB. His zest for life and natural curiosity draw him towards people and projects in which Spohr sees potential for growth. He knows his gifts and likes to share them. Spohr has often taken on too much work and exhausted himself in the process. It is simply part of his nature.

In the 1970's, for example, Spohr took a particular interest in the work of the Montreal choreographer and director, Eddy Toussaint. Toussaint was born in Haiti in 1945. His rich and well-connected family was forced to flee in 1957 when the island fell under the dictatorship of François "Papa Doc" Duvalier. The family settled in Montreal where Toussaint, who had already studied ballet in Haiti, soon became a disciple of Eva von Gencsy. She was a leading exponent of the exciting new form, jazz ballet. One day, von Gencsy told Toussaint that a friend of hers, a very important person in the world of dance, would be coming to visit. "The image I had of an artistic director," says Toussaint, "was of a very severe person, but when Arnold came in he was so charming and very handsome and elegant. We became friends immediately." Toussaint was a great admirer of the RWB and of the way Spohr brought out the best in his dancers. "When you would go to see the RWB you would always have a pleasant surprise."

A decade later Toussaint had established his own small company and invited Spohr to come and see it. Whenever he could find time, from the mid-1970's until the early 1980's, Spohr came to work with Toussaint's troupe in Montreal. "I think he may have been skeptical of what I was doing but he still helped, he always had useful suggestions and made an enormous difference to my company. He is without question the best coach of all time. He taught me so much. If I am still in ballet today it is because of Arnold Spohr."

Spohr took a particular interest in one of Toussaint's emerging young stars, Louis Robitaille. "Louis was not really classically trained," Toussaint explains. "Arnold always found a way to make him look good. He had this understanding of body placement, of detail. He knew how to help dancers draw the audience's attention to what was good in their dancing. He was an absolute magician at that."

Spohr's impending visits would send a wave of anxiety through the company. "Arnold could scream at you in a way that is terrifying," says Toussaint, "but he was never attacking you personally. He was not trying to diminish you but to make you do better. He knows that dancing is something where you have to fight your body every day, however great you are. He really pushes to make you sustain your responsibility to dance. Real artists respect him for that."

Spohr's visits to Eddy Toussaint's company began during some of Spohr's most difficult years in Winnipeg. "He would speak bitterly of the board," Toussaint recalls, "of how difficult it was and how he felt there were people who wanted to take his place. Arnold told me to be careful it did not happen to me. He told me it hurts."

Spohr's visits to the Eddy Toussaint Dance Company ended as the troupe was establishing itself as a contemporary ballet touring company with strong audience appeal and thus a potential rival to the RWB. "He stopped coming when he saw we were no longer the little troupe we had been," says Toussaint. "Arnold was always aware that he was artistic director of the RWB first."

Purple
Passion
Punch

Sergei Sawchyn would have been the last person to deny Arnold Spohr's ability to make the Royal Winnipeg Ballet look its very best on stage. "He was one of the greatest stage directors this country, maybe dance, has seen," says Sawchyn. "He had an enormous capacity for hard work and wouldn't allow anyone else to slack off. He was dedicated, he saw the on-stage whole as being in the tiny details, and he had an intuitive awareness of dance theatre as entertainment. Arnold understood 'show business'."

This did not mean that Sawchyn's working relationship with Spohr became any easier. By his own admission, one of the roles Sawchyn enjoyed most in his years as the RWB's general manager was as a producer. Despite some misgivings about Brian Macdonald's relationship with the RWB, Sawchyn understood his value to the company as a choreographer. Sawchyn worked hard to bring Macdonald's ideas to the stage. "I loved listening to the ideas described, [then] setting out to approach the composers, designers, choreographers, sculptors, painters, dancers and other artists."

Sawchyn had played a major role in producing *Rose Latulippe*. The idea for a full-length ballet based on a French Canadian folk story belonged to Macdonald. He had tried to sell it to Celia Franca at the National Ballet but she turned him down. So, Macdonald approached the RWB. Spohr was enthusiastic and Sawchyn got to work. It was Sawchyn who booked the premiere into the Stratford Festival for the summer of 1966. Harry Somers had been Macdonald's first choice of composer, but when Somers proved unavailable Macdonald turned to another Canadian, Harry Freedman. Sawchyn recalls tracking

Freedman down at a Christmas party in Toronto and later gathered Macdonald, Freedman, and designer Robert Prévost, in a Montreal hotel room. "I more or less locked them in until they'd mapped the whole thing out."

Rose Latulippe did not turn out to be the huge success everyone had hoped for. Spohr still feels the choreography was good. The problem, he thinks, was the aesthetic conflict between Macdonald's folk-inspired story and choreography and Freedman's very contemporary score. Certainly, to judge by the company's performance in a 1967 CBC televised production of *Rose Latulippe*, the dancers gave it their all, particularly David Moroni in his lead role as the satanic character who lures away the innocent girl. The film, CBC's first colour special, still gives a good sense of the RWB's depth of talent and performance power in this period.

Sawchyn also worked closely on the development of Macdonald's 1970 hit, *A Ballet High*, one of the world's first rock ballets. Again, the idea came from Macdonald. He and Sawchyn were driving together and Macdonald suddenly asked: "Have you ever seen a class in New York?" As Macdonald's mind began to race, he went on to imagine a morning ballet class, with tired dancers and hung-over musicians, perhaps even a saxophonist coming in to play. "I want to make a dance with that atmosphere for the kids," Sawchyn recalls Macdonald explaining, "something with a big rock band on stage." Sawchyn told Macdonald about an innovative rock band in Toronto that had just played New York's Carnegie Hall. "Lighthouse!" Macdonald exclaimed. "That's who I want to use."

After selling out in Ottawa, *A Ballet High* caused an equal rush for tickets when it opened at Toronto's St. Lawrence Centre. Within two days the scheduled week of performances was sold out, and people were still lining up. Sawchyn had to persuade the dancers to agree to a one-week contract extension and deal with the band's New York agent who wanted more money. Finally the extension was negotiated. Spohr remembers helping to paste up posters around the city to announce the holdover. Nathan Cohen of The Toronto Star declared that it was the first genuine holdover for dance in Toronto history. Macdonald's agent saw *A Ballet High* in Toronto and wanted to tour it with the RWB for a year. "I'm not sure who nixed that idea but I kick myself now," says Macdonald, "for not having had the sense to put my own company together."

Sawchyn's involvement in the evolution of Norbert Vesak's first ballet for the company, *The Ecstasy of Rita Joe*, was so crucial that Spohr himself insisted that the programme credits should include the line, "Produced by J. Sergei Sawchyn". Vesak's 1971 work began with a request two years earlier from the Indian Brotherhood of Manitoba for a ballet to mark the centenary of a major land treaty settlement. Spohr had already earmarked Vesak as a choreographer he wanted to introduce to the RWB. Vesak received an initial call from Spohr on December 19, 1969. Vesak was at a low ebb. It was the very day he had announced the closing of his Western Dance Theatre in Vancouver. "I was wiped out financially and emotionally," Vesak later recalled. The commission from Winnipeg saved him.

The production committee was inclined towards a ballet based on an Indian legend. Spohr was resistant. "I said to myself, over my dead body. We'd already had one Indian ballet and it wasn't that great." Spohr became more interested when Vesak suggested adapting George Ryga's searing stage drama, *The Ecstasy of Rita Joe*. He was even more interested when Vesak floated the idea of trying to involve Academy Award nominee Chief Dan George. "I totally succumbed to the idea," says Spohr. "The clincher for me was Chief Dan George. He was up for an Oscar for Little Big Man and this could mean good box office for the company." Sawchyn took Vesak's ideas and ran with them.

The multi-media ballet that resulted – dance, film, voice-over, and Anne Mortifee's singing – became an RWB signature piece. Instead of ending up, as Spohr had feared might happen, with a pastiche of dancing round a campfire, he got a dance drama that spoke to the heart and carried a powerful social message. Ryga's play examined the familiar plight of the urbanized native, caught in limbo between two cultures. Like the play, Vesak's tragic ballet carried a visceral punch.

Sawchyn had reason to be gratified by his involvement in these landmark productions. His title of general manager hardly seemed adequate. Some people even thought Sawchyn wanted to run the company. Says Dick Foose, "He was competing with Arnold for the position of Most Important Person." It did not improve their relations.

"I think Arnold felt threatened by me and I grew resentful of him," says Sawchyn. "... Arnold saw me as threatening, not in that I would be a new artistic director, of course, or not even that I'd push him out for somebody new. It was more subtle than that. He didn't necessarily feel left out or inadequate to the task, but much of what went on no longer involved him or a committee. All the new opportunities placed new demands on him. He could not remain calm at the centre of the storm, unless it was between acts, behind the curtain."

The tensions between the two became more than just the "creative sparks" that Kathleen Richardson thought so productive. Sawchyn, and his best ally on the board, Sol Kanee, had already nicknamed Spohr "Nutty Arnold". Sawchyn says Kanee, in private conversation, would even talk of getting rid of Spohr for someone who, in Sawchyn's words, "could play all the innings".

The board was in all likelihood loathe to lose either. Spohr was clearly tired and worn. He had recently been off for two months with pneumonia. Sawchyn was hoping the board would persuade Spohr to take a year's sick leave. The idea went nowhere and it was not long after that Sawchyn began thinking it might be time to quit. "It seemed to me then," says Sawchyn, "that the more Arnold got, the more he demanded. I used to say to Jim Cameron that we had created our own Frankenstein monster here!"

Sawchyn was feeling under-appreciated. He was also going through an ugly marriage breakup. His last big project at the RWB was a 1972 visit to Australia. It was an eleven-week tour, under the auspices of the young Australian impresario, Michael Edgley. The tour was undertaken without a cent of Canadian government funding. Edgley was enthusiastic about the RWB. During the 1972 tour he was already talking about a return visit. However, when the final tally was made, Edgley discovered he had lost money. As he explained to the company, it would be impossible to tour them in Australia again without major international guest stars. The RWB never returned. For the dancers, however, the 1972 tour was one of their most pleasurable to date. Spohr says he drank more champagne in Australia than he had in his whole life.

Instead of a one-night-stand, bus-and-truck trek across North America in winter, the dancers crossed the equator in late January to bask in an Australian summer. They stayed a full two weeks in their first stop, Brisbane. Queensland's Gold Coast is susceptible to cyclones and one hit during the RWB's stay. There was extensive flooding. One of the local musicians playing for the company had to swim to reach his car, parked on higher ground. He wrapped his cello in plastic and floated it beside him. "He made it just in time," says Spohr approvingly. "That was definitely devotion beyond the call of duty."

The company continued to St. Kilda in Melbourne, then to Canberra and Sydney. In Sydney, the RWB played in competition with The Australian Ballet. The Australian company was performing Frederick Ashton's *Cinderella*. Robert Helpmann, a ballet icon in Australia, and Ashton himself, were dancing the Ugly Sisters. Despite initial fears, both companies played to near-capacity houses, although a critic noted that it was about time The Australian Ballet took its cue from the RWB and tried for more adventurous programming. From bustling Sydney, the RWB ended its tour in the more staid serenity of Adelaide.

Once again, Spohr was happy to listen to what the impresarios had to say. "They know their local audience. It makes sense to listen." In Michael Edgley's case, however, Spohr begged to differ. Edgley had already insisted on guest stars, Francesca Zumba and Patrice Bart of the Paris Opera Ballet, to add a bit of dazzle. In Edgley's judgement, Macdonald's humorous ballets were fine. Even Agnes de Mille's Lizzie Borden axe-murder ballet, *Fall River Legend*, which the company had acquired in 1969, was acceptable. What concerned Edgley was Macdonald's more reflective *Shining People of Leonard Cohen* and Vesak's *Ecstasy of Rita Joe*. "This time I insisted", says Spohr, "and guess what, those ballets were our biggest hits in Australia." Critics especially applauded Anna Maria de Gorriz' portrayal of Rita in *Ecstasy*, a role originally intended for Christine Hennessy until she and her husband, fellow RWB member Winthrop Corey, decided to have a baby. It was the role of de Gorriz' career. Chief Dan George, whose recorded voice was heard in the role of Rita's father, was so impressed that after seeing de Gorriz perform, in appreciation, he symbolically adopted her as a grandchild.

Everywhere the RWB went it was given a warm welcome and although, typically, the critics varied in their opinions of particular ballets, they fell over themselves to praise the dancers. The newspaper headlines were a publicist's most fervent dream: "Tradition is tossed aside", "Ballet is dazzling", "Wild cheers for ballet", "Ballet of brilliant versatility", "Don't miss these Canadians".

Spohr's role was not overlooked. "The true power which gives individuality to this rather special company," wrote Beth Dean of The Sydney Morning Herald, "is director Arnold Spohr's refreshing point of view. Unafraid of using the classic ballet idiom to speak of the many worlds of man through dance, he includes an enviable list of renowned choreographers." The vigour and range of the three programmes Spohr had assembled for Australia drew repeated praise, perhaps best summed up by a headline over Ian McIntosh's glowing review in Adelaide's The News: "New zest by Winnipeg troupe may bring rebirth of ballet".

Sawchyn told Spohr he was leaving when the company was safely up and running in Australia. "He took the news quietly. I think he was both afraid to see me go and happy it was over. He stiffened his lips, and jutted his lower jaw. I could tell he knew he would have to get through another setback, just as he had for his whole lifetime until then."

Sawchyn's decision to leave at the end of the 1971/72 season was generally recognized as a major loss. The April, 1972 edition of Ballet-Hoo, the RWB's own magazine, ran an affectionate article about Sawchyn. The title "A Showman in Ballet" was printed under a graphic representation of a clown face, a reference to Sawchyn's next assignment as assistant to the president of Canada's Conklin Shows.

The story included tributes from Michael Edgley, the Chicago Lyric Opera's Danny Newman, a guru of audience development and subscription selling, and from Spohr himself. "Sergei Sawchyn is one of the finest general managers a company could have." Spohr concluded: "He will be missed – his contribution to the Royal Winnipeg Ballet never forgotten, always felt, seen and acknowledged."

What Spohr did with his private copy of the article is far more revealing. It is heavily marked in red ink with circles, underlinings and occasional marginalia. They are unmistakably his and suggest Spohr's mixed emotions. There is a little boxed editorial note in the article that reads: "When Sergei Sawchyn heard that BALLET-HOO was doing a story on him, he insisted that the 'pimples' be included along with the 'polish'. He's still the boss." Beside it Spohr scribbled "our problem". Later, where the article describes Sawchyn's success in soliciting sponsorships to underwrite tickets to the ballet for seniors and people on welfare, Spohr wrote in capitals, "MY DREAM HE HAS HELPED REALISE IT & VICE VERSA".

Sergei Sawchyn was arguably the most forceful and dynamic manager Spohr ever worked with. He set an example that his successors often found hard to match. But Sawchyn also left a legacy. He built an effective administration and helped turn the RWB into a highly professional organization. As the years passed, a legendary glow illuminated Sawchyn's years with the RWB, just as one had already enveloped Spohr's directorship. How comfortable Spohr felt with this competing star in the firmament of the RWB is a question he prefers to avoid.

The board hired Robert Dubberley to succeed Sawchyn. He had a varied fifteen-year background in theatre and came to Winnipeg from Toronto where he had been assistant general director of the St. Lawrence Centre for the Arts. Before this Dubberley had worked at the Confederation Centre in Charlottetown and taken its hit musical, Anne of Green Gables, on tour across Canada and to Japan. Dubberley seemed ideal for the RWB, but he was on his way out within a year and a half.

In 1972, Dubberley was not the only new face around the RWB's Portage Avenue headquarters. There were many new dancers as well. As the 1971/72 season drew towards its close, Spohr had decided it was time for "a house cleaning". There were dancers whom he did not think were working hard enough and others who were simply spent.

He asked Richard Rutherford to do the dirty work. "We were still on tour as I recall. Arnold was unhappy with a lot of the dancers but he was not good at getting rid of people. Usually they drifted away of their own accord. I told him not to keep them hanging around, but then I ended up having to fire them. Arnold just sat across the room." Naturally the blood-letting was not pretty. "Veronica Graver went hysterical," says Spohr. "Michael Manning thought he was terrific and I had some nerve for letting him go. The audacity of me, and on and on he went. I had to take his wounded ego missiles." By the end of it, eleven dancers were gone – close to half the company.

By this time Rutherford was part of Spohr's artistic team. In 1970, at the age of thirty-five and after thirteen years as a dancer with the company, most of those years as its leading male star, Rutherford had decided to retire. He already had a job lined up. The RWB board had invited him to become an associate artistic director. "I assumed it was Arnold's suggestion. He needed the help." Rutherford gave his farewell performance on October 10 of that year and the following night the RWB staged a special "Salute to Richard Rutherford". From the unusual comfort of a seat in the theatre, he was able to enjoy a gala performance that included guest dancers from the National Ballet and Les Grands Ballets Canadiens. Agnes de Mille, a great Rutherford admirer, was in attendance and made one of her memorable speeches. Spohr committed his admiration to print. "Rutherford," wrote Spohr in the gala house programme, "has the God-given gift of an inner magnetism, intelligence and the natural sense of dance ... His body is like a fine instrument that responds at will to anything a choreographer or director wishes to express." Intent on drawing a moral from Rutherford's achievement, Spohr continued, "We need people of imagination and drive with the will for great sacrifice ... Success knows no short-cut."

Rutherford's good friend David Moroni chose the gala as the occasion of his own official farewell performance. In six years with the RWB, Moroni – with his brooding, Byronic good looks – had grown to be a valuable leading dancer. He had the unusual distinction of having had his publicity portrait stolen from a theatre lobby display more times than any other company dancer. In 1970, Moroni was only thirty-two and had a lot of dancing left in him, but he also enjoyed teaching. He therefore heeded Spohr's request to retire early from the stage in order to head a formally constituted Professional Division of the Royal Winnipeg Ballet School. In fact, both Rutherford and Moroni did later return to the stage. Rutherford filled in for an injured dancer during the Australian tour and made a brief official return in 1975 to star in a Vesak ballet called *In Quest of the Sun*. Moroni was back in 1972 to portray the eccentric dancing master in the company's first full-length classic, *The Nutcracker*, choreographed by John Neumeier.

It was Spohr's American critic friend, Olga Maynard, who recommended Neumeier. Neumeier, of German-Polish descent, was born in Milwaukee but had forged a promising career as a dancer and choreographer at the Stuttgart Ballet. By age twenty-five, Neumeier was already ballet director in Frankfurt, where he remembers getting a letter from Sawchyn in August, 1970. Sawchyn asked him to create a work for the RWB. For weeks there was no reply. Then a letter came from Neumeier explaining that as much as he would be honoured to create a work for the company, the rehearsal period Sawchyn had suggested would be too short. Perhaps, wrote Neumeier, the company would be interested in one of his existing ballets. The letters continued to flow between Frankfurt and Winnipeg. The RWB, Neumeier recalls, wanted something "dancey". Sawchyn sent a full kit of background information about the company and Neumeier consulted with one of his dancers, Beatrice Cordua, who had performed briefly with the RWB. It was not until the following spring that it was agreed that Neumeier would stage his ballet *Rondo*, a work for sixteen dancers. From Neumeier's description, Sawchyn thought the work would fit nicely into a programme scheduled for July at the National Arts Centre. The other ballets would be Vesak's *Rita Joe* and a comedy by British choreographer Walter Gore, *The Last Rose of Summer*.

Rondo was very new. Neumeier had created it in Frankfurt in 1970 as part of a trilogy under the banner "Invisible Frontiers". *Rondo* had been shown nowhere else. The ballet used an eclectic recorded score, "a collage" in Neumeier's description. Following classic rondo A-B-A-C-A musical form, his score and choreographic theme evoked contrast and evolution. There were harmonious songs in the A sections – William Cornyshe, Mahler, Simon and Garfunkel – with disruptive contemporary electronic music in the B and C sections. The ballet, in Neumeier's programme note, "explores in pure dance terms and images a common theme: conventions, the invisible frontiers of a culture and their influences on individuals." Its movement range was wide. At one point the dancers crumpled to the floor and rolled themselves off stage. It was a great ballet but not, Neumeier is convinced, quite what the RWB expected. "I think there was a terrible misconception about Rondo. They had expected a classical ballet and had already cast it. They were in shock when they saw the movements. I remember seeing it described in the theatre marquee as 'a classical romp' and told them to take it down."

Spohr was not around when Neumeier arrived to set the work in early July, 1971. It was Rutherford who served as his régisseur and the two got along famously. In Rutherford's recollection, Spohr and Neumeier did not meet until the opening in Ottawa. "We were standing backstage and Arnold, wearing this white velvet jacket, came loping towards us. 'Who's that?' asked John. 'Mr. Spohr,' I replied. I can still remember John letting out this deep sigh." Says Neumeier, "Beatrice Cordua had warned me that he was a very extravagant and extreme individual, but I was still not completely prepared for his bigger-than-life way of coming at you."

Rondo was warmly received but the much-anticipated *Rita Joe* with its powerful Canadian theme was the big audience hit of the programme. It took time before audiences came fully to appreciate the choreographic inventiveness of *Rondo*. Spohr, however, was immediately enthusiastic and soon travelled to Frankfurt to see more of Neumeier's work. Neumeier was planning to replace Todd Bolender's old Frankfurt production of *The Nutcracker*, a ballet he says he generally detested. "It was only as a way of giving my dancers more performances." Neumeier had decided to throw out the traditional Christmas party that opens the ballet so that it would be appropriate for any season. Spohr said he was also looking for a *Nutcracker* and asked Neumeier to provide it. Neumeier was initially reluctant. "I didn't think of the company as particularly classical." His Frankfurt production was given its premiere in October, 1971 and the Bavarian State Opera Ballet in Munich wanted it too. "Winnipeg was like an out-of-town tryout in a way," says Neumeier. "They were the first to use the Jürgen Rose designs. Winnipeg was the confirmation that this piece could develop."

Neumeier had sent his assistant, Ray Barra, ahead to set the ballet and later came himself for two rehearsal periods. "Initially I must admit that Arnold seemed to me so superficial and trivial but eventually I began to realize the truth, that there was this great focus, this respect for choreography. We also shared this enormous respect for Vera Volkova. She was my great inspiration and he was fascinated by her. Also I could tell he was really looking for choreography as an instrument to develop his dancers, a thing I respect so much." Spohr attended Neumeier's rehearsals and, as usual, made notes. "He was so interested in knowing, in taking care of the ballet. He placed a great deal of emphasis on the word of a choreographer regarding his work."

The RWB gave the premiere of *The Nutcracker* on December 26, 1972, with the famous French ballerina, Violette Verdy, as guest star in the role of Louisa. The whole production caused a sensation in Winnipeg – eight sold-out performances – and a flurry of interest across North America. *The Nutcracker* had become a money-spinning Christmas industry for companies across the United States. In Canada, both Les Grands Ballets Canadiens and the National Ballet already had lavish traditional productions – Celia Franca's also featured Jürgen Rose designs – but nothing as conceptually innovative as Neumeier's. Neumeier's version opened with a surprise birthday party for the young Maria. Her brother Fritz has invited his cadet friends, among whom is Gunther, the suitor of Maria's elder sister, Louisa. Louisa has invited her dancing master, Drosselmeier, who gives Maria a pair of pointe shoes. These trigger the second-act dream world where Maria imagines herself rehearsing and performing.

The Nutcracker represented an enormous advance for the company in every respect. One of the features that attracted Spohr was the fact that it offered stage experience to students in the professional school. Unlike many traditional versions of *The Nutcracker*, Neumeier's uses adult dancers to portray the children but, with a total cast of forty, it did require supplementing the regular company with fifteen advanced students. Spohr also saw Neumeier's *Nutcracker* as a ballet that would appeal to family audiences. In 1974, the production was televised by the CBC. It was to serve the company well for many years at home and on tour but, over time, in a small market such as Winnipeg, its drawing power with hometown audiences began to wane. Over time, the RWB found it could not rely on the production to be a dependable cash-cow as could other companies with more traditional versions.

In many respects, Neumeier's *Nutcracker*, stripped of the mice, snowmen, shepherdesses and other saccharine accoutrements popularly associated with traditional versions, was more a ballet for serious dance lovers than for a broadly based holiday season crowd. As Calgary Herald critic Carol Hogg later noted, Neumeier's version "has a touch of bittersweet, where the old one was pure icing". After a quarter century of service, the RWB finally decided to replace the Neumeier version and reverted to a traditional production, adding its own homespun twist. It was none too soon for Neumeier. Other than receiving the occasional royalty cheque, he had almost forgotten the RWB still performed the ballet and certainly believed it was far past its "sell-by" date.

Spohr saw Neumeier as part of a process of choreographic renewal for the RWB. Following the success of *The Nutcracker*, Spohr was looking forward to a productive relationship that would include the creation of new works. As confirmation of the importance the company attached to the connection with Neumeier, the RWB named him as one of its official choreographers. Early in 1973, plans were already being discussed to add his full-length *Romeo and Juliet* to the repertoire. Neumeier, however, did not view his relationship with the RWB as exclusive. At almost exactly the same time, he agreed to stage his *Don Juan* for the National Ballet in Toronto. Two more Neumeier ballets, *Twilight* and *The Game*, both created in Germany, were added to the RWB's repertoire. In January, 1974, they were programmed with *Rondo* as a full-evening trilogy called *Pictures*. At the time, Spohr told William Littler: "I think John Neumeier is the greatest thing going." But, although he continued to be billed as company choreographer for several years, no more Neumeier ballets were added to the repertoire. "When I moved to Hamburg, I became so totally absorbed somehow it all stopped," says Neumeier. "Then, Arnold discovered Oscar Araiz, which I suppose supplanted my role." There may have been more to it than that. While it is true that his job in Hamburg was consuming, Neumeier also had reservations about the RWB's classical abilities. Writing to de Mille in 1976, Spohr refers to Neumeier's misgivings and then defends the way the RWB danced his ballets. "So I do get annoyed," he told de Mille, "for our kids do succeed with his ballets because of the way we rehearse, and the truth of what he wants, we bring to them. No one needs to be condescending or cruel. If they don't like us, or what we do, then don't work with us."

Neumeier's visits to the RWB, few that they were, had un-expected consequences. Neumeier has a natural and very special charisma, a gentle power that draws people to him. Add to this the challenges of his choreography and inspirational way of working and it is not hard to understand why several of the RWB's dancers would want to join him in Hamburg. And they did, notably Salvatore Aiello and Marina Eglevsky. In all, eight dancers vanished from the roster at the end of the 1972/73 season. Sheila Mackinnon retired from dancing to join Spohr's artistic staff. Petal Miller left for England. Madeleine Bouchard and her husband, Attila Ficzere, went to San Francisco. In general, Spohr was philosophical about losing dancers but in this case the timing was bad. The situation was made more difficult by the fact that even in late May, Spohr had no clear sense of who was leaving. To add to his problems, the dancers' union contract had not yet been renegotiated. "We had one of our busiest years ever coming up, including a big South American tour, so I was traumatized with fear. I thought I would go insane with worry. This was my worst and only year that I felt nearly desolated and stranded. I felt like running, but I have never run away from anything."

As usual, Spohr's ingenuity and handy list of contacts came to the rescue. Through a variety of promotions and hirings from the school and beyond, Spohr finally had a company he felt he could hone into shape. "By the time the big tour came in the spring of 1974 I had my new stars ready to conquer South America." They included the eighteen-year-old Bonnie Wyckoff.

Wyckoff had already risen to principal rank with the Boston Ballet where she had danced the lead in de Mille's popular slice of Americana, *Rodeo*. Wyckoff was already thinking of moving on. She was young and wanted to see the world. She asked de Mille for advice. "Ever attentive to what might eventually serve her own interests," Wyckoff recalls, "she said she would be setting *Rodeo* on the RWB the following year and that I should contact Mr. Spohr." Wyckoff sent her résumé off to Winnipeg but heard that there were no vacancies. Wyckoff and her partner, Anthony Williams, had left Boston to dance with the Gulbenkian Ballet in Lisbon and had scarcely arrived when they found a telegram waiting from Spohr. He wanted to audition them. Spohr made a side trip from a holiday in Spain, saw them for two hours on a Sunday evening and flew out the same night having hired both. Wyckoff still remembers the purple suit Spohr wore that day and a conversation over dinner. "He seemed to be perpetually bubbling over, unable to contain his own exuberance, then suddenly shy and self-conscious for about three seconds, then carried away again with whatever idea his enthusiasm had got hold of. I just loved the way he spoke from the heart." Wyckoff emerged as one of Spohr's most incandescent artists. "Little Miss Sunshine", was Spohr's summation of her character. Wyckoff and Spohr soon established an affectionate bond and to this day she remains one of his most fervent admirers.

Spohr earned a new admirer when, after years of trying, he managed to bring Margot Fonteyn to Winnipeg in September, 1973 to appear in the company's first local shows of the season. The fifty-four-year-old Fonteyn was past her prime, but her name was still synonymous with ballet. A large RWB delegation and small army of press photographers were at the airport to greet her. "How long do you intend to keep dancing?" a reporter had the temerity to ask. "I hope to dance through this week," Fonteyn promptly replied. With her partner, Heinz Bosl, Fonteyn delighted six sold-out houses. The RWB's subscriber base was now close to 9,700. The demand for the remaining seats far exceeded supply. The opening night crowd was so excited that it burst into applause seven times as Fonteyn danced one of her classic showpieces, the Aurora pas de deux from *The Sleeping Beauty*. At the end, she was fêted with armloads of roses. Before leaving Winnipeg, Fonteyn wrote Spohr a card expressing, "my deep admiration of the work you are accomplishing and your devotion to dancing." He still keeps it.

By the time the RWB left for South America in April, 1974, the company had already had an exhausting year of touring. Spohr blames general manager Robert Dubberley for overbooking the company, but judging by the response from South American audiences, the dancers clearly had energy in reserve.

In earlier years, the RWB had danced in Jamaica, Puerto Rico, Venezuela and the Dutch Antilles, so its veteran members knew something about the climate and about the friendly, excitable audiences. Dealing with the complex logistics and associated hazards of touring were as familiar to the RWB as the cheering crowds and positive reviews that usually followed. Even so, the 1974 tour was remarkable – fifty performances in nine countries throughout South and Central America and the Caribbean, all in the space of ten weeks and with a travelling repertoire of thirteen ballets, including a selection of pas de deux. The RWB had by now presented its credentials as a cultural ambassador on three continents, but never in so many countries in such a short space of time.

In Bogota, Colombia, almost 2,600 kilometres above sea level, the dancers had oxygen tanks standing by in the wings. In Brasilia, the new national theatre was unfinished and the company was compelled to perform for 8,000 people in the city's Gymnasium, a sports arena. Even then, the specially erected stage was not ready and the RWB crew had to pitch in to finish the job. In Mexico City, as in Brasilia, it appeared most of the government was in attendance, from the president on down. In Buenos Aires, principal dancer Sylvester Campbell had to be rescued by police from a mob of fans. He and Bonnie Wyckoff were such hits in Rio de Janeiro that they were obliged to give an encore of Jack Carter's *Pas de Deux Romantique*. In San José, Costa Rica, the dancers almost cried. "We were going to perform in a sort of arena or horse palace," says Spohr. "It was rotten and filthy and smelled so bad. In the girls' dressing room there was no light bulb and only one small table that collapsed when the girls put their makeup kits on it."

Spohr has poignant memories of the company's stop in Managua, the capital of Nicaragua. An earthquake had devastated the city on December 23, 1972, killing more than 20,000 people. The effects were still very evident. "It was so sad to see all the destruction," says Spohr. "There were still huge cracks in the ground. Our hotel and the theatre seemed to be the only things that had been restored. Canada had donated three fire trucks as part of the international relief effort. One day they came to the hotel, loaded us all up and took us on a tour of the city. We went by all the fire stations and the men were lined up outside. One fireman with tears in his eyes embraced each and every one of us, repeating over and over again, 'muchos gracias Canada'. Our advance advertising read, 'Canadian Ambassadors Coming to City'. Again, we seemed to be Canada's number one goodwill."

The RWB's visit to Cuba presented its own diplomatic hurdles because there were so many American dancers in the company. It took a lot of negotiating with the State Department in Washington to secure the necessary permits. The RWB was the first North American ballet company to visit Cuba since the Castro revolution and there were long lineups outside Havana's Mella Theatre. The Cuban audience giggled when the lovers stripped down to their underwear for the bedroom scene in *Rita Joe*. Otherwise, as elsewhere on the tour, Vesak's ballet garnered many curtain calls. However, Globe and Mail correspondent Lionel Martin noted that some of the ballet's social meaning was probably lost on the Spanish-speaking audience. Why, he asked, had the company not thought of making a Spanish-language version of Chief Dan George's narration?

Vesak's second work for the RWB, *What to do Till the Messiah Comes*, unveiled in the winter of 1973 to great acclaim, was also a major hit throughout the tour. When the full ballet was no longer performed, *Belong*, a pas deux extracted from it, remained hugely popular. Vesak's ballet took its title from a popular book published in 1971 by American self-realization guru, Bernard Gunther, the inventor of Esalen Massage. Its collage score mixed the music of composer Phillip Werren with the rock sounds of Canadian groups Chilliwack and Syrinx and its touchy-feely theme managed to hit just the right chord with younger audiences.

Robin Boyd, a Canadian travelling in South America at the time, saw the RWB dance in Buenos Aires and was so proud that he sent a letter to the Winnipeg Free Press. "No country has better ambassadors than these," wrote Boyd. It was *Messiah* that really got to him. "I had tears in my eyes. Such a complete and truly sensual rendering of life, performed as only those who have felt the extremes can do. I count my seeing this as a unique experience in my young years." For Spohr, the great friend of audiences, this was the very best kind of review.

Spohr came back from the tour with a good deal more than vivid memories and the obligatory souvenirs. On his first journey to South America in 1964 he had noted a picture of Oscar Araiz, a twenty-three-year-old dancer and choreographer who had put together his own touring troupe. Spohr did not see the company or meet Araiz, but somehow the name had registered. During the 1974 tour, in Buenos Aires, he was told he should see the work of an interesting Argentinean choreographer. "I went to this old dusty theatre. It seemed only a quarter full, but the choreography was so strong. It was Oscar's." Then, in São Paulo, Spohr watched another company rehearsing Araiz' sensual pas de deux *Adagietto* and fell in love with it. He finally met Araiz in Rio de Janeiro and immediately invited him to Winnipeg. Spohr had "discovered" yet another choreographer. It was the start of his Araiz binge.

"Discover" is a relative term. Spohr was correct to a degree, albeit from a geographically prejudiced viewpoint. Araiz was already well known in South America. When the distinguished German critic Horst Koegler finished compiling his Concise Oxford Dictionary of Ballet in 1976, Araiz, with more than a dozen works to his credit, occupied substantially more linear space than either the entry for Arnold Spohr or the Royal Winnipeg Ballet. What Spohr did was to introduce Araiz to North American audiences, in the process attracting the attention of Robert Joffrey in New York. Generally, Spohr was unconcerned when other artistic directors picked up on the fruits of his choreographic reconnaissance. "I wasn't bitter about it. If everybody else wants them then I figure we've helped them. It's wonderful to have the achievement of discovery." In the case of Joffrey, however, Spohr was later to have cause for regret. But first he had to get Araiz to Winnipeg and, with the company's financial situation in a perilous state, it was not so easy.

As a fund-raising prospectus of 1974 documented, the RWB had gone through a period of dramatic expansion, but its financial foundations remained insecure. From 1965 to 1974 the cost of the company's operations increased by 504 per cent. Had it not been for a substantial increase in grants from government sources, particularly the Canada Council, the accumulated deficit would have grown at a similar pace. As it was, by early 1974 the company deficit stood at approximately $300,000, close to twenty per cent of its annual operating budget. The same year, the Washington Ballet, with a deficit of similar proportions, had gone bust. The most glaring deficiency during the same nine-year period was the puny growth of corporate, foundation and individual giving – a mere fifty-six per cent increase, from $77,802 to $121,583. With a few notable exceptions, the members of the RWB board were models of parsimony, perhaps lulled by the complacent assumption that when things got really tough there always seemed to be an anonymous donor to save the company from ruin.

Red ink had flooded at a particularly alarming rate during the 1973/74 season and Robert Dubberley was gone long before the company left for South America. Plans to take the company to downtown Manhattan in the 1974/75 season were put on hold and a management committee took over the running of the company until a replacement for Dubberley could be found.

In its moment of distress the RWB decided to turn to an old friend, Jim Cameron. He had quit in 1972 soon after the departure of Sergei Sawchyn. Cameron was working for Madame Tussaud's wax museum in Niagara Falls, Ontario, when he got a call from Sawchyn to say that Kathleen Richardson was trying to get in touch. The two eventually met in Toronto and Richardson told Cameron they needed him to come back and manage the company – so he did.

Cameron earned a reputation for being blunt to the point of rudeness. "Jim was straight-shooting," says Sheila Mackinnon. "He said what he thought, but at least he wasn't devious." Some of the dancers thought Cameron regarded them as dispensable line workers. However, unlike Sawchyn, Cameron had no aspirations beyond getting the finances in order quickly. It meant drastic budget cuts, a bailout from the Manitoba government and, as so often happened in such circumstances, a helping hand from an "anonymous" donor.

Spohr knew about the company's mounting money problems

while still in South America. In typical fashion, he worried that he was to blame. "Arnold took too much responsibility," says Cameron, "as though the debt were all his fault." However, when Spohr got back to Winnipeg he did tell Cameron about this wonderful choreographer he had found in South America. "He has a near-perfect pas de deux," Spohr explained. "Too bad we don't have the money to bring him here." Cameron was impressed. "Here was a case of Arnold being ready to sever his right arm to keep his fingers out of the cookie jar. Tell me of another artistic director who could have restrained himself in that circumstance."

Cameron somehow found the money and Araiz' *Adagietto*, set to the haunting fourth movement of Mahler's Symphony No. 5, was danced by RWB principals Louise Naughton and Craig Sterling later the same year in Winnipeg to ecstatic audience acclaim. It almost upstaged what Cameron considered to be his major coup. He had secured the recent Soviet defector Mikhail Baryshnikov and American Ballet Theatre's Gelsey Kirkland as guest artists. It was to be the launch of their relatively short but headline-making partnership. Since this was also the launch of the RWB's thirty-fifth anniversary season, the board invited Gweneth Lloyd and Betty Farrally to join the celebrations. It was the first time the two women had been in Winnipeg since Farrally's dramatic departure seventeen years earlier.

In retrospect, Cameron may not have done Spohr as big a favour as he first thought. Spohr proceeded to load up on Araiz ballets – eight in all by the end of the 1976/77 season – to the point where RWB dancers joked among themselves that perhaps the company should change its name. Only one of the eight works, the 1976 *Mahler 4: Eternity is Now*, was actually created for the RWB. Some of the Araiz ballets enjoyed well-deserved success. Others were less favourably received and eventually triggered a backlash among Winnipeg subscribers. Spohr's motive was practical enough. He wanted to stock the repertoire with Araiz ballets while the choreographer was a relative unknown in North America and the works still affordable. He also believed that Araiz' contemporary style suited the RWB's image as an artistically adventurous troupe. But, had the Canadian choreographer Norbert Vesak not offered the same?

After his initial success with the RWB, Vesak's career had blossomed. He had moved to the United States in 1970 to become ballet director at the San Francisco Opera and then directed the Metropolitan Opera Ballet in New York from 1973-1980. Yet, despite Vesak's busy career, Spohr's decision to focus on the work of Oscar Araiz appears to have diverted him from pursuing a promising relationship with Vesak. Vesak continued to be listed as a company choreographer but it was not until 1975 that he returned to create *In Quest of the Sun*, the work that brought Richard Rutherford out of retirement. It turned out to be a costly flop.

The ballet was inspired by the fatal encounter between Spain's conquering Francisco Pizarro and the sixteenth-century Inca god-king, Atahualpa. The board of the RWB already had misgivings. *Whispers of Darkness*, a work Vesak had created for the National Ballet the previous year using the same expensive New York designer, Ming Cho Lee, had been an embarrassing failure. The board also disliked Vesak's original title, *Inquest of the Sun*. He was told to come up with something "less morbid". Following this unfortunate experience, it was another six years before Spohr invited Vesak back. He created *Meadow Dances*, an ensemble work with featured solos, duets and trios, set to the evocative Songs of the Auvergne. *Meadow Dances* was Vesak's last work for the company. He died in 1990.

• • •

By this stage of his career, Spohr's position in the broad ecology of the RWB had altered radically. He had emerged as an extraordinarily effective director and played a central role in transforming the RWB into an international phenomenon. Meanwhile, the marketing skills of Sawchyn and Cameron had helped furnish Spohr with a public image, a nimbus that journalist Ted Allan once aptly described as a "vaporous body of fact, fiction and fantasy". Spohr found no reason to dispel it.

In 1976, Grant Strate, the National Ballet's first resident choreographer and the founding chairman of York University's dance department in Toronto, wrote: "The phenomenon of Arnold Spohr demands a new definition of the role of artistic director." Spohr indeed viewed his position as an all-embracing one. His natural curiosity disposed him to be interested in every aspect of the company. From a practical standpoint, Spohr liked to feel he had a basic understanding of what every job entailed so that no one could tell him something was impossible. He had grown up in the company at a time when everyone was expected to lend a hand. Even when the RWB acquired a sizeable staff, Spohr was never hesitant to offer his assistance. At a staff meeting, Jim Cameron remembers mentioning that he urgently needed the help of a skilled bookkeeper. A few days later Spohr showed up at Cameron's office door. He explained that he had a break between rehearsals and had "come to help with the books". Cameron was touched by the offer but politely declined.

The company had expanded on every front and was growing into a complex organization. Spohr believed it was an important part of his role to see that all these different elements functioned together harmoniously and were focussed on the company's fundamental mandate. Simply stated, this was to present dance and dancers that audiences would flock to see. The key, in his mind, was to assemble a strong team. "I didn't mind delegating at all," says Spohr, "but you have to have the right people." Increasingly, he would voice his frustrations about people who were not "pulling for the team". His ideal was to be surrounded by competent staff in every division and by a dedicated board of directors.

"With Arnold," says Pamela Ouzounian, "you really felt the company had a leader." Ouzounian began her career in the arts in 1972 by working as a receptionist with the RWB. "He was always so open and so present. Arnold would be in everybody's office and he knew everyone's name. He was genuinely interested and so passionate about everything."

It was not uncommon for Spohr to deliver little homilies on the subject of co-operation. He would sometimes chide staff in one department for failing to communicate information to all the others. For him, the RWB was an organism. The connections between its constituent cells were vital. His own commitment to the company's welfare was passionate and profound. His ambition was boundless. He looked for a similar passion and commitment in everyone else. It was hardly surprising that some fell short of Spohr's exalted expectations.

Spohr believed himself to be totally selfless and would grumble if he thought other people were letting their "egos" get in the way. But, in the process of expending so much nervous energy and anxiety on what he saw as the company's welfare, Spohr allowed his own health to suffer, with unfortunate consequences for himself and the RWB.

Spohr did not look after his health wisely. His culinary skills were at best rudimentary. He had an imprudent, though not uncommon, weakness for fatty foods. The result was that Spohr's nutritional condition was less than ideal. He developed a form of colitis and, although even he cannot be sure when it first happened, there were small harbingers of a heart condition. This made the natural stresses of the job all the harder to bear.

"Arnold must have resigned a thousand times," jokes Kathleen Richardson. His threats of resignation became so commonplace, they were not taken seriously. Spohr's "burnouts", however, did become a cause for concern. When they occurred, he found the only way to recover was to go away quietly, sleep, meditate and let nature, with appropriate pharmaceutical and naturopathic support, take its course. Spohr explored various therapies. Shiatsu proved effective, but little could help his chronically overstressed condition. Spohr started wearing sunglasses indoors, for a while under a big floppy Beatles-style cap, and occasionally he would even doze off in rehearsal. "We'd see Richard Rutherford nudge him," says Peter Garrick, a dancer of that era. Spohr felt he needed a warm escape far away from Winnipeg. In the mid-1970's, he bought a condominium in Fort Lauderdale, Florida. Often, it seemed his friends and relations got to use it more than he did.

One of Spohr's major concerns was the welfare of his dancers. However impossible it was to achieve, his characteristic impetus was to try to make everyone, especially the dancers, happy. "If they're happy," says Spohr, "they will dance well." He still remembers an occasion during the company's visit to Caracas in 1966 when Sawchyn had arranged to have a live performance taped for Venezuelan television. It had not been cleared with Canadian Actors' Equity. The dancers were told they would not receive additional payment because there was no extra work involved. "They virtually walked through it," says Spohr. "It was embarrassing and should never have been allowed to happen." When money was tight, which it most always was, Spohr's main worry was the dancers. "If the company gets too much money," he once wrote, "it's sometimes thrown for a loop. Frankly, I enjoy the challenge of making do with what is available, except the one real advantage of more money is to pay the dancers higher salaries."

Spohr's relationship with his dancers had also evolved psychologically. The metaphor he most often invoked when talking of the structure of the organization was that of a tree. In terms of the people in it, he preferred to speak of family. "We were all 'the kids'. Arnold was the father figure," says former RWB communications director Lendre Rodgers Kearns. "It was how he saw his world."

For Spohr, the concept of the RWB as a family, dysfunctional as undoubtedly it sometimes was, remained fundamental. "As a company works together as a family, so its members draw on one another's strength. This relationship helps them conquer adversity."

The metaphor of family was particularly applicable to his tight-knit group of twenty-five dancers. As the years flew by and Spohr got older, the average age of his dancing company remained much the same. The subject of Spohr's precise age remained a mystery to most. His own antipathy towards getting old, combined with a measure of personal vanity, disinclined him from revealing how old he really was. In 1976 he was officially said to be turning fifty and since this worked in his favour by three years, Spohr was happy to go along with it. That December a demi-centennial birthday celebration was duly convened. There was even a congratulatory telegram from Canada's ballet-loving, occasionally pirouetting Prime Minister, Pierre Elliott Trudeau. Those who knew the truth saw no point in spoiling the fun.

When Spohr began as director, he would not have been old enough to be any dancer's father. By the late 1970's he was old enough to be father to them all, which is just the way he saw himself, or to be more exact, the way Spohr thought they saw him. As he later wrote: "My concern is for the individual members of the company because I regard them as family. Each of the dancers genuinely appreciates and depends on that personal interest in their welfare and artistic development. They regard me as a kind of father figure."

Spohr certainly was not reluctant to accept such a role. It filled his strong emotional need to nurture. In the studio, Spohr expressed his fatherly concern in the way he helped his "kids", by whatever means necessary, to achieve their artistic potential. Outside the studio it was expressed in gifts, kind words and an easy familiarity uncommon among ballet company directors. Once during a tour, when the mood had turned negative, Spohr managed to find a different stuffed animal for every dancer and distributed them with a mind to which animal best suited each personality. Joost Pelt still remembers his lion. "Dancers saw it as a warm gesture," says Pelt, "but I don't think they fully understood. Arnold tried to use whatever he could to express his feelings."

Bill Lark recalls how Spohr would sometimes give money out of his own pocket to needy students in the school's scholarship programme. Sheila Mackinnon says some people exploited Spohr's natural generosity. "He wanted so much for everyone to be comfortable in their own lives," she says. "It was a fierce love." If a dancer were sick, Spohr would be constantly attentive. "One time," says Lark, "I had this chronic diarrhea. I was wasting away. Arnold called his nurse sister Erica. She called me and told me it sounded like ulcerated colitis and made me an appointment. She was right. I was off for four weeks and Arnold was all the time calling to see how I was. He was always the loyal one."

Spohr loved to tease and he loved to joke and neither the teasing nor the joking was always appropriate. Peter Garrick still remembers a couple of particularly crass examples. Garrick was blind in his left eye and in fact had an artificial one. "We were in Paris and I'd met this beautiful girl. We were coming out of the theatre together, just a few paces ahead of Arnold and Richard Rutherford. Suddenly I heard Arnold shout, 'What do these French girls see in all the one-eyed people?' Richard was so embarrassed he came to me later and apologized for Arnold. Then another time, years later, I told Arnold about this programme to teach ballet to blind children. He just laughed at me. For someone so smart he could do some pretty dumb things. All the same, you really felt he cared about you, and the art."

Then there was the Purple Passion Punch. According to legend the concoction had been devised by Spohr himself, although he has no recollection of it. In any case, nobody could figure out what went into the mix, but it was, by general account, nasty. Spohr's reputed concoction would appear at the RWB's annual Christmas party, along with a tree and the gifts he had bought for company members. One year all the girls got a bottle of some atrocious cologne. Some of them used it as bathroom deodorant. "In my day we rather dreaded it," says Sheila Mackinnon. "We were dead tired and often only had Christmas Day off. We all went because we knew he needed it more than we did." Gordon Wright remembers the way Spohr would prepare. "We'd be on tour and you'd be in downtown god-knows- where and there he'd be, hunting for little gifts to stockpile for Christmas."

Not all the dancers found it easy to deal with the intensity of Spohr's desire to make the RWB one happy family. "We used to sit and joke about it," says Marina Eglevsky, "but you felt you had to go along with it or you could hurt his feelings. One year I opened my present. It was a belt. Arnold started coming over to me with a big smile on his face, so I tried to put it on but it broke in my hands and fell on the floor. I looked at it, horrified."

A Volatile Brew

The RWB's administration and technical staff had grown throughout the Sawchyn years and beyond in response to the company's emergence onto the world stage. So too had Arnold Spohr's artistic team.

From his official retirement as a dancer in 1970 until the end of the 1972 Australian tour, Richard Rutherford had served as Spohr's associate director. After helping "clean house", he surprised Spohr by announcing that he too was leaving. Rutherford had fallen in love with Australia and wanted to spend some time there. Long-serving ballet mistress Gywnne Ashton, who latterly also worked as Spohr's assistant, had left the previous year. Eugene Slavin, who had arrived as a dancer in 1967 and became ballet master alongside Ashton the following year, left in 1972.

Spohr then hired two Americans, the gentle, likeable Vernon Lusby and, from the dance department at York University, Frank Bourman. Lusby, who first worked with the RWB as Agnes de Mille's rehearsal assistant, was given Rutherford's old title of associate director. Bourman, a debonair man with a mellifluous voice and faintly mysterious air, was initially billed as ballet master. Then in December, 1972, Rutherford returned unexpectedly from Australia. Kathleen Richardson had assured Rutherford there would always be a place for him. The following February, the board executive decided to rehire him with his old title, associate director, as of June 1, 1973. Since Spohr already had a new "associate director", Vernon Lusby, he asked the board to give Rutherford some other title. Rutherford ended up in the newly created position of production coordinator. "I was never sure what it really meant," says Rutherford.

"Basically I just did the same as before, taking rehearsals and doing the scheduling."

The 1975/76 season introduced a flurry of titular changes that suggest the emergence of an informal hierarchy. Bourman jumped from "ballet master" to second billing under Spohr with the puzzling title of "associate artistic director". Since Spohr had gone back to being simply "Director", it was not clear with whom Bourman was supposed to associate – the board perhaps? Lusby came next in the billing, still with his title of associate director. Now he shared it with two others. Rutherford had been given back his old title as associate director and it was added to the invented title of production co-ordinator, given him in 1973. Finally, David Moroni, who since 1970 had steadily been developing the RWB school's professional programme, was also made an associate director. It would have been hard at the time to find any ballet company with so many associate directors. Spohr makes light of this sudden flowering of associates. "Titles! Everyone wants a title. I was the director. That's all that mattered. We just gave other people titles to keep them happy."

But were they all happy? In 1975, Spohr was entering his eighteenth season as director. He had taken the RWB to a high plateau and it was not clear if either he or the board knew exactly where to take the company next. Even if Spohr gave no serious indication of wanting to move on, the fact that he was now delegating his duties more widely than ever inevitably caused some people to speculate about the succession.

Moroni had his hands full fighting to win Canada Council support for the professional school. Although the RWB's general recreational school usually made a small profit, it was not sufficient to underwrite the professional programme. In 1975/76, for example, the general school showed a $16,685 profit, but the professional division was $76,115 in the red. The Council had informed the RWB that it should not assign company operating funds – and by implication part of its Council grant – to the activities of the professional school. The independently constituted National Ballet School in Toronto had been receiving Council support for more than a decade. So, in 1973, and again in 1974, the RWB applied to the Council for similar school funding. Ludmilla Chiriaeff's nine-year-old École supérieure de danse du Québec applied at the same time.

The Council needed to have the new applicants assessed before a grant decision could be made and hired the British dance educator and historian, Peter Brinson, to survey the schools. When this news slipped out, it immediately triggered a reaction within the leadership of the Dance in Canada Association, established in 1972 as an umbrella service organization. Brinson was friends with the National Ballet School's founding principal, Betty Oliphant. Oliphant was close friends with Monique Michaud who, in 1972, had become head of the Canada Council's newly established Dance Section. For a number of observers, such as Grant Strate, a Dance in Canada Association board member, it looked like a set-up. The suspicion was that Michaud intended to make Oliphant's National Ballet School the official professional training institution for all of Canada. According to Strate, Brinson admitted as much in a phone conversation. Strate, who was in principle opposed to such a centralizing policy, confronted Michaud about the issue in a private meeting at her home in Ottawa. As Strate recalls in his memoirs, Michaud showed him the door.

By 1975, the Canadian dance community as a whole had become turbulent and highly politicized. There had been an extraordinary growth in creative activity across the country. New companies had emerged, all clamouring for Council support. The Dance in Canada Association effectively became their political mouthpiece and was strongly critical of what many of its members regarded as the Council's tendency to protect a small group of established clients. At a conference in Chicago in November, 1975, Monique Michaud explained to the assembled delegates that the Council was con-sciously exercising a form of "birth control" within the Canadian dance community. To the new claimants for Council support, it looked like a closed shop.

Spohr had been an enthusiastic supporter of Dance in Canada in its formative years and served a term on its board of directors. Although he did not always like or understand the often intellectualized work being produced by the new breed of creative radicals, Spohr believed in their right to pursue their artistic ideals. As Dance in Canada became more openly critical of the Canada Council, Spohr's involvement with the Association alarmed the RWB's general manager, Jim Cameron. As he advised the RWB board, it was important to maintain good relations with the Council and these might be jeopardized if Spohr was unwittingly drawn into Dance in

Canada's squabbles with Ottawa. The political atmosphere was thus dangerously fraught when Brinson began his assessment of the three professional ballet schools in Montreal, Toronto and Winnipeg.

Peter Brinson's report did not specifically endorse a plan to anoint the National Ballet School, but his conclusions indirectly supported its claims to the lion's share of Council funding. Brinson was unimpressed with what he judged to be the idiosyncrasies of Chiriaeff's eclectic methods. In Winnipeg, Moroni had become a self-proclaimed disciple of the great Russian teacher Vera Volkova. Brinson, however, questioned the extent of Moroni's understanding of her methods. Brinson described the existing standards of professional training as "dangerously uneven". He felt that the National Ballet School should be recognized and appropriately funded as a "centre of excellence", with the other two professional schools as effective satellites.

In 1976, the National Ballet School saw its Council grant almost double to $600,000. The other two professional schools were offered a token $10,000 each. This was half the amount requested by the RWB. Moroni felt so despondent, he told the board he intended to resign. Both he and Spohr felt slighted, but took the money anyway. Chiriaeff declined.

For Moroni, the Brinson Report and the Canada Council's apparent favouritism towards the National Ballet School became a lingering grievance. More generally it created a problematic political backdrop against which the RWB's relations with the Council were in future to be played out. If the RWB's professional school was to be handicapped, then by implication so also was the company. It sometimes looked to the RWB as if the Council failed to recognise fully the company's achievements and right to evolve artistically and to expand.

As for other possible heirs to Spohr's directorship, Richard Rutherford claims to have had no aspirations in that regard. Increasingly, however, he felt that the RWB held no future for him. He needed a change and made a break for Ottawa in 1977. Within a year, he was hired onto the staff of the Canada Council.

Lusby, meanwhile, had developed a drinking problem and could no longer be considered a contender. He had become, in Spohr's words "a lost soul". In the spring of 1977 Lusby's contract was not renewed. That left Bourman. He certainly did see a future for himself in Winnipeg, not least because Spohr had told him so.

Although many of the dancers found Bourman hard to work with, Spohr appears to have trusted him and gave Bourman increasing responsibility. In the spring of 1974, Spohr asked the board to make Bourman's position more permanent. The executive then instructed the general manager, Jim Cameron, to prepare, "a definitive report on the contributions of each of Mr. Spohr's senior assistants." Some board members may have been wondering why Spohr needed so many.

"In my years," says Bourman, "I took the company out on tour more often than Arnold. Sometimes he would fly in for the major cities. I think he wanted the excitement and recognition." By his third season with the RWB, Bourman had it written into his contract that, in Spohr's absence, he was empowered to make all artistic decisions on tour. Bourman says his own expanding role at the RWB caused a cooling of his relations with Moroni. "We had started out friendly, but as Arnold appeared to favour me, David became unsettled. I think, even then, he wanted to be Arnold's successor. In the end we weren't speaking."

Spohr concedes that at one point he "may" have told Bourman that he was the obvious candidate to succeed him. Bourman recalls it more emphatically. "Arnold told me I was his successor if anything happened. He led me to believe he was in a place to make that decision." It looked as if something might happen. Spohr's health problems got no better, the burden of the job no easier. Spohr, however, did not have the authority to name an heir. When Bourman approached the board for clarification, its response disturbed him. "I was told I could be acting director if something happened to Arnold, but no more." By 1977, Bourman decided it was time to withdraw. "I would have stayed if I could have changed things, but there was a lot of dissension and back-stabbing going on. Things were falling apart in the company."

Much of the underlying tension can be explained by the RWB's continuing financial situation. Spohr worried that if the dancers were not better paid he would have trouble keeping them. He was still itching to take the company to New York so he could show off his Araiz acquisitions before anyone else scooped him. The Joffrey Ballet put an end to that hope by staging Araiz' eccentric *Romeo and Juliet* in 1977. This did not make Spohr's relations with the management any easier or improve his health. Evelyn Hart, then a young company member, recalls returning from a tour to find Spohr waiting at the airport to greet his flock. "He looked ashen, absolutely terrible. We really worried about his health." So did Spohr.

Jim Cameron was a conscientious general manager. He wanted the company to dance its way out of debt. In this regard he had the support of the board, especially Sol Kanee. Cameron's stringent approach to controlling the budget, which included delaying the New York visit, began to make Spohr wonder if the company would remain stuck on its current plateau. He became susceptible to the possibility of finding someone more amenable than Cameron. A potential candidate soon emerged – a charming, apparently cultivated and smoothly ingratiating young American called Edward A. Reger, known as "Chad".

More than twenty years after his departure from the RWB, the mention of the name Chad Reger still elicits strong and almost consistently negative reactions. Some board members say they were duped, others claim they never trusted him. There are former dancers who believe Reger contributed to a growing state of internal unrest that ended in tumult and unhappiness. Spohr prefers to forget it all.

An aura of mystery, of incomplete elements in a story that never quite seemed to add up, clung to Reger even when he was with the company. Reger's own account of his life – rich parents and influential connections, a law degree from Yale, his life in dance – seemed almost too good to be true.

Reger's first contact with the RWB was as an occasional student in the school, when and for how long nobody can recall. For a time, Reger worked as acting general manager at the San Francisco Ballet; or was it the SFB school? Today little about Reger's background seems concrete. When Jim Cameron decided he needed an assistant to help with fund-raising, Spohr suggested Reger. Content to hire someone Spohr clearly liked, Cameron brought Reger on board in May 1975. He says it was a big mistake. According to Cameron, Reger was never any help to him as an assistant general manager. Spohr, meanwhile, thought Reger was wonderful. He was full of ideas and shared Spohr's dream of taking the company to New York, even if it meant incurring a loss.

Peter Garrick had quit dancing and become company manager just before the RWB's appearance at the Israel Festival in August,

1975. He had great respect for Cameron and none for Reger. Garrick still believes Reger turned Spohr against Cameron. The dancers, so often away on tour, were aware that all was not well back home. In typical fashion, they tended to blame their hardships on Cameron. Reger, with his own direct experience of dance, seemed more sympathetic. In an undated card to Spohr, most likely from a 1976 tour, Bonnie Wyckoff wrote: "I am aware of the struggle that is going on now within the administration of the company – i.e. Cameron, Chad, you and the board ... I am very concerned for the future of the company, and this seems a <u>critical</u> time of power-struggle. They must all be made to realise that as long as <u>you</u> are the dominant influence in this organization (whether through you, or the authority <u>you </u>delegate) the R.W.B. cannot help but to grow to be the most unique, progressive and creative ballet company in existence."

By December, 1977, Cameron, outmanoeuvred, decided it was time to withdraw. He signed his letter of resignation two days before Christmas. Garrick remembers Cameron telling him: "Chad's got my scalp on his belt." Spohr says he wanted to be rid of Cameron. "In many ways Jim was excellent. His big problem was his rude manner."

Cameron pleaded with the board not to give Reger the crown. "Kathleen Richardson said if we don't, Arnold Spohr will quit," recalls Cameron. At the executive meeting that accepted Cameron's resignation, Reger was made acting general manager. By the time the souvenir book for the 1977/78 season appeared, Reger was full-time general manager and was receiving same-line billing with Spohr, a distinction never accorded to Reger's predecessors in the job. Garrick left soon after Reger's promotion. "I knew Chad was a phony and that he would get rid of me anyway."

The change also solidified Bourman's determination to leave. "I was not very pleased with the transition from Jim to Chad. Jim had no bedside manner but he was conscientious. Chad was personable but not trustworthy." The news of the change prompted Wyckoff, more optimistically, to send Spohr another card. "Really, you can't imagine what a relief it is for us to know that at last, maybe there is a chance for 'artistic' and 'administration' to begin to focus in the <u>same</u> direction, with the same goals and hopes." The "maybe" proved to be a prudent qualifier.

It may not have been apparent to Spohr at the time, but the power balance between him and the board had shifted decidedly in his favour. Spohr had quite reasonably grown far more confident of his abilities and even more skilful in getting his way. A clear instance was his success in giving the company's repertoire a more contemporary, serious-minded slant. There were certainly a number of board members who worried that the RWB might be drifting from its populist tradition, yet Spohr had shown himself to have an uncanny instinct for reading the climate of the times. So, who were they, as volunteer board members, to fight him? "Arnold was like a magician who could almost hypnotize an audience through his own passion," says former board member Irena Cohen. "It was all emanating from him."

The curious contrasts in Spohr's personality – strength and vulnerability, innocence and astuteness, confidence and insecurity – worked in his favour. They drew people to Spohr and made them eager to help. John Graham, who became the RWB's president in 1973, says Spohr's own personality affected the board's willingness to go along with his ideas, if sometimes apprehensively. "Arnold seemed to be easily bruised or upset. You felt sorry for him. He cared so much and worked so incredibly hard, you wanted to help him make his dreams come true."

Spohr had also earned the right to be heard. The company's success was proof of that. The board also appreciated Spohr's willingness to work within the company's financial limitations. "He was a genius at figuring out how to make our money go a long way," says Richard Kroft, Graham's successor as president. "You felt you were dealing with a financially responsible person. The spending claims often came from people other than Arnold." Kroft's respect was such that he actually suggested in 1977 that Spohr should routinely be invited to meetings of the inner sanctum, the executive committee. "As a board we were part of his team. Of course, all the ideas did not spring out of his head, but to me Arnold was the central reality of the RWB. We all knew that Arnold was the guy responsible when that curtain went up and that he would not let us down."

This shift in the balance of power does not mean that Spohr's relations with his board were always harmonious. Winnipeggers were becoming weary of a diet laced with Araiz ballets. In the 1976/77 season, subscription sales had fallen to 6,200. The board became assertive. "We had to tell Arnold 'this stuff isn't selling' and suggested more classics," says John Condra, president from 1977 to 1980. "He was mad at that and I think he even resented me for a time.

Part of Arnold's insecurity meant he didn't want to feel undercut. We forced him to refocus. It took him time to get over it, but he came around."

Araiz had not entirely monopolized the repertoire. After its RWB debut in 1973, de Mille's *Rodeo* became an audience favourite and company signature piece. The ballet fitted the spirit of the RWB like a glove. The following year, Spohr acquired a major work cast in a starkly different mold, German choreographer Kurt Jooss' trademark anti-war masterwork of 1932, *The Green Table*. It was magnificently staged for the RWB by his daughter, Anna Markard. In contrast to the high-spirited sentimentality of *Rodeo*, Jooss' intensely dramatic ballet provided a jolt of reality.

Spohr, at his presenter's request, included *The Green Table* in the touring repertoire for the 1975 Israel Festival, but it appeared redundant to the local inhabitants. As Leible Shanas, a Winnipegger who had emigrated to Israel twenty-seven years earlier, urged a local reporter, "tell them that they don't have to come from Canada to show us the horrors of war." The Israeli audiences wanted diversion and amusement of the kind so shamelessly provided by Paddy Stone's new ballet, *The Hands*. Max Wyman, in his history of the RWB, called it "as trivial a piece of television variety-show entertainment as anything in the repertoire." The Globe and Mail's John Fraser wrote that Stone's ballet had "all the substance of candy floss". Whatever critics may have thought about *The Hands*, for Israeli audiences in 1975 it was the perfect escape from the harsh realities of everyday life.

Spohr also gave opportunities to emerging choreographers. Edmonton-born Larry Hayden made his RWB debut in 1974 with *Moments*, a promising if predictable rendering in movement of Dvořák's Serenade for Strings. In 1976, Salvatore Aiello made his choreographic debut with *Solas*, a solo for his wife, Marina Eglevsky; the couple had returned from Hamburg the year before. Spohr also had a variety store of works in the repertoire with which to balance his programmes. Even so, by 1977, Araiz held a dominant position.

From June 12-25, 1977, Spohr was back in Russia, this time as an official guest of the Soviet government to attend the Third Moscow International Ballet Competition. It was a welcome escape from the worries at home. He was delighted to discover that American bronze medallist Yoko Ichino, partnered by former RWB principal Sylvester

Campbell, had chosen to dance the *Belong* pas de deux from Norbert Vesak's 1973 RWB creation, *What to do Till the Messiah Comes*. As Spohr reported on his return, *Belong* caused "a great stir" among the audience.

Back home, Spohr assembled a new artistic team. David Moroni now became "associate artistic director" – Bourman's old title. The dancers Salvatore Aiello and Bill Lark joined Sheila Mackinnon on the roster of régisseurs and Hilary Cartwright was appointed company teacher. Cartwright had been a dancer in The Royal Ballet and in its touring troupe. Back problems had compelled her early retirement from the stage in 1968 and she began a new career as a teacher and ballet mistress. Cartwright and Moroni had met in London. They liked each other and shared a similarly rigorous approach to teaching. In 1976, Moroni invited her to work as a guest teacher in the RWB school's professional programme. Spohr was impressed and brought Cartwright into the company.

What the board did not yet know was that Spohr was already planning for his succession. Although Cartwright's title in 1977 was simply that of company teacher, she insists that Spohr had told her that the position was effectively to be that of associate director. In 1977, Cartwright was given same-line billing with Moroni. The prospect of being much more than a ballet mistress was the reason Cartwright had agreed to stay in Winnipeg. She considered the dancers inadequate in terms of their classical base but was confident this deficiency could be corrected over time. "It seemed to be a company so ripe with promise," says Cartwright.

Spohr's plan, as she remembers him explaining it, was to pass the day-to-day artistic operations into the hands of her, Aiello and Moroni. Spohr was to take on an ill-defined advisory role. "I was really impressed that he wanted to step down," says Cartwright. "Not many artistic directors can recognise when their time has come."

Cartwright respected Moroni as a teacher and shared Aiello's ambition to see the RWB grow in new directions. Aiello had emerged as the company's most compelling and versatile male principal but, at the age of thirty-three, was looking to his future. Like Cartwright, Aiello did not always agree with Spohr's choice of repertoire or way of working with dancers. However, according to Marina Eglevsky, Aiello saw an opportunity to grow into a new role under Spohr's tutelage. "Sal simply adored Arnold and Arnold loved him."

It was not until February, 1978, that the board was apprised of Spohr's intentions and then only because he accidentally let the cat out of the bag during a media interview. Spohr had to explain himself. "He told us," says Richardson, "that he'd settled the future of the company and to his great surprise the executive said you can't do that. It's just not on. Of course, Arnold did everything with the best interests of the company at heart."

It seems odd that Spohr would not have told the board sooner, or that the board could have been unaware of the assumptions under which Aiello and Cartwright were working. Spohr had certainly shared his plans with people outside Winnipeg. In late January, 1978, he explained in a letter to a prospective choreographer that Aiello, Cartwright and Moroni would be taking over as co-directors. Spohr stated emphatically: "The choice of what will be done next year will be theirs, with my advice." The same day, Spohr wrote similarly to Paddy Stone in London. A year earlier, Stone had been pitching a proposal for a ballet version of the Gilbert and Sullivan operetta, The Mikado. This time Spohr's language betrays a note of personal uncertainty. "They have worked extremely well together, so I may as well move on or I will work here forever. So we will see what will happen." By March 8, however, suitably chastened by the board's reaction, Spohr appears to have acknowledged that the RWB's destiny was ultimately out of his hands. In a letter to the British ballet teacher, Allan Hooper, Spohr wrote, "Where the Company will move to is the board's decision."

Although board members now knew what Spohr had been planning without their knowledge, they were still uncertain about the next move. For some, the thought of an RWB without Arnold Spohr was unimaginable. For many board members it was all they had ever known. "He was the company," says John Condra. "If Arnold went it was a whole new ballgame." There were others on the board who thought it might indeed be time for a change of leadership, but not in the way Spohr envisaged. "Although Arnold kept persisting," says Condra, "we told him it wouldn't work. We thought if he did quit, we weren't going for a troika."

Spohr is vague about exactly what he was thinking, but quitting altogether was almost certainly not his intention. Installing a single successor might have backfired if the candidate had proved too assertive. The idea of placing the RWB in the care of three people rather than one could be read as Spohr's shrewd way of ensuring his own continuing involvement. Spohr's self-identification with the company's fortunes made it impossible for him to conceive of a total separation. He also believed it was vital to maintain continuity.

However, Spohr was still determined to find a means of lightening his burden which, with a one-week engagement at New York's City Center 55th Street Dance Theater close at hand, seemed especially onerous. In an interview that ran in The New York Times two days before the company's opening, Spohr told Jack Anderson: "Though I think the time has come for someone else to take over the job of running the company, I'll still be around – just as Frederick Ashton and Ninette de Valois are still around at the Royal Ballet."

From Spohr's perspective, New York was a chance for another breakthrough in the company's development, akin to Jacob's Pillow, or its gold medal triumph in Paris. It had been a long fight to secure the engagement and Spohr wanted to show off his company in its current contemporary persona, in a repertoire that was fresh and different. Unlike the National Ballet of Canada, which had won admission to the Metropolitan Opera House on the coat-tails of Rudolf Nureyev, the RWB was going to sink or swim in New York on its own. Spohr was going to prove that the "prairie freshness" for which the company was already widely known was backed by artistic substance. The ballets of Oscar Araiz were the key. One of the reasons Spohr had been pushing hard for New York was because the RWB's exclusive North American performance rights on the Araiz works would expire at the end of the season.

When the trip to New York had been announced in the summer of 1977, Spohr already knew that The Joffrey Ballet was preparing a staging of Araiz' full-length *Romeo and Juliet*. It was a pity the RWB would be denied the honour of introducing the South American choreographer to New Yorkers. Spohr could only hope that *Romeo and Juliet* would leave the city clamouring for more from Araiz. After The Joffrey unveiled its production in October, 1977, Spohr could no longer count on that. The ballet got mostly negative reviews. Araiz' attempt to reveal the different facets of Juliet's personality by using three different dancers for her character came off as clumsy and confusing. Spohr was alarmed. Should he or shouldn't he stake the RWB's reputation on a choreographer whose work was now suspect in New York? Spohr sought advice from people he trusted, worried endlessly and then decided to do what he had intended all along. Spohr settled on three programmes, opening with an all-Araiz evening which comprised of a reworking of Gian Carlo Menotti's *The Unicorn, the Gorgon and the Manticore* and *Mahler 4: Eternity is Now*, a ballet that reflects on the themes of life and death. Next came a programme made up of Vesak's *What to do Till the Messiah Comes* and two more Araiz' works, *Family Scenes* and *Rite of Spring*. For his third programme, Spohr dropped the Vesak and added Araiz' popular pas de deux, *Adagietto* and an old RWB warhorse, Macdonald's *Pas d'Action*.

Spohr knew well enough that, as the acknowledged dance capital of the world, New York would require an all-out effort. The RWB had not been looking its best and Spohr was determined that it should. He forgot about his usual mid-winter break and returned to the rehearsal studio with a vengeance. His presence had the dual effect of snapping the dancers back into peak form but also of making them very nervous.

The trip was already budgeted at a deficit – $100,000, to be guaranteed by Kathleen Richardson – but that did not stop Chad Reger from making sure the company arrived in style. Even before the curtain went up on March 28, there was a celebratory dinner at the exclusive Russian Tea Room. The guest list included everyone from government officials such as Thomas Enders, the United States Ambassador to Canada, and Robert Steen, Winnipeg's mayor, to the celebrated former ballerina, Alexandra Danilova. Even David Yeddeau, one of Spohr's "Holy Trinity" from the 1950's, had flown in from Toronto for the event.

Back in Winnipeg, by the next morning, the local citizenry was reading about the near capacity opening-night crowd, the numerous curtain calls and the glamorous parties. The story was filed before the New York reviews had appeared. For Winnipeggers, the delay was a cliffhanger. Some of the dancers stayed up late to catch the early reviews. Generally, they had reason to be pleased. Clive Barnes, now working for The New York Post, hammered Araiz but had kind words for the dancers. Anna Kisselgoff, who had succeeded Barnes at The New York Times, was equally delighted by the dancers and had more thoughtful and positive things to say about Araiz. Just as Spohr had hoped, Kisselgoff noted the RWB's progress. "The main change is not only in the quality of technique but – based on this first glimpse –

in the company's very self-image." The RWB had moved on from its populist phase to "more ambitious, even more intellectual, goals". Barton Wimble of The Daily News wrote that the company had taken New York by storm and compared it very favourably with "the huge and heavy Edwardian machine that is the Canadian National Ballet." To Wimble, the RWB was "quite simply one of the finest ensembles of young dancers in the world today."

As the week continued and more reviews appeared, tickets became scarce. Clive Barnes returned twice. Although he did not warm to Araiz, suggesting that Spohr had been unwise to place so much trust in the choreographer's work, Barnes continued, like other reviewers, to praise the dancers.

The overall success of the RWB's New York season gave Spohr a much-needed fillip. "I was very nervous about New York," Spohr confided to Bill Como in a letter that May. "It took us such a long time to get there. I did take a gamble with all of Oscar's works, but that is where we are at this time. I felt very content after our New York engagement. We actually did it. New York made me feel very ful-filled, because we have come a long way since the messy, dis-organized state I inherited in 1958."

New York also fuelled the ambitions of Aiello and Cartwright. To them, New York represented a watershed. It was like a coming of age. They believed this was the moment for major artistic renewal, but that would depend on a clear resolution of the leadership issue. Rumours can be toxic and there were plenty of them flying around the RWB that early spring of 1978.

The uncertainty was taking its toll on the dancers, who had already drifted into two broad camps. Some found working with Aiello and Cartwright a pleasant change from Spohr's impassioned approach. Others missed the individual care and attention he brought to the studio. To them it seemed as if the old familial spirit of the RWB was slipping away. The board was still resistant to the idea of a triumvirate and, with a mounting deficit, was in no mood to embrace Aiello and Cartwright's expansive dreams. On April 18, John Condra received a strongly worded letter from Monique Michaud, head of the Canada Council's Dance Section, expressing the Council's "grave concern" over the company's financial plight. What the board wanted was for Spohr to state his intentions clearly. By April 20 he had obliged.

Spohr announced that he would remain as artistic director. As he explained in his letter to Bill Como: "Now I am ready to tackle new challenges, so it is always a beginning. We are never there." Spohr also indicated that Aiello and Cartwright would continue as his associates, but it was far from clear whether they were willing to stay, or if the board was willing to accommodate them. It was the end of May before it was announced that Aiello, Cartwright and Moroni would serve as associate directors for the upcoming 1978/79 season. The actual division of responsibility would effectively be what it had been the previous fall. The board accepted the arrangement begrudgingly and the internal wrangling over contract terms and pay dribbled on into June.

As this was going on, two dancers decided to quit. Frank Garoutte had been planning to retire, but he told reporter Janice Keys that the current internal state of the RWB had cemented his decision. Eric Horenstein had been plagued with injuries but, as he also told Keys, "… if there had never been a question of Spohr leaving, I would probably have stayed on." Garoutte and Horenstein were not alone. Sheila Mackinnon also found the company's unsettled state intolerable. She disliked Chad Reger and was frustrated by Spohr's apparent detachment. "When I left, Arnold wasn't doing much of anything. His whole life was turning upside down. It was as if he had reached a fork in the road that he didn't want to face. Hilary, Sal and David were playing the dancers off against each other. Arnold did nothing. His attitude seemed to be 'I'm going to sit back and let them hang themselves.'" Perhaps Spohr was wiser than Mackinnon thought.

For the moment, it looked as if some sort of order had been restored, but the reality behind the scenes was very different. Spohr signed a new contract on July 14, 1978 that ran until April 30, 1979. Whatever unrecorded conversations may have occurred outside the boardroom, it is clearly apparent that Spohr had expressed an intention to relinquish the directorship at that point. When the board executive met on July 18, 1978, John Condra reported that Spohr had agreed that a search committee should be set up "in order to find a replacement". Noting how little time this allowed, Condra urged the board to begin the search immediately. In an August 10, 1978 letter to David Leighton, president of the Banff Centre, Spohr himself seemed unsure of the future. "I'm looking forward to seeing you next time I'm around, who knows, I don't know where I will eventually be, but I'm sure I'll always be part of the Banff Centre and maybe, as I'm a fatalist, become a catalyst there."

Officially, Spohr was back in the saddle. For how long was a question many were asking. His apparent lack of resolve created the perfect environment for more speculation and rumour. It was as if a vacuum had replaced what had once been the vibrant heart of the organization. In those circumstances it was hardly surprising that others tried to fill it. It meant that the new season, the RWB's fortieth, was to be even stormier than the last. When it was over, the company would find itself in disarray with its public image seriously damaged.

The 1978/79 season was now planned to be one of retrenchment. Before New York, the production committee, at Spohr's prompting, had proposed Dutch choreographer Rudi van Dantzig's *Romeo and Juliet* as a highlight of the fortieth anniversary season, at a cost of $102,000. Many board members believed that Winnipeg audiences would respond positively to full-length story ballets, but *Romeo and Juliet* would have to wait.

The accumulated deficit had now reached $303,000. The financial situation had not been helped by poor *Nutcracker* sales at Christmas. Subscriptions had again declined, now to only 5,000, not much more than half their historic peak. In a September, 1978 interview with The Winnipeg Tribune's Richard Garlick, Spohr conceded that he had to win back his local audience. "It's our fault. We've always found something new and exciting and that's what I'm looking for now. People need change, but it costs a lot of money to get a new ballet." In October, Spohr told Maclean's magazine, "We've been out conquering the world, but we haven't conquered Winnipeg. It's a challenge."

There was to be limited touring and only two additions to the repertoire, a restaging by Cartwright of *Les Sylphides* and a new ballet by Aiello. He ended up providing two. The rest would be revivals, including such well-tested, light-spirited ballets as *Les Patineurs*, *Rodeo*, *Aimez-vous Bach?* and *The Hands*. Only two Araiz ballets were scheduled for Winnipeg, *Adagietto* and *Family Scenes*.

As to the question of his own leadership, Spohr told Garlick that he still wanted to shift some of the load, but could not say when that might be. "Right now, I don't know what I'm doing." Spohr was reluctant to comment on the touchy subject of the general manager, although privately his initial enthusiasm for Reger had given way to scarcely veiled suspicion. The October story in Maclean's stated baldly that the attitude of many RWB workers towards Reger was "one of barely restrained hostility". Spohr dealt with the issue obliquely. "Eventually," he told Maclean's, "I'm sure we'll get the person, an experienced person."

The home season opened in high style. Agnes de Mille – disabled from her 1976 stroke but still lively in spirit – was in attendance for a revival of *The Bitter Weird*. Aiello contributed a solo, *Reflections*, and Cartwright's staging of *Les Sylphides* was also unveiled. As the season progressed, however, the situation deteriorated. Spohr seemed withdrawn, even disinterested. "He confused everybody," says Cartwright. Most of the running of the company was left to her and Aiello. Cartwright says they tried to draw Moroni more closely into the leadership team but could not get him involved. Moroni said he preferred to concentrate on the school. "Frankly," says Cartwright, "Sal and I thought he felt a bit jealous of us."

The dancers, meanwhile, continued to worry about who really wielded authority. Who was going to do the hiring and firing and in what direction would Aiello and Cartwright move the company? In the spring of 1978 some of them were fearful that Cartwright wanted to move the RWB in a more classical direction. By the fall, the rumour was that Aiello wanted the company to become even more contemporary. The RWB's very identity was weighing in the balance. Moroni was certainly not in favour of a further move towards contemporary work. A major objective of his professional training programme was to provide the technical grounding that would allow the RWB to perform more classically demanding work. Moroni had already provided the company with a number of promising talents, most notably Evelyn Hart. Moroni remembers Hart calling him while on tour to complain about the contemporary repertoire. This, she told Moroni, was not what she had joined the company for.

Confusion and suspicion began to combine into a volatile brew that threatened to rip the company asunder. Aiello and Cartwright, away on tour with the company, heard rumours that a plan was afoot to oust them. When they returned to Winnipeg they tried to meet with Spohr but, says Cartwright, he avoided them. Moroni suddenly turned cool towards them. "I somehow felt," says Cartwright, "that while we were away he was instrumental in stirring things up."

The board appears to have been unaware of the seriousness of the situation, but they had read the less than laudatory reviews from the tour and noted that the company was not performing with its usual zest. Early in 1979, they asked Spohr to return to the studio. This was too much for Cartwright. Spohr had agreed to leave the dancers to her and Sal. "I was furious with him. I told him it was a total betrayal." In March, Cartwright announced that she would leave at the end of the season. Aiello held his fire. "He did not approve of Arnold's methods any more than I did," says Cartwright, "but Sal believed he could work around them."

Reger, meanwhile, was busy hatching plans for a return to New York. In January, 1979, Reger told the executive that there was a possibility of a season at Lincoln Center's New York State Theater that July. The RWB would appear with Nureyev in the world premiere of Rudi van Dantzig's *Ulysses*. It was even possible, Reger told the board, that the production might be broadcast live. Furthermore, there was a chance that Nureyev would perform as a guest of the company in Winnipeg in October. Reger warned those assembled that it was crucial to keep the matter private for the moment. In early March, Reger told the executive that a deal with the Niederlander producing organization was confirmed for July 17-29. The New York billing, he said, would be "Rudolf Nureyev appearing with the Royal Winnipeg Ballet". Spohr told executive members that he felt New York was a gamble the company must take. He outlined the repertoire. There would be no Araiz. Spohr explained that profits from the engagement would underwrite *Ulysses*, which the RWB could then tour to major cities on both sides of the Atlantic.

The executive was thrilled and voted to accept the deal, subject to the company solicitor checking to see that the contract was airtight and that *Ulysses* stayed within budget. Reger was even accorded a vote of "thanks and commendation" for putting "this imaginative package together". For the executive, the prospect of getting Nureyev to Winnipeg was almost more important than sending the company to New York. Nureyev could make money for the RWB at home. New York was a risk. The executive wanted to see the ink on the Winnipeg part of the deal, which would require a separate contract negotiated directly with Nureyev's personal manager. Reger's inability to provide convincing proof that he had the requisite signed contract in hand for Nureyev's engagement in Winnipeg may, according to some insiders, have played a key role in Reger's unexpected departure that April.

In the midst of all this, a situation potentially damaging for the RWB erupted. On February 22, 1979, seven men were arraigned in Winnipeg on charges of buggery and gross indecency. One of them was a member of the RWB board of directors, who was also in a relationship with a company dancer. He had been swept up in an extensive police investigation into alleged sexual offences involving juvenile males. Four years earlier a police crackdown in Ottawa had uncovered what the media dubbed "a homosexual vice ring". One of the accused had jumped to his death. With this tragic incident still in mind, rumours of a police witch-hunt traumatized Winnipeg's gay community. There was alarming talk of a master-list of twelve suspects, some of them prominent Winnipeggers, apparently leaked to the same local reporter who had first written about the invest-igation. Police denied all knowledge of such a list. However, concern about impending further arrests was very real.

The impact could have been monumentally disastrous for the RWB if the circle of suspicion, fuelled by public hysteria and rumour, had been allowed to grow and implicate others associated with the company. It did not happen.

Compared with the media frenzy that had accompanied the alleged anti-gay police witch-hunt in Ottawa, the Winnipeg situation was covered less sensationally. John Condra, the incumbent RWB board president, used his considerable influence to contain the potential fallout. "There were a lot of scared people in the city at that time," says Condra.

Meanwhile, there was a potential hitch in the plan for New York. The dancers' union contract would expire on June 30, 1979. On April 2, the RWB entered negotiations with Actors' Equity. It was to be a bitter process. The dancers wanted wage parity with the National Ballet over three years, as well as a cost-of-living clause. The board was determined to fight both demands. If the New York engagement were to proceed it would require extending the existing contract, or negotiating a special deal to cover the necessary weeks of extra work. Reger must have known this, but the issue was not raised at the negotiating table. Instead, the Equity office got a call from Reger in New York. Reger said he needed a swift agreement from the dancers in order to clinch the engagement. Niederlander, now aware of the dancers' contract dispute, had insisted on a clause making the RWB liable for any losses in the event that the company cancelled. Bernard Chadwick, Equity's executive secretary, told Reger it would be impossible to arrange an extension on such short notice.

The full board met on April 18. Some of them were worried about the liability clause in the Niederlander contract for New York. At the same meeting it was announced that on April 10, Reger had given written notice of his resignation, citing the illness of his father and the need to help with the family's business interests in Pittsburgh. The resignation was accepted "with regret".

There were many, including Spohr by this point, who were happy to see Reger go. "I wanted the board to get rid of him. I was so distracted trying to deal with the Chad situation and cover for him," says Spohr. "They let him go benevolently." The company declined to comment on rumours that Reger had been forced out. "There is no question that the board felt another upset would be bad," says Lendre Rodgers Kearns who, as the RWB's director of communications, was responsible for managing the company's media image. "The company was at a low point. They didn't need trouble." Certainly there was no sudden march to the door. Reger remained at his desk for two more weeks, still dealing, as it was reported, with the New York engagement.

The pressure was now on the dancers to agree to a contract extension. Their attitude towards an appearance with Nureyev in New York was mixed. On one hand it appeared to be a great opportunity. On the other, there was the risk of being totally overshadowed. The whole atmosphere was vitiated by the board's obdurate refusal to include a cost-of-living clause in a new master agreement. The dancers knew Spohr wanted the company to perform in New York with Nureyev, but were in no mood to compromise. Already split in their personal allegiances over the lingering leadership issue, the dancers were now split again, on different lines, over New York. It was a sorry mess. By May 1, the New York deal was off. The next day the company opened its final Winnipeg performances of the season.

Spohr was furious and was not inclined to moderate his emotions. "I could hardly see straight because of what they were doing to me." He vehemently denies it now, but at the time Spohr was variously heard to blame the company's troubles on a number of "bad seeds" among the dancers who had "ruined everything". Some of the dancers believed Spohr had even drawn up a blacklist of names of those who were to be punished. Bill Lark remembers that he and some of his colleagues could never figure out how the administration always seemed to know what had been said during the dancers' private discussions. They suspected a mole.

This was hardly the prelude to what was supposed to be a happy family gathering – the RWB's fortieth birthday celebration on Saturday, May 5. Despite internal ructions, the company gave a stirring performance and Aiello's new showcase for the company's men, *Journey*, was a particular success. Spohr had judiciously programmed *The Hands* as a closer because he knew it would end things on a buoyant note.

Offstage, however, the situation was far from buoyant. Rumours were already circulating about an impending crop of dancer re-signations. A group of nine dancers had requested a meeting with members of the board. The meeting was held in the theatre's Green Room, following the closing Sunday matinee performance. Several of the dancers had heard that they were being described as "bad seeds". Spohr did not know the meeting was taking place. He was mingling cheerily with guests attending a wine-and-cheese reception out front as the dancers backstage poured forth their grievances. They were angry about being stigmatized. They were angry with management. They wanted an assurance that Spohr would no longer conduct rehearsals, otherwise they were quitting. "There was no conspiracy," says Rodgers Kearns. "The dancers did not have a singular point of view. They simply wanted to make sure the board understood their concerns. They wanted to have a voice."

According to witnesses, Kathleen Richardson thanked the dancers for their comments and wished them well for the future. John Condra suggested they go away and think about it. By the time the dancers arrived at the reception, emotions were running high and spilled over into tears. It was the last time the company would be together that season before splitting into two groups, one to perform at the Vancouver Children's Festival, the other to travel to Mexico. Some of them knew they might never meet again.

The Winnipeg Free Press reporter, Barbara Cansino, broke the news of the nine dancers' resignations the next morning. Cansino also reported that Neal Kayan, the RWB's music director since 1971, had been forced out. "I go with great anger, great regret," Kayan told

Cansino. The next day the newspaper reported that a tenth dancer was quitting. Once again the RWB became the subject of an editorial cartoon. On May 9, the Winnipeg Free Press ran a cartoon by Kuch showing a woman in a great hurry. In the cartoon the woman, wearing a feathered hat and floral-print dress, is seen striding forward. Her left hand grasps the wrist of an alarmed and airborne little girl in pigtails and tutu, clutching a pair of pointe shoes. In her outstretched right hand the woman holds a copy of the newspaper. The headline reads: "Tenth Resignation Rocks Ballet". A ballet mum, as the cartoon implied, knows a good opportunity when she sees one.

The RWB did its best to control the damage, but it was too late. Dancer Bill Lark spoke openly of his sense of betrayal and contempt for the way the management and board had behaved. Others pointed out that each dancer had particular, in some cases very personal reasons, for leaving. For some it was clearly about Spohr. Others just wanted to move on because it was time. Harry Williams, one of the departing dancers, told The Winnipeg Tribune: "Would you please get it across to people that it's not a mass exodus conspiracy of some kind."

Spohr tried to put a brave face on things but privately he was devastated. "It was terrible for him," says Rodgers Kearns. "Arnold is so open, so unprejudiced. He's like a puppy and simply believes in absolute good in everyone; until he's proven wrong." Aiello was also upset, but for different reasons. He still held the post of associate director and had plans for the company's future. Aiello hoped something could be done to reverse the exodus. "I just cannot stand and watch all these dancers leave this company," he told the Winnipeg Free Press. "I just will not stand for it." According to the report, Aiello and Marina Eglevsky would be leaving unless something was done. For her part, Eglevsky was shattered by the New York fiasco. She had dreamed of dancing with Nureyev and the chance had been taken away from her. "I was beyond hurt over that," she says. Aiello even spoke of forming a company with the dancers who were leaving. Two of the departees had been quoted as saying that they would stay if Aiello were put in charge, but Aiello insisted he was not trying to oust Spohr. "I don't think Arnold should leave. I don't think he can leave. I don't want him to leave."

Aiello, who died in 1995, always denied that he had tried to stage an outright coup. He also denied having given the board a him-or-me ultimatum, although Aiello did concede that he had proposed a number of suggestions to Kathleen Richardson which, in essence, would have returned Spohr to an advisory role. Marina Eglevsky says her husband believed there was a future for him working with Spohr, but it was not to be. Spohr still describes Aiello's actions as "terribly treacherous". Condra says he and Richardson went to Spohr and told him they were behind him. "But, we said if you want your job you better get your act together. It was a major crisis."

Both Aiello and Spohr were away while the media had been reporting daily on the crisis. Aiello had gone to Montreal to stage a work there. Spohr was with the RWB group at the Cervantes Festival in Mexico. The two finally met in Winnipeg on May 18. By then the board executive had voted unanimously to support Spohr as artistic director. Five days later, the board decided not to renew Aiello's contract. Moroni, the lone survivor of the sometime triumvirate, was confirmed as sole "associate artistic director".

Within two weeks Aiello had found a job at the North Carolina School of the Arts in Winston-Salem. Eglevsky hated the city and left for New York. This was the start of their personal estrangement. "We were both stunned and disillusioned," says Eglevsky. "I was so upset by everything that had happened. All these factions; people trying to get power. It ruined my career." Several weeks later, Aiello had harsh words for the board. "The nucleus of the company," Aiello told reporter Janice Keys, "outgrows the director and the board every so often and then it's either they go or the nucleus goes ... The board can manipulate Arnold and that's why they want him. They found it more difficult to manage Hilary and me."

The body count by the end of the fortieth anniversary season was awesome: eleven dancers, the general manager, music director, two associate directors and Mark Porteous, the young company manager and a keen supporter of Aiello. "I don't agree with what's happened," Porteous told Keys, "especially what happened to Aiello and the way the board handled that. He's a great loss."

There was residual internal fallout. Rodgers Kearns who had until this point worked well with Spohr, found him cool towards her. "We were 'bad friends' for a couple of years," she says. It was only later that she discovered why. "Arnold and I were on a plane together. He gave me a big hug and told me that David Moroni had said I was disloyal." Rodgers Kearns, despite attractive outside offers, remained with the RWB until 1988. "I stayed around for one reason only and that was Arnold Spohr – his joyousness, his sense of wonder and playfulness, his ability to have faith in every human being."

At the calamitous end of the 1978/79 season, Moroni vividly remembers finding Spohr in his director's office. "I caught him crying. He looked absolutely shattered. Arnold didn't know what he was going to do." Moroni pointed out that more dancers were staying than were leaving and that there were talented dancers in the school who could be hired. Moroni also had suggestions about replacement régisseurs. Spohr began to bounce back. "Arnold thrives on chaos," says Moroni. "It ignites his energy. Nothing revives him more than the feeling that he is going to be the knight in shining armour."

Spohr remembers Moroni telling him that he would have to prove himself all over again. But Spohr says that he was not deeply concerned. "I really had no worry, because I had the future prepared for three or four years ahead."

By late May, Spohr was already announcing his hiring plans. By the time he sat down to write the report that would be submitted on his behalf to the annual general meeting in June, his old optimistic hyperbole was flowing freely. Even the financial situation was on the mend. With the help of a Manitoba Arts Council deficit reduction grant, the RWB could look forward to starting its forty-first season with an accumulated deficit of $111,000, a far more manageable sum than the $303,000 it had been a year earlier. The rebuilding work was not going to be easy, but Arnold Spohr had a choreographic mission to Amsterdam on his immediate agenda and could also look forward to refreshing his spirit in the cool, clean air of the Canadian Rockies.

10

The Banff Connection

The zenith of a grand jeté at The Banff Centre in Alberta is about as high as any dancer can hope to soar in Canada but, then, the jump begins at more than 1,350 metres. Dancers tend to tire sooner on the stage of Banff's Eric Harvie Theatre because the air is noticeably thinner.

Dance has been part of The Banff Centre for close to seventy years. For almost half that time there was a mutually beneficial connection between the summer dance programme and the Royal Winnipeg Ballet. The connection was established when Gweneth Lloyd began teaching in Banff in the late 1940's and remained strong until Arnold Spohr relinquished direction of the dance summer school in 1981. The involvement of Betty Farrally, almost until her death in 1989, symbolized the continuation of an important historic bond. Spohr still maintains a lively interest in Banff.

By the time professional dance companies began to emerge in Alberta in the 1960's, the Banff/RWB connection was well established. Sometimes the Albertans felt excluded from what they viewed as home turf. After all, for years the provincial government footed most of the bill. Nevertheless, the people who guided the affairs of The Banff Centre saw no reason to meddle with an arrangement that added so much lustre to the institution's international image. How else would dance luminaries such as Vera Volkova or Agnes de Mille have been lured to Banff? Who but Spohr could have turned the annual student performances into gala events that attracted critics from across North America? Dance at Banff has continued to thrive under new leadership, but only because of the strong foundation laid by Lloyd, Farrally and Spohr.

From its earliest days, the University of Alberta, founded in 1908, had a vigorous mission to reach beyond its original Edmonton campus, to bring learning to the people of the province. A Department of Extension was established in 1912 and Albert Edward Ottewell, teasingly nicknamed "Tiny" because of his huge stature, became its first head. Under Ottewell, university faculty members were sent out as itinerant lecturers, armed with notes, slides and projectors. Ottewell himself joined the team, driving to remote farming communities in a Model-T Ford Coupe that listed heavily to the driver's side under his substantial bulk.

In November, 1927, near the end of Ottewell's tenure, the University of Alberta found a new way to extend its reach by launching its own radio station, CKUA. The success of the university's extension programmes attracted the attention of the Carnegie Foundation of New York. In 1932, with the Foundation's support, the Extension Department, by then under the direction of Ned Corbett, assisted drama groups throughout the province to produce plays. The following year the university went a step further and decided to launch a summer drama school. After some debate it was decided to locate the school in one of Alberta's most popular tourist destinations, the Township of Banff in the Canadian Rockies. The Banff school board provided access to local classrooms. A creaky wooden building known as Bretton Hall served in the early years as a theatre. Thus was born what grew to become the now autonomous Banff Centre, since 1947 magnificently located on a sixteen-hectare campus, nestled on the slopes of Tunnel Mountain and commanding splendid views of the Bow Valley.

It is not entirely clear when dance was first incorporated into the summer programme, but classes in eurhythmics were taught by Regina's Grace Tinning in the early to mid-1930's. In 1941, Gweneth Lloyd wrote to Donald Cameron, who had become head of the Banff Summer School in 1936, to suggest the addition of ballet. Five years later, Cameron invited Lloyd and Mara McBirney, a respected teacher from England who was soon to settle in Vancouver, to come to Banff and advise on the general development of dance. The two women soon persuaded Cameron to make ballet training a priority.

Lloyd agreed initially to act as an advisor in Banff. The following summer, on Lloyd's recommendation, Joan Stirling, one of her recently retired Winnipeg Ballet dancers, arrived to teach what the calendar of the then Banff School of Fine Arts described as "Basic technique of the Ballet on the system of the Royal Academy of Dancing". In 1948, Lloyd sent another Winnipeg Ballet star, Jean McKenzie. McKenzie was also scheduled to teach again in the summer of 1949, but, when she was unable to come, Lloyd replaced her. The following summer, Lloyd officially began a seventeen-year reign as co-head of the dance programme at Banff, sharing the title with Betty Farrally. The two women were not Banff's only connection with the Winnipeg Ballet. The University of Manitoba's John Russell, who played such a crucial role in the RWB's early history, had already begun teaching in the theatre department at Banff. Russell was followed in 1953 by John Graham, another invaluable Winnipeg Ballet board member who, with occasional gaps, remained a key member of Banff's theatre faculty until 1983.

When Lloyd and Farrally finally severed their connections with the RWB in 1957, it did little to weaken the link between Banff's summer dance programme and the company the two women had founded some 1,400 kilometres away. The first summer after Spohr became the RWB's director, he arranged for several of his dancers to study in Banff. "For many years," Spohr explains, "the programme was like a school for us and stayed that way until we started our own summer school in Winnipeg. We got a lot of dancers from Banff."

In 1961, Brian Macdonald introduced jazz-ballet training and it remained part of the curriculum for many years. Sometimes ballets created by Macdonald, that eventually found their way into the RWB repertoire, travelled to Winnipeg via the Rockies. *Prothalamion*, a ballet Macdonald first made for television, was presented by the Banff students in 1962, before it reached the RWB. The same summer Macdonald's immensely popular *Aimez-vous Bach?* was choreographed for Banff summer students. Macdonald staged it two years later for the RWB.

When Lloyd decided to retire from Banff in the summer of 1967, it was a logical step, at least from the Centre's perspective, to invite Spohr to succeed her. Spohr was prepared. From 1960, with the RWB board's consent, he had been teaching each summer at the Nelson School of Fine Arts in British Columbia. In 1964, Spohr was formally named director of Nelson's dance department. "I had accepted the offer of starting the department in Nelson because I was still looking for a source to get dancers from ... until a proper professional school in Winnipeg could be set up." In the mind of The Banff Centre's director, Donald Cameron, installing Spohr would add enormous prestige to the programme and cement a fruitful relationship with the RWB.

The relationship with Banff also appealed to Spohr, particularly because it would immerse him in an environment where leading teachers and artists in all disciplines would be gathered. The RWB board of directors, however, had reservations. The company was in overdrive. Spohr was already stretched to the limit. Also, the RWB had a school of its own. The board did not want Spohr to be placed in the position of serving two masters. Specifically, the board pointed out to Donald Cameron that Spohr's commitments to the RWB would always take priority. Writing to Cameron on behalf of the board, Sawchyn pointed out that Spohr would not be able to guarantee his personal attendance for any specific time. "He will, however, spend as much time at the Banff School as is possible in the light of our various commitments, and he will certainly advise as to matters of faculty, curriculum, guest artists, teachers, etc."

There was also the issue of Farrally. "I asked her to work with me at Banff," Spohr recounts, "but Betty said she couldn't do that after having been my boss for so many years. So I immediately said she could work with me as co-director, and that settled it." Spohr was full of ideas and had the connections to help realize them. Farrally's organizational sense and long experience working at Banff offered a practical balance.

From the late 1950's, Lloyd had regularly invited notable guest teachers from the Royal Academy of Dancing in England to teach in Banff. Among them were Louise Browne, Maria Fay and Julia Farron. Spohr was also a firm believer in the importance of exposing dancers to the best teachers. Since his own teaching methods had already moved well beyond their RAD roots, Spohr decided, with Farrally's agreement, to invite leading ballet teachers from other training systems to give master classes. Spohr believed the master classes would attract professional dancers to Banff.

Perhaps Spohr's most spectacular coup in this regard was to bring Vera Volkova to teach in Banff for the summers of 1969, 1971 and 1972. Spohr later used his diplomatic connections to bring a Bolshoi teacher to Banff by writing directly to Robert Ford, the

Canadian ambassador in Moscow. It took four years of trying, but finally Natalia Zolotova, like Volkova an expert in the Vaganova system, arrived in 1977 and returned two years later. Teachers from the RWB, such as Gwynne Ashton, Frank Bourman and David Moroni, were also frequently part of the summer faculty in Banff. Others who had begun in Lloyd's day – Sonia Chamberlain and Eva von Gencsy – were also invited back. Earl Kraul, the former National Ballet star, taught at Banff in the 1970's and once missed a morning class because an immovable mother bear and her cub had taken up temporary residence on the porch of his chalet.

Performance had long been an important component of the summer programme in Banff. For several years the young company of Banff dancers even toured. The performances gained a new lustre under Spohr's direction. From the start he was intent on raising their profile. By the time Spohr became co-head of the programme, Banff had built stage facilities that would make this possible. The well-equipped 1,000-seat Eric Harvie Theatre had opened with a ballet performance in 1967. A smaller studio space, the 250-seat Margaret Greenham Theatre, was inaugurated two years later. As Spohr wrote in 1970 to David Leighton, The Banff Centre's newly installed president: "We try to make our division the best in the world. Even if we may not succeed we may as well try. I believe in reaching for the top – nothing else will do."

Having found a way to attract professional dancers to Banff, Spohr saw it as a logical step to include them in the performances. As he told Ken Madsen, a senior member of the Banff administration and key supporter of the ballet programme, "I feel we should do this because they inspire the kids and raise the standard." In 1973, still intent on giving the summer programme an increasingly professional character, Spohr proposed inviting an established company to take up residence in Banff for at least part of the summer. Since neither his own busy RWB nor the National Ballet seemed likely prospects, Spohr agreed to sound out Ludmilla Chiriaeff at Les Grands Ballets Canadiens in Montreal, but his personal loyalty to an old friend and dance partner intervened. In 1972, Eva von Gencsy had co-founded Les Ballets Jazz in Montreal with her former student, Eddy Toussaint, and with Geneviève Salbaing, a former dancer with excellent connections among the Montreal business elite. Chiriaeff, so Spohr understood, saw Les Ballets Jazz as competition. Von Gencsy had already brought her company to study and dance in Banff. As Spohr told Leighton, having von Gencsy and Chiriaeff at Banff at the same time "might be unpleasant". As he added, "I do wish to keep Eva happy for she is very important to the dance department and we are very lucky to have her back, bringing the jazz standard up and really stimulating the dance department with her personality and charm."

One of the most memorable dance performances at Banff during the Spohr years came in the summer of 1976. Aaron Copland, the American composer, had agreed to spend two weeks with the music department. It seemed only fitting that the students in the dance programme should perform *Rodeo*, the famous ballet score Copland had written for Agnes de Mille in 1942. After considerable negotiation, de Mille herself agreed to come to Banff and supervise the final rehearsals. The opening night was a gala occasion. A capacity audience stood and cheered as Copland and de Mille, both living legends, took their bows. To everyone's delight, de Mille made a little speech.

The great lady was delighted by all the attention. "I was treated as though I were the Queen Mother and I couldn't have been happier," she informed Spohr. The students, said de Mille, "did marvelously". De Mille claimed, however, to be far from happy with the two RWB dancers brought to Banff to dance the principal leads. "The boy I thought had promise but had been very badly coached. As for the girl I simply don't know. She struck me as being very nervous and moderately gifted but uncertain in her work."

This was not the first time Spohr had had to deal with de Mille's temperamental outbursts. When she had briefly passed through Winnipeg in 1973 to take a look at final rehearsals for the company's first production of *Rodeo*, de Mille had also objected to the lead casting, particularly for the role of Champion Roper. She had frothed and fumed and threatened, but Spohr had stood his ground. As he pointed out to de Mille then, and again in 1976, it was Vernon Lusby, her own approved régisseur, who had taught *Rodeo* and approved the casting. Although not averse to ranting and raving himself, Spohr would not tolerate an outsider, even someone as famous as de Mille, coming in and belittling his dancers, his family.

Spohr responded in a forceful letter to de Mille, defending his dancers and rebuffing her attack in a little homily that only he, with total sincerity, could have written: "I believe in honesty with courtesy, no destructive element involved. Life, especially dance, is difficult and traumatic enough without adding ugliness."

Generally, Spohr's programming policy for the Banff performances followed the same principles he applied in Winnipeg. There were two levels of performance, a workshop, which included the younger students, and the more glamorous shows that formed part of the annual multi-disciplinary Banff Festival. Without forgetting that the prime consideration was to give the summer students a valuable learning experience, Spohr also wanted to give audiences a good show. The broad formula was to offer something classical, something contemporary and something light and frothy, often a jazz ballet, to send everyone home smiling. Lloyd had followed a similar approach, except that until the later 1960's it was she who provided most of the choreography, with occasional contributions from Brian Macdonald. Since Spohr had long abandoned his own choreographic career, he preferred to use Banff as a place to try out emerging choreographers.

In the mid-1970's a plan was devised to ensure the presence of new choreography in the Banff summer dance programme by incorporating an annual award in the form of a creative residency. Largely through the skilful fund-raising work of Ken Madsen, Lila Lee, an Edmonton philanthropist, agreed to underwrite the costs of bringing a different choreographer to Banff each summer to create a work for the students. The award, which includes a cash prize as well as the residency, was launched in 1978 when Mauryne Allan choreographed a work titled *Spring* to Vivaldi's The Four Seasons. The award, which continues to this day, was named for Mrs. Lee's late husband, Clifford E. Lee, and was the first occasion that the family's philanthropy had been directed towards the arts.

Sometimes the Banff Festival performances did not work out to Spohr's satisfaction. David Leighton remembers one such occasion vividly. He and his wife Peggy were hosting an opening-night party at their home, just a short walk down from the theatre. Spohr was among the last to arrive. As Leighton came to the door to greet him he innocently asked, "So Arnold, what did you think of the show?" With that look of disgust that has frozen generations of dancers in their tracks, Spohr ventured only three loudly declaimed words: "Largo! Largo! Largo!"

Although it meant carving time from an already busy schedule, Spohr felt it was important for the Banff students to know something about the heritage of ballet. He occasionally invited distinguished critics as guest lecturers, including the noted American writers, Doris Herring and Olga Maynard. Herring came to Banff in 1971 and Maynard taught for three consecutive summers, 1973-1975. In 1974, having learned that the American Dance Festival in Connecticut had launched an ambitious summer course for critics, Spohr even suggested establishing a similar programme in Banff.

His motives were promotional as well as idealistic. Teaching students ballet history was valuable. The same was true of teaching dance critics how to do their job better. What more effective way to spread the word about ballet at Banff than to entice as many critics as possible to the slopes of Tunnel Mountain? In reference to Olga Maynard, Spohr frankly told Madsen: "Everybody wants her because she does these good articles for the magazines." Eva von Gencsy corroborates Spohr's observation. "Olga Maynard saw Les Ballets Jazz dance in Banff and wrote a beautiful article about us in Dance Magazine." Spohr, of course, was canny enough to reassure Maynard that his motives were pure. In January, 1974, he wrote to her: "My admiration for you is not for what you can do for me or the Royal Winnipeg Ballet, it is for what you are as a person and the talent you have."

Spohr's years as co-head of the Banff summer school coincided with some of his busiest years as director of the RWB. Combined with his own personal need to take time to recuperate from a gruelling workload, the result was that he often found it difficult to commit to spending the full summer in Banff. Farrally was a constant, a bastion, but in order to cover his own absences, Spohr received Leighton's agreement to appoint Frank Bourman as a third co-head, beginning in 1975. Bourman continued to work in Banff, even after resigning from the RWB to join Minnesota Dance Theatre.

Whenever possible, Spohr would at least try to be in Banff to supervise final rehearsals and give the students and choreographers the benefit of his magic touch. David Leighton summed it up in a September, 1976 letter to Spohr: "You always come in at the end to cut out the unnecessary, trim it down and give it its final polish that makes the difference between a good show and one that is just amateurish. We need you, and the choreographers need you, heaven knows."

When he was in Banff, Spohr did not limit his interest to the senior students most likely to develop into professional dancers. Spohr has always been willing to share his passion for dance with anyone who shows even a glimmer of interest and promise. As a teacher he recognizes that although many of his students will never become professional dancers, they could potentially become informed devotees of the performing arts, perhaps even donors, arts administrators or volunteer supporters.

Elizabeth Fawcett, who went on to become an arts administrator, learned her love of dance from Spohr while a summer student at The Banff Centre. "He was never condescending to anyone, even though he knew most of us were never going to be professionals. He just made you want to dance and do your best for him." Even among students such as the young Fawcett, who freely admits she studied dance just for fun, Spohr held nothing back. "He had boundless energy. He seemed to leap all over the studio from one student to another. To this day I can still hear him saying, 'Now girls, lead with the sternum; remember sternum and hips'. Another time he was teaching us about characterization and he stalked about the room pretending to be a giant spider."

At its peak in 1969, the dance programme at Banff had an enrollment of 276 students. The programme's popularity meant that classes were becoming overcrowded. In 1972, it was decided that enrollment should in future be limited. In any case, enrollment significantly declined during the 1970's. It was becoming apparent that Banff's summer dance programme was losing some of its edge.

The broadening interest in ballet that had begun in the late 1960's was reaching a crescendo a decade later. Ballet summer schools were mushrooming across North America, all competing for students and teachers. The Banff programme still had the added appeal of a high-profile performance component and Arnold Spohr's illustrious name at its head. However, the cost differential between Banff and other summer schools put it at a disadvantage in terms of attracting students. Combined with Spohr's increasing absences, it was enough to convince the Banff administration that it was time for a change. They decided that Brian Macdonald would assume the leadership of a revamped summer dance programme, to be divided into two distinct streams, one for the training of younger dancers and the other designed specifically for young professionals and dancers on the brink of a career.

1981 was Spohr's last summer as co-head. Farrally stayed on to work with Macdonald, who remained head of the programme for the next twenty years, passing the torch in 2002 to his wife, Annette av Paul. The change in leadership, however, did not end Spohr's relationship with Banff. His roots there went too deep. Most summers since he retired from Banff, Spohr has travelled to the Rockies to observe the progress of the dance programme and to visit old friends. Macdonald always made a point of ensuring that the students, most of them easily young enough to be Spohr's grandchildren, knew who he was and what he had done for dance.

The Road
to Swan Lake

In the fall of 1966, a young aspiring ballet dancer in Columbia, South Carolina, was looking for an affordable summer school where he hoped to get some intensive training. He came across a brochure advertising a course to be taught by members of the Royal Winnipeg Ballet in Nelson, British Columbia. The student was Peter Garrick, the dancer with the artificial eye. Garrick had seen the RWB during one of its American tours and had fallen in love with the company. "For me it was what dancing was all about."

Garrick arrived in Nelson the following summer with high expectations. Then Spohr came in to teach class. "I was all nervous and I remember thinking that this man didn't look anything like what I'd pictured a ballet director to look like." Class began and Garrick was dipping into his pliés when suddenly he felt a slap on the back. It was Spohr. "You're terrible, you're horrible, you're too far forward." The barrage of criticism went on for the duration of the class. Garrick was feeling humiliated and demoralized. Then, as he was leaving, Spohr said, almost casually, "You're not so bad really."

Garrick later learned that there was a scholarship programme at the RWB school. He wrote to Spohr expressing interest and still clearly remembers the impact of a particular phrase in the encouraging acceptance letter from Spohr. "If everything works out with your eye, you have an excellent opportunity for a career for dance." Says Garrick, "I don't think he'd muddled his prepositions. He really meant it; not a career *in* dance but a career *for* dance. I've never forgotten it."

Arnold Spohr has never stopped working *for* dance and, in the fall of 1979, there was much rebuilding work to do. High turnover in the roster of dancers was something Spohr had dealt with before, but the internal turmoil of the previous spring had been different. Although Bonnie Wyckoff returned following an unhappy year with The Joffrey Ballet, Spohr's principal ranks remained sorely depleted. He had complained bitterly about the extensive media coverage during the crisis. "Why do they have to stir up trouble? What business is it of theirs?" He overlooked the fact that, as a publicly funded company, his artistic custodianship of the RWB was a matter of public interest. Spohr may also have forgotten that the company's many donors and fans also felt a measure of ownership and a real concern about the future of the RWB. Whether he wished to recognise it or not, the whole credibility of the RWB, and by implication Spohr's own reputation, were on the line.

Spohr, however, knew he had a trump card. In fact, he thought he had two. Their names were Evelyn Hart and David Peregrine. Both had been shaped as classical dancers by David Moroni. He and Spohr saw a bright future for Hart and Peregrine, perhaps even a glowing partnership that would capture public interest, just as the partnership of Karen Kain and Frank Augustyn had at the National Ballet. Spohr maintains that his decision to remain in 1979 was largely determined by the need to nurture the artistic development of Hart and Peregrine. Spohr had no confidence that this would have happened under Aiello's leadership.

Peregrine, a year older than Hart, had joined the RWB a season before her, in 1975. Three years later, both became soloists. Spohr promoted Hart to principal rank in 1979 and Peregrine a year later. Spohr had no way of predicting just how much and how quickly they would deliver on the talent he so clearly recognised. However, when Hart and Peregrine returned from two international ballet competitions in 1980, laden with medals, he was ready to act. The following year the RWB was finally able to afford Rudi van Dantzig's *Romeo and Juliet*, with Spohr's hottest properties in the title roles. It was the start of a new golden age.

The decision to stage a full-length *Romeo and Juliet* took many people by surprise. It seemed a significant departure from the RWB's tradition of presenting diversified programmes of mixed repertoire. Spohr continued by adding *Giselle* in 1982 and five years later, during his penultimate season, *Swan Lake*. The RWB, however, did not give itself over entirely to full-length productions. During Spohr's last nine seasons as director, he added a total of thirty-one ballets to the repertoire, covering a gamut of choreographic styles, from George Balanchine to Paddy Stone. Spohr did not discard popular works from the past. He brought the RWB's old friend, Alicia Markova, back to Winnipeg to stage *Les Sylphides.* Hits such as Stone's *Variations on Strike Up the Band* and *The Hands* were still in service more than a decade after their creation. However, of Spohr's thirty-one additions in this period, only eight were original, commissioned works.

Some people contended that Spohr's decision to move into full-length ballets was simply a device to keep Evelyn Hart in Winnipeg. It was not long before critic Stephen Godfrey described the RWB as "The Evelyn Hart Travelling Troupe". There were those who even argued that the RWB should have stuck with its traditional programming format and allowed Hart to find a company better suited to her artistic needs as a classical ballerina. Spohr, however, genuinely believed that the RWB should find a way to nurture Hart's extraordinary talent and it was clearly in the company's interest to do so. Hart herself was aware of the perception that she effectively ruled the company. In a 1982 interview with Dance in Canada magazine she demurred: "Regardless of what anyone thinks, I don't have Arnold Spohr wrapped around my finger."

Spohr had broader concerns than the welfare of a single ballerina. Both he and the board acknowledged the company's need to bolster its fortunes and rebuild its Winnipeg audience. By the fall of 1979, the deficit was rapidly shrinking, but so too were subscription sales. The board had discussed the market appeal of staging full-length ballets long before Hart appeared on the scene. The 1963/64 souvenir book promised a full-length *Coppélia*, but it never materialized. Proposals for full-length works had come and gone, usually because the company could not raise the money to finance them. In 1966, the RWB was able to tap special government Centennial funding to present its first full-length ballet, Macdonald's *Rose Latulippe.* Six years later it staged *The Nutcracker.*

In 1979, Spohr was also thinking of the RWB school and about what the programming of full-length ballets would mean for the overall evolution of the company. The RWB could confidently look forward to a more reliable stream of well-trained young dancers. There could only be one Evelyn Hart, but that did not mean there would not be other talents for whom full-length ballets were the ideal showcase. Spohr had all this in mind as he plotted a path forward in the summer of 1979, but his immediate need was simply to get the RWB up on its feet again.

David Moroni had found two competent régisseurs for Spohr, both former RWB dancers, Marilyn Lewis and Cathy Taylor. Lewis, the wife of newly promoted principal dancer Joost Pelt, returned after an eleven-year absence. Taylor had been teaching in the RWB school for the previous two years. The principal male ranks were augmented with Michael Bjerknes from The Joffrey Ballet. There were several internal promotions and an influx of six dancers from the school, including André Lewis, who, besides Spohr, is to date the only dancer to have risen to become the company's artistic director. To help hone his noticeably younger troupe, Spohr brought four international guest teachers to Winnipeg in the three months leading up to the first performances.

Kerry Duse, associate conductor under the departed Neal Kayan, was made music director. The RWB hired Max Tapper as its go-getting development director. Spohr also had a new general manager to work with, one for whom he had great hopes, William Riske.

Bill Riske had fallen in love with theatre as a boy in Edmonton. He was a twenty-one-year-old stagehand at Neptune Theatre in Halifax when he heard there was a vacancy for a soundman at the RWB. Riske joined the company in 1970, just in time to take the technically complex *A Ballet High* on tour. The next year he was promoted to stage manager and began to put down roots, marrying company pianist Barbara Malcolm in 1973 and starting a family. In 1976, Riske was promoted to production manager and eventually to the post of associate general manager under Reger. Spohr, who had actively supported Riske's ascent at the RWB, now urged the board to promote him once more. Riske was not officially signed as Reger's successor until October, 1979, but he had already been busy picking up the pieces and laying the groundwork for the company's financial recovery. Nobody had ever taken on the RWB's top administrative job with as deep an understanding of the company's inner workings as Bill Riske. "Bill was a more than capable manager," says Rodgers Kearns. "He was exactly the right manager for the time. He knew how to manage growth. When Bill needed to cut he was never penny wise to be pound foolish."

Riske survived for thirteen years, a record so far unsurpassed in the history of the RWB. Riske could be difficult and was not a natural communicator, but he was capable and deeply loyal to the RWB, and that was enough for Spohr. At last, Spohr believed he finally had a general manager whom he could trust to put the company's interests above everything else.

The headlines for the RWB's Winnipeg opening in October, 1979, were just what Spohr needed. "Royal Winnipeg Ballet looks as strong as ever", declared the Winnipeg Free Press. The Globe and Mail headline read, "Royal Winnipeg recovers on point and on time". There was concern among some of the critics that the company's male corps was not as strong as it sometimes had been. Reviewing a revival of Araiz' *Women*, The Globe and Mail's Stephen Godfrey noted the absence of several departed dancers whose mature artistry he sorely missed. Overall, however, the critics responded well to the talent Spohr had assembled. The inclusion once again of guest artists, this time from American Ballet Theatre, also added some welcome dazzle. Danilo Radojevic, a 1977 gold medal winner in Moscow, and Marianna Tcherkassky, drew repeated bravos for the classical excerpts they danced at each performance.

There was frequent praise for Bonnie Wyckoff, much missed by her fans during the previous season. They did not have Wyckoff back for long. At the end of the 1979/80 season Wyckoff left to join Oscar Araiz, a choreographer she idolized, at his new post as ballet director in Geneva. Unlike several of her successors in the company's senior female ranks, Wyckoff would not have to compete for the limelight with Spohr's budding star, Evelyn Hart.

The reception for Spohr's new addition to the repertoire, Hans van Manen's *Songs Without Words*, was muted, but then so is the ballet. It is a romantic work, danced barefoot by four couples to ten Mendelssohn piano solos. The ballet's poetic, contemplative mood is not the bravura dancing that rouses a crowd. However, *Songs Without Words* was important to Spohr. It marked the start of what he already called his "Dutch connection". Spohr had been planning this long before the travails of 1979. Spohr's Dutch connection was a choreographic vein that added the visceral strength of modern dance to the framework of ballet classicism, free of mannerisms and direct in approach. Spohr had been longing to tap into it.

Rudi van Dantzig's recent masterpiece, *Four Last Songs*, set to

Richard Strauss' famous Vier letzte Lieder, was slated for the RWB's April, 1980 performances and Spohr was already eyeing van Dantzig's *Romeo and Juliet*, with the hope of presenting it in the spring of 1981. Van Manen would be returning in his Latin mode the following season with *5 Tangos* and, although he was Czech by birth, Spohr was also angling for Jiri Kylian whom he considered Dutch by aesthetic. In total, by the time Spohr retired, his Dutch connection had yielded nine ballets – three each from van Manen and van Dantzig, two from Kylian and one from Nils Christe. Although American critics especially have tended to deride the Dutch choreographers as typical exemplars of "Eurotrash", the works Spohr introduced generally suited his dancers and extended their expressive range. Spohr did not allow his Dutch choreographers to dominate the repertoire. He sprinkled their works judiciously.

Spohr was not just interested in Dutch choreographers. He was also drawn to the more extravagant passions of Venezuelan-born American choreographer Vicente Nebrada, a former member of the Joffrey and Harkness companies. In 1979, Nebrada had brought his Ballet Nacional de Caracas to New York with great success and Spohr had already engaged Nebrada as a choreographer for the following season. Over the next three years Nebrada staged two of his ballets – one of them, *Our Waltzes*, soon became an RWB signature piece. He also created two works for the RWB, including, in 1982, a version of Stravinsky's *Firebird*.

The theme of productive renewal in the RWB was echoed again by the media when the company took *The Nutcracker* on a short Western tour in December, 1979. Now that Spohr was back in full stride, he felt more comfortable in discussing what had happened the previous spring. He described the mass departures of May, 1979, as "getting rid of the cobwebs and clearing the air". In an interview with The Vancouver Sun's Wayne Edmonstone, Spohr explained: "I prefer to think of what we're offering as the work of a fresh company with a new lease on life."

New lease on life perhaps, but much work was still needed to bring the RWB back to full strength. When Rudi van Dantzig had arrived in Winnipeg in the fall of 1979 to work on *Four Last Songs*, he had found the quality of dancing uneven. "Not very good technically, but eager," as he now recalls. In January, 1980, when the objective eye of The Houston Chronicle's Ann Holmes surveyed the RWB, her comments were astute. "The total image of the company reflects acute judgement at the top where Arnold Spohr, as artistic director, chooses attractive programming. The two evenings were nothing if not engaging and entertaining. The depth of dance quality is a somewhat different matter ... There is a discernible weakness through the company's ranks, but the choice of works and the casting adroitly attempts to veil this fact."

Spohr was not blind to the deficiencies. He continued to use his unique skills as a ballet master to make the company look the best it could and by the season-closing performances in 1980, the dancing had noticeably improved. So had the company's balance sheet. The RWB ended the fiscal year with a surplus of $478,489 on a $2,092,300 operating budget. The outstanding accumulated deficit was retired and $239,843 was appropriated to reserves for a future building relocation and for new repertoire. Stringent cost controls had played a part, but it was a deficit reduction grant from the Manitoba Arts Council that had crucially helped the RWB lever its vigorous fund-raising activities.

The artistic director's report that Spohr submitted to the 1980 annual general meeting reflected his satisfaction with the RWB's dramatically improved condition. "Imagine, in one year, with togetherness, we are flying high. With constant refuelling and care of our organization, we should stay there ... I want you to know that I am back in a most positive way ... After 24 years, our house really looks shiny and bright and in order. It has taken a good while." Spohr was the one who needed refuelling. His health now failed him at the worst possible moment. Hart and Peregrine were off to compete in Japan and Bulgaria.

The decision to send Hart to Varna, Bulgaria, had been made in 1979, but in February, 1980, it was also decided to enter Hart and Peregrine in the World Ballet Concours in Osaka. The Japanese competition had none of the prestige of Varna, but since it was being held almost a month earlier, Moroni believed Osaka would provide useful experience before the main event. Spohr had already been preparing the dancers for Varna and readily agreed to the proposal to enter them for Osaka. There was one small hitch. "Guess what? They'd left it too late and I had to get on the phone early one morning from on tour in Halifax to Masako Ohya and be nice to her so she would let us in." Spohr had fortunately added Ohya, the organizer of the Osaka competition, to his list of friends when they had met three years before in Moscow. Again, Spohr's impeccable connections proved their value. Hart and Peregrine were in, but Spohr was too burned out to join them. He was so ill that Moroni had to replace Spohr on the company tour. Bill Riske arranged for Frank Augustyn to coach Hart and Peregrine in the *Giselle* pas de deux.

Hart and Peregrine returned from Osaka early in June with bronze medals. The RWB's principal pianist, Earl Stafford, received an honourable mention. To Spohr's delight, Norbert Vesak, whose *Belong* the duo had danced in Osaka, earned a gold medal for choreography. There was more of the precious metal to come. Spohr now says he had expected his dancers to do well in Varna, but even he did not anticipate the riches they brought back. Hart won the gold medal and a special award for exceptional artistic achievement. Peregrine, the only male non-Communist Bloc competitor to win a medal, returned with a bronze. Stafford was gilded for his piano accompaniment and once again Vesak took the gold for *Belong*.

This triumph was more than Moroni and Spohr could have ever dreamed of. It rocketed Hart into the international limelight. The RWB now had a veritable star. The company's communications department, under the dynamic leadership of Rodgers Kearns, knew how to market Hart to the hilt. Hart had the celebrity to sell a show and therefore became of immense importance to the RWB. Artistically she towered over everyone. The prospect of losing Hart to another company appears to have caused the board more anxiety than it did Spohr.

Spohr had a very special relationship with Hart. "They were kindred spirits," says Rodgers Kearns. The two were both obsessive perfectionists, nervous and insecure by disposition and utterly consumed by dance. Dance gave meaning to their lives. Their similarities initially drew Hart and Spohr together and in the end pushed them apart. Spohr was more tolerant of Hart's demands, her anxiety attacks and extreme need for emotional support, than were many of his colleagues.

In 1981, when Hart had been wounded by a review of her portrayal of Juliet, Spohr asked the Manitoba Theatre Centre's artistic director, Richard Ouzounian, what he thought of Hart's acting ability. Ouzounian told Spohr that he was impressed. "Then please write and tell her," said Spohr. "Coming from you, it will mean a lot to her."

Says Ouzounian: "Arnold understood Evelyn's vulnerability. I thought to myself what a really great person he is."

"For me, she was worth the effort," says Spohr. "I see Evelyn dance and I have tears in my eyes. It's so uplifting. Of course, she used the RWB for her own convenience because Evelyn couldn't find what she wanted in another company. We gave her the care and the time she needed." The relationship between Hart and the RWB developed into a classic co-dependency.

In the fall of 1980, Spohr was able to show off his gilded star in the RWB's second United States tour of that year. The itinerary included a brief return to New York City, but this time to a less prestigious venue than City Center. The RWB danced two performances in the Bronx, in the new 2,300-seat Lehman College Center for the Performing Arts. Clive Barnes once again had reservations about the repertoire but he was bowled over by Hart and his words – "she has the ineffable image of greatness about her" – have hovered over Hart like a halo ever since. Jennifer Dunning from The New York Times was just as impressed. Barton Wimble of The Daily News observed that there were fewer noticeable solo talents in the RWB than during its 1978 visit, but, in praising Hart, ventured that she "probably won't stay very long".

The trip to the Varna competition in 1980 had other far-reaching consequences for the RWB. During the competition, Hart and Peregrine had taken daily class with the Bulgarian, Soviet-trained teacher Galina Yordanova. Hart was thrilled with Yordanova's classes. Throughout her career, Hart has always searched for guides to lead her to new artistic levels. She moves serially from one mentor-teacher to another and Yordanova was next in line. Moroni, one of Hart's earliest guides, was also impressed with Yordanova. Moroni watched her teach class in Varna and knew instantly that he wanted to bring Yordanova to Winnipeg. In early December that year she made her first visit to Canada to teach in the RWB school's professional programme. In the years that followed, Yordanova became a regular fixture on the guest teaching schedule. Many of the company's dancers, led by Hart, also became disciples of Yordanova. Her classes were notoriously demanding – dancers did not so much "take" them as "survive" them – but the impact on the classical standards of the professional school and company became in-creasingly apparent.

Spohr had always dreamed of the day when the RWB might be ready to dance *Swan Lake*, arguably the greatest of all the full-length Russian classics. With Hart in full bloom and Yordanova at hand, the day suddenly looked closer. *Swan Lake* was definitely something Spohr wanted to make happen while he was still director and it was not long before his plans assumed definite shape. Until this point it would have seemed folly for the RWB to contemplate staging *Swan Lake*. Setting aside the cost, *Swan Lake* requires a large corps as well as technically accomplished principal dancers. Now, however, the pieces were falling into place. There were enough senior dancers in Moroni's school who, with adequate preparation time, could supplement the regular company in full-length productions. As the RWB moved to a more stable financial footing under Riske's management and Tapper's corporate fund-raising efforts, the issue of cost appeared less of an insurmountable barrier. Spohr knew it would take several years to bring the company and school to the required level. He would have to win approval from the still very active RWB production committee, but *Swan Lake* was no longer just a dream. In the meantime, *Romeo and Juliet* and *Giselle* would be important stepping stones.

The production committee wholeheartedly agreed that full-length productions were needed to help win back the Winnipeg audience. The committee, however, was not about to rubberstamp Spohr's plan for van Dantzig's *Romeo and Juliet* before the full board had had a chance to see what it was buying. A video recording was requested from Amsterdam, but when the tape eventually arrived in the spring of 1980, only five board members showed up for the screening. John Condra was concerned that the RWB would be competing with the National Ballet's much larger 1964 production by John Cranko. One board member suggested that audiences might be happier with something bright and cheery such as *Cinderella* or even another *Hansel and Gretel*. But, as usually happened, Spohr got his way and *Romeo and Juliet* was approved by the end of June.

By the time van Dantzig came to work on *Romeo and Juliet*, he already knew the company's strengths and weaknesses. In Evelyn Hart, van Dantzig was sure he had a star he could count on. Van Dantzig had taken full measure of her talent when he visited Winnipeg to set *Four Last Songs*. Now, Hart was to become van Dantzig's "dream Juliet", one he was willing to compare with the legendary Soviet ballerina, Galina Ulanova. By now, van Dantzig had also had a chance to observe Spohr in action. The two had first met three years before in a restaurant when van Dantzig was staging his *Ramifications* for the Houston Ballet. "I'd just arrived, was jet lagged, drank a coffee and heard a loud voice through the room, 'Aren't you Rudi?' Then Arnold asked me if I could come to Winnipeg too."

In Winnipeg, Spohr watched the rehearsals. "I recall Arnold drifting in and out," says van Dantzig. Spohr was not the répétiteur assigned to van Dantzig's ballets although, as the choreographer dryly remarks, "I think he later took over when he wanted, or felt like it." The two had very different approaches. "Arnold was a dedicated director/ballet master but from a much older generation, with a different taste and outlook on things."

Van Dantzig first choreographed *Romeo and Juliet* in 1965 for the Dutch National Ballet, using the full company of sixty-five. Rather than edit the ballet for Winnipeg, van Dantzig gave individual corps members several different roles. It made for many rapid costume changes in the wings. Van Dantzig saw advantages in the multiple casting because it kept the corps focussed and involved throughout the ballet. However, he was still short of dancers. The answer was Moroni's professional school. By the time *Romeo and Juliet* received its North American premiere in Winnipeg in September, 1981, the RWB school's professional division had been in existence for more than a decade. A majority of the company's dancers had received all or at least the final part of their training in the school. Now, for *Romeo and Juliet*, Moroni was able to supply a dozen of his senior students to augment the company. With the addition of three RWB artistic staff members in character roles, this brought the total cast to thirty-nine. Although it was on a smaller scale than the Dutch original, the RWB's *Romeo and Juliet* had a clarity that helped focus the drama and make the company's production distinctive. Spohr was not setting the RWB up in competition with the National Ballet. He was offering audiences something different.

Winnipeggers were astounded by the sheer visual impact of *Romeo and Juliet*. The production was beyond anything they could have anticipated. Spohr had found Toer van Schayk's original designs unduly dark and dour and had convinced him to introduce more vibrant colours. The Winnipeg audiences embraced Evelyn Hart as a star to rival anyone the National Ballet could put on stage. In 1981,

Romeo and Juliet was by far the biggest and, with a final price tag of more than $190,000, the costliest production the RWB had yet undertaken. Just as Spohr and the board had hoped, the ballet drew Winnipeggers back to the company. *Romeo and Juliet*'s six initial performances were sold to capacity and the production helped boost the list of season subscribers to almost 8,400 – double the figure it had been after the troubles of 1979.

"Romeo and Juliet" is a brand that sells itself, so in a way what critics thought was irrelevant. Their differing opinions, however, did have bearing on Spohr's artistic judgement. Local critics, particularly in smaller cities, often have a tendency to root for the home team. Outsiders are a more reliable barometer and their reactions to *Romeo and Juliet* were mixed.

In 1965, the Dutch National Ballet asked van Dantzig to choreograph *Romeo and Juliet* because the company was unable to acquire any of the existing productions. Full-length spectacles are not van Dantzig's natural choreographic métier and the prescriptive nature of Prokofiev's score leaves little room for manoeuvre. As some critics noted, there was an academic predictability about much of the choreography. It tended to undermine some of van Dantzig's dramatic innovations. These included drawing a class distinction between the feuding Montagues and Capulets, reducing *Romeo and Juliet*'s high mortality rate by sparing the life of Count Paris and introducing symbolic death figures. John Ayre in Maclean's magazine had reservations about Hart but praised the production's "astonishing vibrancy and success". He deemed it, "the perfect vehicle for the dramatic power that was always obvious in the shorter works but never fully exercised." However, in a review for Dance in Canada magazine, critic Leland Windreich neatly encapsulated a fundamental problem. "As a company project it leaves one feeling that Canada's most innovative ballet organization has been asked to perform in someone else's old-fashioned, cast-off and inappropriate shoes."

That was in 1981. Over time, however, the RWB subtly modulated its *Romeo and Juliet*. Whether van Dantzig approved or not, Spohr applied his particular gift for bringing vibrancy to a work, to the point that the ballet began to look very much the company's own. When the RWB toured its *Romeo and Juliet* to Toronto in the spring of 1983, Alina Gildiner of The Globe and Mail noted: "In the hands of a lesser company, this production might seem leaden and dramatically ponderous. But the RWB knows how to handle it deftly, how to display its depth." The occasional complaints that van Dantzig's *Romeo and Juliet* dragged on too long were remedied more than a decade later when the RWB made about fifteen minutes-worth of cuts to avoid running into orchestra overtime. "The shortening," insists van Dantzig, "meant a big loss of impact."

When CBC Television recorded the RWB's *Romeo and Juliet* in 1982, Spohr himself appeared with the company for the first time in almost a quarter century to perform the character role of Friar Lawrence. It was not a great performance. "I fear I wasn't very happy with his interpretation," says van Dantzig. "It was too vain, too smiley, too self-aware also." Spohr remembers having trouble getting down on his knee at one point in the ballet. "He was so nervous and stressed out," remembers Hart.

The Canada Council did not greet the addition of *Romeo and Juliet* to the RWB's repertoire with enthusiasm. Even before the premiere, a warning note was sounded. In April, 1981, Monique Michaud wrote to the RWB's new president, Leon Rubin. Beneath the officialese, the gist of the letter was plain enough. The RWB had built its reputation on its ability to tour economically. The Council, as Michaud explained, would never consider intervening in artistic decisions. The RWB, however, should not look to the Canada Council for extra money if its intent was to finance full-length productions. Instead, the company must "give thought to means to cope with this departure from its traditional format."

As far as RWB board members were concerned, the Canada Council was most definitely trying to intervene. Like all true Winnipeggers, they were not about to kowtow to Ottawa. Their regional pride was offended. They were sure Michaud's real agenda was to protect the National Ballet's effective monopoly as the Canadian purveyor of full-length classics. It was the start of a continuing series of not always friendly exchanges between the RWB and the Council. These skirmishes dogged Spohr's final years as director, although for the most part he left it to the board to do the fighting. "Kathleen Richardson did not mince her words," Michaud recalls. Spohr's personal relations with Council staff remained cordial. He and Michaud had known each other for many years. "Arnold was well liked at the Council," says Michaud. "I never felt any personal animosity. The differences were between our two boards. Arnold had always been keen on original repertoire. That's what the Council liked. It felt each of the ballet companies had its own strengths and wanted each to play to its strengths."

• • •

In the spring of 1982 Spohr became one of four recipients of the twenty-seventh annual Dance Magazine Awards. These are given by the American publication to honour individuals who have made outstanding contributions to the world of dance. The awards do not come with a fancy medal or a fat cheque. Recipients are given a framed photograph with an engraved citation. However, as peer awards they are highly prized. The cumulative list of winners is a veritable Who's Who of dance. Spohr was not the first Canadian to be recognized. Toronto-born Melissa Hayden, who had become a star in Balanchine's New York City Ballet, won the Dance Magazine Award in 1961. Spohr, however, remains the only Canadian to have earned it by staying and doing his work at home, a fact that made him justifiably proud. "Everybody always complains about having to work in Canada," he told a TV interviewer at the time, "and about having to go elsewhere to make it. And so, here am I, working in Winnipeg, and I've achieved this award just working in Canada."

A crowd of more than 500 gathered in New York at the Sheraton Centre's Royal Ballroom for the May 3 presentation ceremony. Many of Spohr's friends had travelled from afar to be with him, but his American friends handsomely outnumbered them. Everyone, it seemed, knew Spohr and wanted to speak with him. In his introductory remarks, Dance Magazine editor-in-chief William Como described Spohr as "the best-loved man in Canadian dance". Spohr was the last to receive his award. Paul Taylor presented modern dance choreographer Laura Dean. Lucia Chase presented American Ballet Theatre star Fernando Bujones. Lee Theodore, founder of the American Dance Machine, received her award from Hal Prince. Then it was Arnold Spohr's turn and Agnes de Mille rose to speak.

The fact that she was seventy-six and partly paralyzed by a stroke had in no way dulled de Mille's appetite for a captive crowd. She had dressed for the occasion in a long-sleeved, frilly cream-white gown. De Mille went on and on, playing for laughs and mostly succeeding by making fun of Winnipeg, its northern remoteness, the cold, and the

Spartan conditions she had endured there on her early visits. After holding forth in this manner for almost as long as the three previous presenters combined, de Mille finally got to the subject of Spohr, briefly paid tribute to his genius as a régisseur, then lapsed into a condescending and inaccurate account of the early years of the RWB. It was an embarrassing display. If she had looked at Spohr's face, de Mille might have noticed the famous "camel look".

Finally, Spohr was free to make his acceptance speech. Briefly setting aside his notes, Spohr gently squelched de Mille with a mix of sarcasm and irony, delivered with perfect timing and calm dignity. "Well here I am (*pregnant pause: laughter*) from my igloo (*another pause: more laughter*), from the Klondike. All the cats, dogs, whatever, have frozen to death. Somehow I survived ... Thank you, Agnes, for your kind and glorious words." Point made, Spohr then returned to his notes, recounted the tale of de Mille's gruff rebuff of his first attempt in 1961 to meet her, thanked everyone with Academy Award copiousness, including the Canada Council, and sat down to a heartfelt round of applause.

The citation on his framed photograph read: "To Arnold Spohr, whose courage, determination, organizational skills, and singular artistic taste have galvanized Canada's Royal Winnipeg Ballet into a company of international stature, a joyous achievement which has enriched immeasurably our world of dance."

There were more awards the following year – another doctorate, this time from the University of Winnipeg, and a Diplôme d'Honneur from the Canadian Conference of the Arts – but the Dance Magazine Award still has special meaning for him.

Spohr did not have time to tarry in New York. He was soon back in Winnipeg for the May 5 world premiere of Nebrada's *Firebird*. Despite the orchestral glories of its 1910 Stravinsky score, making its traditional good-versus-evil, fairy-tale plot work choreographically has always been a challenge. If it were conventionally prettier, Stravinsky's music might work well as a ballet for children. From what some critics could judge, this had been Nebrada's aim. Nonetheless, the audience loved his *Firebird* and gave the ballet a long standing ovation. The reviews were also enthusiastic. The critics were impressed by the spectacle of Astrid Janson's translucent sets and fantastical costumes and by the magic of Tony Tucci's lighting. They were less enamoured of Nebrada's often dull choreography.

After a scorchingly erotic pas de deux for Hart, the Firebird, and guest artist Zane Wilson as the Prince, there was little of choreographic interest besides the antics of various serpentine nasties and darting dragonflies. The choreographic shortcomings of Nebrada's *Firebird* attracted a good deal of negative attention during the RWB's fall 1982 visit to London, but for the moment it looked as if the company had scored another popular hit.

With two trips across the Atlantic, 1982 was an exceptionally busy travel year for Spohr and the RWB. The first was a two-week tour to Cyprus and Greece in July. The two Greek tour venues – Athens and Salonica – were outdoors but in Nicosia the dancers had the advantage of an air-conditioned theatre. They gave a benefit performance for the Cyprus Red Cross. For audiences in Nicosia, the arrival of the RWB, tired after an exhausting flight via Amsterdam and Athens, was an extraordinary and much appreciated event, but for Spohr the company's performances at the Athens Festival were the highlight of the whole tour. The RWB was the first Canadian company to appear at the festival. "We danced in the ancient Herod Atticus Theatre," remembers Spohr, "right in the shadow of the Acropolis. It's a huge amphitheatre. You could look up and see the Parthenon. It was like being connected with all that history, dancing there under a starry sky." The RWB's performances were such a success, the company was immediately asked to return. "It was a high," Spohr told a reporter. "We've conquered Greece now."

The overseas autumn tour was a much bigger and critically testing venture. The company had not been seen in London since the Commonwealth Festival of 1965 but many of the same critics were still writing. This time the RWB was staying for two weeks and performing in the original home of The Royal Ballet, the 1,500-seat Sadler's Wells Theatre with its rather cramped, raked stage. The company's arrival was well publicised, with advance features appearing in both of Britain's leading dance magazines. Hart and Peregrine had already appeared together in a London gala the year before and this helped heighten expectations. Organizers of the London visit even managed to arrange a Royal opening gala with Princess Anne in attendance.

Spohr took a repertoire sufficient to stock three different programmes. It covered a wide spectrum of RWB history, including works by de Mille, Balanchine, Vesak, Neumeier, Araiz, Nebrada and, of course, a representative sampling of Spohr's new Dutch connection. With so many strongly opinionated critics in attendance, there was inevitably a diverse range of opinion concerning the merits and demerits of individual works, but as the first week wore on, a consensus began to emerge. The company looked strong, it was more classically secure, but the repertoire overall did not do justice to the dancers' abilities. Several critics commented on the fact that the RWB did not have a house choreographer who could place a distinctive imprint on the company. Throughout the London run, Hart was repeatedly singled out for praise. By London standards, the season was a critical success and although the Sadler's Wells Theatre was only sold to about sixty per cent of capacity, the RWB did considerably better than most visiting foreign troupes.

From London, the company travelled on to dance in five German cities, including Frankfurt and Stuttgart, before heading off in early November to the most exotic and what should have been the warmest stop on the whole tour, Cairo. Visits by foreign ballet troupes were a comparative rarity in Egypt. In 1982 they were particularly hard to arrange because Cairo's opera house had burned down six years earlier. The RWB was therefore required to perform in what was known as the Balloon Theatre, a fragile-looking version of a geodesic dome with a tent suspended inside. The company's performances were intended to raise money for the rebuilding of the opera house.

The RWB had worried that it might have to contend with hot weather. Instead, it arrived in the midst of a cool spell. London had been warmer. Worse still, the rain, which on average deposits little more than an inch a year on Cairo, decided to fall in far greater quantities all at once, turning to hail for its grand finale. The interior of the 1,500-seat theatre was drenched, including the stage, and the water was still dripping. The rain had also seeped into the lighting board. According to their union rules, the dancers were not obliged to perform if the temperature dropped below twenty degrees Celsius. It was only thirteen degrees. The scheduled opening looked impossible. "But the kids took a vote," says Spohr, "and said they'd dance, and everyone worked hard to get the theatre dried up as best we could. They ended up giving a terrific show and the audience loved it."

The theatre was in such disrepair that in any case only about half the seats were usable and the opening-night audience was a select invited crowd of about 400. Many of the women had brought their fur coats. Several of these found their way backstage to keep the dancers warm during inactive moments. "It was a case of us pulling through for Canada," says Spohr, "and showing what you can do when you all work as a team."

Accounts vary as to why Norbert Vesak's popular pas de deux *Belong* was not performed as scheduled. One theory has it that the Egyptian censors ruled the dance too erotic and under-clad. The more likely alternative theory is that the stage was too damp and cold for anyone to be expected to lie and roll on it. The temperature rose for the remaining Cairo performances and the demand for tickets was so great that even the most dilapidated seats were sold.

There was more excitement before the RWB opened its final engagement of the overseas autumn tour in Belfast. The dancers arrived intact, but rough conditions in the Irish Sea almost left a truck carrying shoes, costumes and other supplies stranded on the wrong side because the ferry service had been disrupted. The truck finally arrived in Belfast at 6:00 p.m. and was rushed to the opera house by a police escort. One hour and thirty-seven minutes later, the curtain rose on Nebrada's *Our Waltzes*. Says Spohr: "We always know how to pull through in adversity. We should. We've been doing it for long enough."

• • •

For the 1982/83 season, Spohr's twenty-fifth as artistic director, the RWB decided to brand the year as a "Silver Celebration of Excellence". A somewhat stylized black and white graphic of Spohr was featured on all RWB promotional material. It was not the most flattering image and made Spohr look a good deal older than he was. As journalist Ted Allan wryly noted, it gave Spohr the look of "a distracted Roman emperor smiling wanly out from some ancient coinage." But as Allan also observed, Spohr's expression was aptly captured – ambiguous, benevolent and veiled.

Again, the company was enjoying steady growth in its home audience base and, with the lure of another full-length classic, the season drew almost 9,500 subscribers. The ballet was a brand new production of the Romantic two-act classic *Giselle*. Spohr invited the British choreographer and director Peter Wright to stage it. Although Wright had been responsible for the National Ballet's much-praised production of 1970, Spohr did not see this as an impediment. By this stage in his career, Wright was an acknowledged expert on *Giselle* and had staged the ballet successfully for several different companies. He was therefore the logical choice.

By the end of 1982, Hart had almost succeeded in her goal of breaking free from her imposed partnership with Peregrine. The two dancers, both protégés of Moroni, had been thrust together and although the Winnipeg public seemed to view them as an ideal stage couple, Hart felt she deserved a more artistically compatible partner. Spohr was not resistant to hiring guest partners for Hart. They would add more glamour and excitement for the audience but, as the board was aware, Hart's partners would come at a cost. It was accepted as the price of keeping her happy. Hart's choice of partner for *Giselle* was a dancer she had met at the Dutch National Ballet in Amsterdam, Henny Jurriens. To soften the implied snub to Peregrine, Spohr invited the National Ballet's Veronica Tennant, a noted exponent of the role of Giselle, to be Peregrine's partner. Although they were only given three performances compared with Hart and Jurriens' four, Spohr accorded Tennant and Peregrine the privilege of inaugurating the production at a matinee on Boxing Day, 1982.

Winnipeggers thronged to see *Giselle*. Tennant and Peregrine received what by Winnipeg standards was a rousing ovation, but it was the evening performance with Hart and Jurriens that generated the biggest stir. The mood in the theatre was electric and by Giselle's suicidal "Mad Scene" at the end of Act I, Hart had moved many of her audience to tears. Her ethereal Act II, with everything flowing like one long poetic line of movement, was the cap to an historic performance. It was more than a great debut. It was the launch of an Evelyn Hart cult.

Hart's success increased the number of outside offers she began to receive. This alarmed the RWB board. They asked Spohr whether he was sure that Hart would honour her contractual commitments to the company. Even before she had made her full-length *Giselle* debut, the National Ballet's artistic director, Alexander Grant, had booked Hart to dance the role in Toronto in February, 1983. Toronto balletomanes had already singled Hart out as a woman to watch and her Toronto *Giselle* was given a rapturous reception. Again, Spohr remained sanguine. When Erik Bruhn succeeded Grant at the National Ballet in the summer of 1983, he and Spohr quickly agreed to work out an exchange arrangement to allow Hart to perform in

Toronto and leading National Ballet dancers to appear with the RWB. Spohr had come to understand Hart very well by now and, as he reassured the board, if they let Hart "do her own thing" she would never desert them. History has proved Spohr right, but the cost in energy and time to the RWB in having to placate and support such a high-maintenance ballerina, however eccentrically brilliant, was considerable.

• • •

Discussion of a gala performance to recognise Spohr's long service to the RWB had begun at the board level as early as 1980. At one point there was talk of holding a celebration in conjunction with the opening of *Romeo and Juliet* in 1981. Various ambitious proposals were suggested for the 1982/83 season, his twenty-fifth anniversary as director. The company thought Harry Belafonte, now an honorary RWB board member, would make a splendid master of ceremonies. There was even talk of inviting a genuine Royal from Britain, but the organizers settled for Ed Schreyer, the Governor General and a former premier of Manitoba. When Peter Wright's company, the Sadler's Wells Royal Ballet, was booked as a guest into the 1983/84 subscription series, the gala got shifted to the fall. Wright, who had a great fondness for Spohr, agreed to make his company available to dance with the RWB in a joint gala performance on October 18, 1983. So, in a way, it would be a "royal" gala anyway.

The gala's financial objective was to raise money to endow a perpetual scholarship in the professional school named in Spohr's honour. Spohr was to be involved in the planning and execution of the evening's dancing. The rest was left to the gala committee and no less than eleven sub-committees, covering everything from pre-show banquet arrangements to protocol. The gala itself was a splendid affair. However, the greatest tribute Spohr could have wished for was the extraordinary commitment of time and effort by countless volunteers from the board, the company and the community, who laboured over many months to make it a success. Tickets for the special pre-performance dinner sold so well that the organizers had to expand the table capacity from 400 to 500 guests. A team of volunteers ensured that every ticket to the actual performance and post-show reception was sold.

The news cameras rolled as the VIPs arrived to dine in style. The guests included Spohr's siblings, Beatrice, Wally, George and Erica, along with official dignitaries, friends and colleagues – past and present. Sergei Sawchyn and Jim Cameron, the former general managers with whom Spohr had sometimes crossed swords, were also there to celebrate his special evening.

The Manitoba Centennial Concert Hall was festively decorated, with a huge suspended photo of Spohr dominating the lobby. The performance was an easily digestible menu of mostly classical excerpts, with the RWB and the Sadler's Wells Royal Ballet giving a joint performance of van Manen's *5 Tangos*. The emotional part of the evening was yet to come. As the audience cheered, each member of the company presented Spohr with a red carnation. When dancer Julie Whittaker spoke, there was rapt silence. "To work with this man is to be touched by the very best. We offer him the ultimate in love and gratitude." Whittaker was in tears as she spoke and Spohr gave her a comforting hug. Then the fun began. A silver Jaguar XJ6 bearing the licence plate "RWB-1" appeared from the wings, driven by a man in a Beefeater uniform. As the driver stepped out to present the keys to Spohr on a silver salver, board member Rod Zimmer slipped a full-length, size forty-four mink coat over Spohr's shoulders. The audience reasonably assumed that the Jaguar was an outright gift. In fact it was only a one-year, sponsored lease. The fur coat, from an "anonymous donor", was Spohr's to keep. By the time the final tally was made, the gala had raised almost $50,000 for the Arnold Spohr Scholarship fund.

• • •

The arrival of *Giselle* in the RWB repertoire, little more than a year after *Romeo and Juliet*, was worrisome to the Canada Council. By now its concerns were public knowledge. The following spring, Timothy Porteous, the Council's director, again reiterated its position, adding that there was concern about the RWB using student dancers to flesh out its large productions. "I guess it depends", Porteous told a reporter, "what the real cost of those extra dancers are, but those dancers are human beings. Surely, the time will come when they'll have to be paid full-time salaries."

The Canada Council's anxiety about the RWB's move into the full-length classics continued to irritate Spohr, but in no way shook his resolve. If anything, it compelled Spohr to examine, articulate and justify his position, in the process mobilizing a multi-faceted argument – a mix of artistic vision and pragmatism – that left him even more confident that he was right.

The Council's scarcely veiled warnings pressed a number of sensitive buttons. The strong streak of prairie independence in Spohr's character resented what he regarded as the Council's centralist dictates. It was not the first time – the ballet survey of 1962, the Brinson report thirteen years later – that cultural mandarins in Ottawa had apparently sought to engineer the evolution of Canadian ballet in a way that potentially thwarted legitimate regional aspirations. There was also Spohr's pride in the achievements of the RWB and his belief that it had earned the fundamental right to grow.

In April, 1986, Spohr set out his arguments forcefully in a letter to the Council's then director, the former diplomat, Peter Roberts. Spohr insisted that his artistic policy, founded on a formula inherited from Gweneth Lloyd, remained unaltered. "The Royal Winnipeg Ballet," wrote Spohr, "is a company with an eclectic repertoire personifying access to everything. Our contemporary choreography and jazz is based on a classical foundation. The requirement for a dancer in the company is a classical technique with tremendous versatility." As Spohr pointed out to Roberts, this formula had become widely imitated in North America. Switching into upper case, Spohr's literary equivalent of shouting, he wrote: "MOST OF TODAY'S COMPANIES HAVE FOLLOWED IN OUR FOOT-STEPS EMULATING OUR FORMAT."

Spohr used historical arguments to counter the Council's suggestion that the RWB was a "contemporary" company. The RWB, Spohr reminded Roberts, had danced *Swan Lake Act II* and *Les Sylphides* as early as the 1950's. "The classics in the past and today were always included." Spohr also pointed out that from the earliest years of his directorship he had sought to develop a strong base of classical training in the company's school. It was with Council grant support, Spohr archly recalled, that he had travelled repeatedly to the great teaching centres of Europe and the Soviet Union to search for and develop a strong classical training system for the RWB. "We are a classical ballet company with an individual identity from our eclectic repertoire. The way we perform is from the molding of teachers, directors, choreographers and coaches brought in at great expense and tremendous appreciation on the part of the Canada Council."

Spohr understood well enough, however, that the Council was not worried about whether the RWB danced the odd short classic here or there. The Council's concern, at a time when its resources were stretched ever thinner, was the financial implication of the RWB's increased emphasis on full-length ballets. Rather than offer solutions for the Council's financial predicament, Spohr preferred to argue both the artistic and practical imperatives that motivated his move into full-length works. He portrayed this as an inevitable process. From the practical standpoint, Spohr insisted that the classics were a sound investment because they promised a much longer shelf life than many of the RWB's contemporary acquisitions and also were popular with the public. He rejected the suggestion that the RWB had placed itself in competition with the National Ballet and its lavish productions of the full-length classics.

"We do not intend to be in competition with the other companies as a large classical company, any more than the symphony orchestra or the legitimate theatres are across the country. Shakespeare – they all do it – not only Stratford. All symphony orchestras play Beethoven, Brahms, etc. We do this as an exercise so that our dancers will be most versatile and achieve the highest standard possible of style and technique in original ballets and the ballets of established, world renowned choreographers, which we have used throughout our existence. Doing the real classics (like Shakespeare for the theatre) gives the dancer a base, a standard to come up to and learn from and grow and expand."

Spohr fleshed out his letter by citing the RWB's many triumphs. He ended on an almost defiant note: "Given the fact that this is a classical ballet company, would the Canada Council begrudge the acquisition of three or four classics over the extended period of forty-eight years of existence?" With or without the Council's blessing, *Swan Lake* was going ahead. Little more than a year later, on May 6, 1987, Galina Yordanova's production was given its premiere in Winnipeg.

Few evenings in the company's history had been anticipated with as much public excitement or as much nervous trepidation backstage. All six performances were sold out well in advance. A great deal of care had been invested in the preparation of *Swan Lake*. The moment of trial had now arrived. Once again, Spohr was putting the RWB's reputation on the line. Critics from across the country had flown into the city of Winnipeg to see the result.

By National Ballet standards, the $250,000 budget for the RWB's *Swan Lake* was small cheese. For the RWB, however, the production was a huge investment. Twenty-two students from the professional school, who had been drilled progressively over more than a year by Galina Yordanova, joined the RWB's twenty-six company dancers. The addition of sixteen walk-on supernumeraries and three RWB artistic staff members in character roles, including Moroni as the evil magician von Rothbart, brought the total stage population to sixty-seven bodies.

It would have been foolhardy to expect any company to step into a masterwork such as *Swan Lake* and make it its own immediately. What was remarkable about the RWB's premiere was how close the company came to achieving this. Spohr had asked Yordanova for a clear, traditional staging in the spirit of the seminal 1895 St. Petersburg production, and that is what he got. While Erik Bruhn's 1967 version for the National Ballet revised and refocussed *Swan Lake* by adding an overlay of quasi-Freudian princely angst, Yordanova opted for a straightforward fairy-tale narrative, with the plight of the swan queen, Odette, as its dramatic core.

As is common with most companies, Hart danced both the roles of Odette and Odile. By this time she had performed them with the Sadler's Wells Royal Ballet. Predictably, given her ethereal qualities, Hart excelled as the bewitched Swan Queen of the lakeside acts. However, it was Svea Eklof, in the second cast, who brought true bravura to Act III's deceiving temptress, Odile. For many observers, perhaps the most remarkable achievement was the female corps de ballet in the "white" lakeside acts. As one critic commented on CBC Radio, "There was hardly a feather out of place. It was ensemble dancing to rival that of companies who have been performing Swan Lake for decades." Globe and Mail critic Stephen Godfrey was similarly impressed. Noting that the corps is the real foundation of *Swan Lake*, Godfrey wrote, "here the RWB showed it was able to pull off the ballet with flying colours."

By the end of the run, the RWB was already settling into its newest production. Winnipeggers had now seen Hart in three of ballet's greatest full-length dramatic roles and were bursting with pride. Spohr knew the company needed more time to master the subtleties of *Swan Lake* and expand comfortably into the production, but already he had good reason to be satisfied.

Just as Spohr was on the brink of entering his final season as director, the RWB had risen to yet another level.

12

Not If
But When

Arnold Spohr's retirement had been a recurrent topic of discussion ever since the crisis of 1978/79. Several times before that troublesome season, Spohr had made noises about resigning, but the threats, for that is what they had essentially been, were interpreted to be tactical rather than serious. He still had work to do.

In 1978, when Spohr made public his intention to "step aside", the response had been different. Some were horrified at the prospect. Others felt the time was right. Even when Spohr had reasserted full control the following year, it was very uncertain how long he would remain. Having placed the issue of his succession squarely on the table, it was impossible to take it back. Spohr's very choice of language in his annual report of 1979, his depiction of David Moroni as "the rightful heir", underlined Spohr's own awareness that he was entering the final phase of his directorship.

From then on, in conversation, Spohr spoke often of the way he was "grooming" David Moroni to take over "in a few years". Reasonably enough, Moroni took the prospect very seriously. It concurred with his own view of how the future should unfold. What neither fully grasped was the determination of the board, when the time came, to assert its own right to settle the company's leadership.

But when, exactly, would Spohr retire? His twenty-fifth anniversary gala in October, 1983 could equally have served as a farewell. It certainly fuelled speculation, at least among outsiders, that the day of his retirement could not be far off. Spohr gave a hint of this in his gala speech. "A company," he told the attentive crowd, "in order to survive, must have continuity. I hope to belong in one way or another for the transitions and be of service as long as I can." Max Wyman, in an affectionate tribute in the gala souvenir programme, recalled a telling comment Spohr had once made. "I hope never to age. I hope to remain young and contribute until I am finished with my life."

As Spohr stood in the lobby of the Manitoba Centennial Concert Hall after the gala performance, patiently working through the long line of well-wishers waiting for the chance to shake his hand or give him a hug, he looked anything but young. By the time Spohr finally joined the party – his party – on the mezzanine level, he had little more sparkle left than the dregs of champagne abandoned by departed guests. The evening had been both emotionally and physically exhausting. If Spohr had announced then and there that he had decided to step down, nobody would have begrudged him. It would have seemed the most natural thing in the world. Duty done; rest earned.

It did not take long, however, for Spohr to bounce back. He has extraordinary powers of recovery. With the light of dawn, he was already busy making sure that appropriate transportation had been arranged to convey Betty Farrally to the airport. If anything, the gala rekindled Spohr's confidence in his ability to continue, particularly when he had a chance to review the copious, adulatory media coverage. There on CBC Television was Wyman stating that the RWB had never been better. "The company is truly at its apogee. This is the best state it's ever been in. It's changed its character a little; it's become more classical, altogether more wonderful. It's a major tribute to what he's done. It's a major achievement." There was Spohr's friend from New York, Bill Como, telling Canadian viewers, "Arnold Spohr is one of Canada's national treasures. When someone says Canada, you think Royal Winnipeg Ballet." There was Evelyn Hart, stating what had been on many minds the night of Spohr's gala: "It's tough to envision the company without him."

The board, however, was already looking ahead. Spohr may have wished to work for the RWB until his dying day, but those entrusted with its continuing welfare were already thinking about his retirement. The first serious discussion of it occurred at a meeting in 1981. Spohr was a contract employee. The job had never offered a pension. However, Spohr's inability to manage his personal finances wisely was well known among his friends and relations. There was serious concern about his future security. Spohr could be a practical realist in terms of accepting the RWB's financial limitations, whatever artistic sacrifices those entailed. "He was pretty good at not going over budget," says Kathleen Richardson. In contrast, personal money management has remained something of a mystery to Spohr. He knows in a generalized way that money is essential, yet ultimately does not accord it that much importance. He derides the habit of one of his former colleagues who, according to Spohr, likes to squirrel away his hard-earned gains in the bank. "What's the good of that?" asks Spohr. Over the years, friends and relations had tried to help Spohr with his financial affairs. For a time, his brother Wally assumed the responsibility. When Spohr's brother George retired from the RCMP and entered the real estate profession, he encouraged his youngest brother to invest in property.

For Spohr money is for spending, largely on other people, something he has always done with flair and notorious prodigality. Spohr was brought up poor and acquired no real concept of accumulating assets or providing for the future. In moments of extremity, like Mr. Micawber in Dickens' David Copperfield, Spohr has always lived in the optimistic belief that something will turn up. Generally, it does.

Spohr's salary in the early years of his directorship was modest, but by the mid-1970's, he was being paid comparatively well. The contract he signed for the period 1973-1976 provided a salary of $25,000 a year, plus travel and other expenses incurred on company business. In the 1973/74 season, Celia Franca, founding artistic director of the much larger National Ballet of Canada, was only making $23,000. In addition to his RWB salary, during the years from 1968 to 1981, Spohr had regular income from The Banff Centre, in return for his services as co-head of the summer dance programme. In the late 1970's, this was close to $800 a week. There had also been the early windfall of a $15,000 Molson Prize in 1970, a sizeable amount at the time. Somehow, the money did not stick.

Spohr must have understood that his RWB job did not come with a pension. The board had blithely assumed that he would make provision for the future. When it became clear that this was not the case, the subject of a pension for Spohr was raised at a board meeting. It was referred to the finance committee for consideration. Two years passed before the committee had solid proposals. One idea was to pay an annual pension to Spohr as a continuing financial obligation from the company's budget. This was soon rejected on the grounds that the RWB might go bust or that a future board could decide to cast Spohr adrift if times got tough. All the pension options were posited on an assumed retirement age of sixty-five. For Spohr that would mean 1988.

Five years is not a long time to finance a pension. The proposed solution involved obligations on the parts of both Spohr and the RWB. Spohr would agree to contribute to a Registered Retirement Savings Plan. The company would accumulate a fund which, on his retirement, would generate regular annuity income. The combination of Spohr's RRSP, his public pension and the RWB's contributions were felt sufficient to support a comfortable retirement. During the presidency of Lynne Axworthy, in one of the rare years that the RWB posted a healthy surplus, the board decided, with Canada Council endorsement, to make a substantial lump-sum transfer to the company's retirement fund for Spohr. Closer to the end of his directorship, when it appeared Spohr's retirement income would still be insufficient, his lawyer negotiated an improved settlement that included a further infusion of capital – contributed by "an anonymous donor".

Effectively, as early as 1983, the board had set a target date for Spohr's retirement. How fully he understood this is hard to determine. Talking about retirement is not the same as living it. The RWB, as Spohr often stated, was his family. You do not retire from your family. Spohr had dedicated his life to the service of the RWB. Surely, as the paterfamilias, he would always have some role. Spohr spoke of the RWB as a team endeavour and sincerely acknowledged the contributions of others, but deep down he found it hard to imagine that its destiny could ever be completely independent of his own. Spohr was the company's beating heart, its soul and its conscience. There were many who felt similarly. They worried about who could even begin to fill the void.

In Spohr's mind the solution, as it had been in 1978, was for him to step aside into an advisory role. The problem was how to define that role. It could hardly be left to Spohr to decide. The RWB was confronted with an ultimately insoluble conundrum.

Nobody can really explain how it came about that Spohr finally announced his intention to retire. At a board meeting in January,

1986, the subject of establishing a search committee for a new director was broached. Spohr, so the board learned, had mentioned that he might retire in the fall of 1987. At the end of the meeting, it was decided that Spohr should put his intentions in writing before a search committee was struck.

Many of the dancers sensed the end was near and believed it was none too soon. The company was no longer the family of kids Spohr had been used to dragooning in his earlier years. The whole ballet world had changed. The dancers of the 1980's were more aware, more self-assertive and less ready to defer. They respected Spohr for what he had achieved, but were less willing to tolerate his emotional outbursts. "He was getting very difficult to work with," says Hart. "The screaming and shouting got worse, he seemed even more obsessive. He was under so much stress – fighting the Canada Council over *Swan Lake*. That took so much courage. He was getting old. He was in pain and running out of energy."

In the end, did Spohr really make up his own mind or was he nudged? According to Hart, Kathleen Richardson canvassed the dancers to get a sense of their mood and needs. What she heard must have had some influence. The best that two senior board members of the time can offer is that Spohr was "encouraged" to make a firm decision. "Let's say his talking and our feelings converged," recalls Joseph Wilder, the board member who chaired the committee to find Spohr's successor. "Thirty years is a very long time for a director. It's not healthy. Every company needs refreshing." The news that Spohr would be retiring was released officially at the company's annual general meeting in September, 1986.

With Spohr's retirement set, the race for his job was on. The board had no intention of following Spohr's desire to see his "heir" automatically inherit the throne. There would be an open competition. The board would be king-maker. Spohr told anyone who would listen how important it was to maintain continuity with the company's heritage. He was wary of the idea of someone being parachuted in from beyond the bosom of the RWB. Spohr spoke darkly of "the unknown factor".

Since the best candidates often wait to be asked to apply, the search process was entrusted to a professional headhunter. His role expanded beyond the simple task of identifying promising candidates to include consulting on the whole transition process. "Arnold was such a central figure," says Wilder, "that it was very important to us for the transition to be handled in as sensible and sensitive a way as possible. We knew it was going to be difficult for him."

Spohr was given vague assurances that he would always be part of the RWB. After some debate, it was agreed that he should be given the title of Artistic Director Emeritus. Spohr was also to be given his own office in the RWB's new headquarters, then under construction. Spohr's office would be, and to this day remains, the only one in the RWB's home where the occupant's name appears on the door in addition to his or her job title. Originally the plan was to locate Spohr's office immediately next to that of the artistic director. When it occurred to the building committee that such close proximity might be unwise, Spohr's office was moved several doors down the hall. Neither the title nor the office was used as an inducement to encourage Spohr to retire. These came only after that decision had been made. According to Wilder, Spohr was never promised a specific role in the affairs of the RWB beyond retirement.

Spohr was not a member of the selection committee, but as short-listed outside candidates arrived in Winnipeg to be interviewed for the artistic directorship, he must have had a very good idea who the "unknown factors" were. Their visits caused a certain amount of consternation among the inside candidates and among those dancers who had already made their choice. For a growing number of them, that person was Henny Jurriens.

Jurriens was born in Arnhem, The Netherlands, on February 21, 1949. He had studied ballet from an early age. In 1966, he joined the National Ballet of Norway but returned home in 1970 to become a soloist, then principal dancer with the Dutch National Ballet. By the early 1980's, Jurriens was being groomed as the likely successor to the company's artistic director, Rudi van Dantzig.

Jurriens first appeared with the RWB in 1982 as the guest partner of Evelyn Hart. The two became close friends and Jurriens often partnered Hart in international guest appearances. While Jurriens' relationship with Hart and the RWB strengthened, his ties to the Dutch National Ballet unravelled. Van Dantzig abandoned his plans to retire and the company's management made it clear that they did not view Jurriens as the natural successor. Jurriens, feeling hurt and betrayed, moved to Winnipeg late in 1986 to become a full-time member of the RWB.

Jurriens was, by this time, already well known and liked by the dancers. He had none of the airs of an imported star. Jurriens was generous, congenial and soon very much one of the family. Spohr was not particularly enamoured of Jurriens' dancing. Although Spohr acknowledged Jurriens' partnering skills, he found Jurriens generally dull on stage. "It's that Dutch thing," he used to say. Spohr took Jurriens because of Hart, but quickly grew to appreciate his even-tempered and well-grounded character. There was even talk that Spohr saw in Jurriens the same qualities that had once convinced van Dantzig to make him his assistant artistic director in Holland.

Officially, in Spohr's cosmology, David Moroni was the heir apparent, but even some board members got the impression that Spohr may have secretly favoured Jurriens. In conversation, Jurriens sometimes confided that his decision to move to Winnipeg was partly motivated by the promise of more than simply a place where he could work through the last years of his dancing career. "We thought Arnold might have made some overtures to Henny," admits Wilder.

In late February, 1987, while the selection process continued, Spohr embarked on his seventh trip to the Soviet Union, this time to offer moral support and very practical assistance to his prima ballerina, Evelyn Hart. Through a complicated series of negotiations involving the Toronto television producer/director Robert Barclay, the Soviet agency GosConcert and the Canadian Embassy in Moscow, it had been arranged for Hart to dance in a Moscow gala as well as with the Odessa State Ballet. Barclay and his crew would turn the proceedings, including a side trip to Leningrad, into a television documentary.

Earlier in the year, Spohr had been receiving treatment for an unusual lump that had appeared in his neck. He was concerned that it might be cancerous and doubted he would be able to travel with Hart. The lump turned out to be benign and a much relieved Spohr packed his bags.

To a seasoned Soviet visitor such as Spohr, the conditions that greeted Hart and her retinue were unremarkable. It was Hart's first visit and she was shocked by the general organizational chaos, poor accommodations and inadequate food. Spohr, on the other hand, thought conditions were better than during his last visit almost a decade earlier. "There has been a great improvement in Russia," he told a Winnipeg reporter. "Things have become much more modern.

The hotels and the service were much better and there seemed to be tremendous freedom."

Apart from Spohr, Hart, Barclay and his film crew, the Canadian contingent included two of Hart's dance partners from the RWB, André Lewis and John Kaminski, as well as teacher/coach Galina Yordanova. In Moscow, Hart rehearsed with Andris Liepa, the rising young Russian star who was to partner her in her classical repertoire. Then, largely to oblige Barclay's needs, the team headed for Leningrad and the legendary Vaganova Choreographic Institute. For Spohr, who had become an indirect disciple of Vaganova's system through his studies with Vera Volkova, it was a symbolic visit. "Here we were, all the way from Winnipeg, with our radiant, golden ballerina, trained in our own school in the Vaganova tradition and visiting the place where it all began." Spohr even talked reluctant officials into taking down a large framed portrait of Vaganova so that he, Hart and Yordanova could pose with it for a photograph.

From Leningrad, the group travelled to Odessa where Hart and Liepa led the local company in a performance of *Giselle*. "They got a twenty-five-minute ovation," Spohr recalls proudly. The crowd that later watched Hart dance on the cramped stage of Tchaikovsky Hall in Moscow was equally enthusiastic, although for a while Spohr worried if the event would ever happen. Hart was part of a ballet gala involving various foreign and Soviet Bloc dancers. "It was almost a disaster," says Spohr. "Nothing had been properly arranged. No thought had been given to making it work as a show. I ended up more or less directing the whole thing with Galina. We even had to call the lighting cues, if you could call it lighting." For Spohr this was all in a day's work, a reminder of the chaotic conditions the RWB had often faced during its early tours.

The media duly noted the group's March 9 return to Winnipeg, in time for the RWB's revival of *Romeo and Juliet*. Hart was scheduled to dance at the March 11 opening but bowed out because of her jet lag. This left Svea Eklof with the unenviable task of trying to excite an audience that had come to see the company's most famous ballerina. As one reviewer noted, the audience was unresponsive.

A month later, Spohr was called to a meeting with a group of Royal Bank officials. He had been a signatory to a letter nominating Gweneth Lloyd for the annual $100,000 Royal Bank Award for Canadian Achievement. "I thought they wanted to talk to me about

Gweneth." What Spohr may not have known was that he had been nominated for the same award several times during the preceding decade. As was soon explained to him, Spohr had been chosen as the award's co-winner for 1987 with Lloyd. The news was formally announced on May 27 – hot on the heels of his third honorary doctorate, this time from the University of Victoria. Spohr later described his initial reaction. "I was dumbfounded, flabbergasted, speechless – an unusual trait for me – and ecstatic, all at the same moment."

From among a very small group of artists ever to win the Royal Bank Award, Lloyd and Spohr were the first and only figures from the world of dance. In making its choice, the award selection committee noted: "From the time he joined the ballet, Dr. Spohr has brought his city, his province and his country accolades and achievements that will long be remembered."

Spohr chose the black-tie award dinner on September 17 as a symbolic public opportunity to look back on his life and to offer his credo. His speech had all the import of a major valedictory. Spohr reflected on his parents, on the sturdy upbringing that taught him the difference between right and wrong, on the importance of team effort and the accomplishments of the company, and on the contributions of staff, dancers and board.

"I have always had the will to achieve the highest standards possible and the intelligence to know that very hard work, openness, flexibility, a positive attitude and desire for personal growth and knowledge must be constant until my dying day. If I wish to fulfil my motto, I must always have much to give. So, I constantly replenish, be it knowledge, physical or mental well-being. And, my true rewards come from the achievements of the dancers, choreographers, staff and board who are establishing and contributing to dance for our country."

The decision to split the award between Lloyd and Spohr aptly recognized the thread of continuity between the RWB's founder and the director who had made the company world-renowned. Spohr had evolved with the times and adapted the repertoire to suit changing audience tastes and the expectations of his dancers. He had seen his dream of a feeder school come true and used its resources to push the RWB in a more purely classical direction. Through it all, however, Spohr had remained true to the ideal of the RWB as a company whose goal was to entertain audiences. Who would now pick up the torch?

As the selection committee reviewed the various candidates, Henny Jurriens' application looked stronger and stronger. Everyone knew that Hart was rooting for Jurriens. For her, Moroni was out of the question. "Evelyn turned on me royally," says Moroni. "I had made the mistake of telling Henny that I did not think she was ready to do *Swan Lake*. She wrote me a letter. I remember she used the word 'divorce'." Hart's opinion, however, did not govern the committee's decision. There have been suggestions over the years that Jurriens was chosen because to do otherwise would have risked losing Hart. Spohr himself believes Hart's partiality was the deciding factor. It is a convenient theory but an implausible one.

By 1987, the board knew well enough that Hart needed the RWB quite as much as it needed her. Despite Hart's frustrations, the RWB was the company in which she could feel emotionally rooted and supported. The board also understood that the RWB would be unwise to pin its fortunes on a thirty-one-year-old ballerina who, however special, had her own personal agenda. They knew she had a history of shifting personal allegiances to which even Jurriens might fall victim. Hart's consuming goal was to dance the repertoire that most fulfilled her artistic needs and if that opportunity arose somewhere other than in Winnipeg she would in any case be gone – but probably not for long.

Henny Jurriens' appointment as artistic director, effective June 1, 1988, was officially announced on November 26, 1987. "Evelyn may have backed the right horse," says Wilder, "but it was the committee that picked the horse." For the selection committee, Jurriens was the candidate who seemed to have it all – artistic experience, sound judgement, a stable character and enthusiasm. Jurriens was already part of the RWB and yet he was also someone whose artistic vision reached beyond the company. "We chose Henny," says Wilder, "because he was by far the best candidate from an artistic point of view."

Wilder's committee exercised great discretion in keeping its choice a secret. The full board was not given the opportunity to endorse the committee's choice until the morning of the announcement. As a courtesy, Spohr was informed in advance and then joined other company members in the big studio at 289 Portage Avenue for the announcement. Whether in his heart Spohr truly approved or not, he was just as demonstrative as everyone else in greeting the announcement. "Arnold's a smart guy and a good politician," says Wilder. "If he was not happy with Henny, he sure made a pretty fast turnaround."

As the cheering died down, Arnold Spohr was left to ponder the inescapable reality that the end of his long reign as artistic director was only months away. These were to be inordinately busy months. The RWB was preparing for two major events. Finally, after almost half a century of nomadic existence, the company was moving into a home it could truly call its own and shortly after would leave on its first Asian tour.

By this time, Spohr had led the RWB on so many foreign tours that he had long lost count of the miles clocked, hotel rooms checked into and out of, strange meals eaten in exotic restaurants and items of luggage lost. The common thread was that whenever he and the company returned to Winnipeg, it was to less than adequate studios and offices in rented premises. From the time Spohr became artistic director, the company had leased space in four different locations and, for as long as anyone could remember, Spohr had been using a combination of persuasion, pleading and pestering to motivate the board into building the RWB a permanent home.

Since September, 1971, the RWB had been based at 289 Portage Avenue. Initially, the former furniture warehouse seemed spacious after the company's Smith Street premises but, as the RWB expanded, it soon outgrew its new home. By the late 1970's, the Portage Avenue space had become a crowded, dusty, mice-infested maze of studios and offices. Small lettering on a street-level entrance, where drunks and beggars sometimes loitered, was all that betrayed to passers-by that at the top of a long flight of stairs could be found Canada's oldest ballet company and the city's most instantly recognizable export. Reports of the building's chronic decay became all too familiar. At a board meeting in November, 1979, general manager Bill Riske brought the alarming news that one of the walls was sinking.

Since the late 1960's, the grand project to find a permanent home for the company had been a recurrent topic of discussion. Committees were formed, feasibility studies were undertaken and pleas for government support submitted. Over time, various buildings in different parts of Winnipeg were suggested for purchase and conversion. As early as 1970, headlines in the Winnipeg papers announced that the federal government was about to contribute $600,000 towards acquiring a site for a new ballet building, most likely to be situated on land between the old Playhouse Theatre and the new Manitoba Theatre Centre. Given its close proximity to the company's home stage, the Manitoba Centennial Concert Hall, the site had obvious appeal for the RWB. Yet, like so many other trial balloons, this one also deflated.

The general sense of renewal that buoyed the company after the upheavals of 1978/79, and the inescapable realization that the Portage Avenue premises were grossly inadequate, helped re-ignite the building project. In the summer of 1980, the building committee, chaired by Richard Kroft, formally agreed on the urgent need for a new company home. The committee discussed funding strategies and the pros and cons of keeping the company and school under one roof. The committee was even willing to consider a site beyond the downtown core.

By 1981, the board had selected the Winnipeg partnership of Les Stechesen and Alec Katz as architectural consultants. Even then, the project lurched along in reaction to the political climate and general state of the economy. In his report to the RWB's annual general meeting of June, 1983, Kroft reflected wearily on "a constant process of rising expectations followed by disappointment and dashed hopes." When the board engaged Stechesen and Katz, it had done so with a new building in mind. Then, daunted by the cost, the focus was switched back to identifying existing buildings for conversion. At one point, the RWB was almost politically pressured into locating itself on the third floor of Portage Place, the downtown shopping centre that was supposedly going to "revitalize" Portage Avenue.

Then the political winds began to blow in the RWB's favour. The plan for a new, tailor-made home was restored and a downtown site was secured at the corner of Graham Avenue and Edmonton Street. On October 3, 1985, on a clear crisp morning, Michael Volhoffer, an RWB stage crew member, took a jackhammer to the asphalt of the former parking lot so that assembled VIPs could take turns moving the exposed earth around in an official ground-breaking ceremony. Spohr, jauntily sporting a hardhat, shared a spade with Moroni, Kroft and Manitoba Lieutenant-Governor Pearl McGonigal. Five-hundred helium-filled balloons were set free to float up and across the

Winnipeg sky, announcing the historic event to the general citizenry.

Construction began the following summer with November, 1987, as the scheduled completion date. Spohr often strolled by the site to see how the work was progressing. By the time it was finished, he was understandably ecstatic. "My life couldn't reach a higher level of peace and joy than this," he was reported as saying. "Now I can settle back and watch the future happening."

The building's exterior, with its post-modern allusions to prairie grain elevators, has a functional look. The mix of tinted green glass, brick, tyndall stone and cladding material in shades officially described as "Lilac Brown" and "Blue Clay", creates a muted effect. Yet, taken as a whole, the building is distinctive enough to proclaim the RWB's presence in the heart of Winnipeg and massive enough to symbolize the company's importance to the life and reputation of the city.

Without question, the contrast to the RWB's former Portage Avenue premises was dramatic. The old building was dark and pokey. Everything was crammed into a meagre 22,000 square feet. Some of the old studios were little better than shoeboxes. The dressing and showering facilities were execrable. The RWB's new home, all 61,500 square feet of it, is filled with light, thanks to a central atrium. This lofty space connects the ten studios on one side with three levels of offices, lounges, dressing rooms, wardrobe cutting and storage rooms on the other. Two of the studios offer a working area as large as the RWB's home stage at the Manitoba Centennial Concert Hall. One of them, a 4,000-square-foot studio on the ground floor, has a raised seating area and is equipped to function as a performance space. There is even a physiotherapy centre. The design included a 160-space multi-storey parking garage to the south of the main building – both a convenience, and as Spohr had correctly pointed out, a source of revenue.

The artistic director was assigned a spacious corner suite on the fourth floor that includes its own private dressing room and shower. Spohr never occupied it. Although he was still officially director for five months beyond the building's opening, he decided it was more sensible to let Henny Jurriens move in. Spohr took premature possession of the much smaller office down the hall, already allocated to him as Artistic Director Emeritus.

As Jurriens commented: "The most important thing about this

new building is that it provides a creative atmosphere. Even if you work in the offices you can look across the atrium, through the windows and into the studios. You never have any doubt why you are here. The whole building is set around the creative side of what this organization exists for, and that is dance."

The building was finished on time and within a very modest budget of less than $10 million. Of that, $2.5 million came from the federal government and another $2 million from the province of Manitoba. That left Kathleen Richardson, as chair of the capital campaign committee, to raise $5.7 million from corporations and private donors across the country. When a black-tie gathering of some 240 guests sat down to dinner on Saturday, January 9, 1988, to celebrate the building's official inauguration, Richardson was able to report that it was 92.4 per cent paid for. She dryly observed that anyone who still wished to contribute was welcome to do so. At the same dinner, Joe Wilder announced that the main company studio was to be named in honour of Arnold Spohr. The atrium was named for Richard Kroft, the board member who had laboured so hard and for so long to build the RWB a home. The actual ribbon-cutting took place the following Monday, accompanied by a fanfare of trumpets. Five days later, almost 2,000 Winnipeggers lined up for the chance to inspect the RWB's new home in the first of several open houses.

• • •

The RWB remains one of Canada's most internationally travelled dance companies. Only the smaller Les Ballets Jazz de Montréal has danced in more countries around the world. With some sixty years of practice, the RWB has perfected touring to a fine art and is renowned among presenters and theatre crews for its professional efficiency and friendliness. In August, 1984, after the Olympic Arts Festival in Los Angeles had closed, the local crew who had worked with all the various visiting dance troupes at the Pasadena Civic Auditorium decided to hand out its own medals. The RWB had shared the spotlight with, among others, Dance Theater of Harlem, Sankai Juku and the companies of Twyla Tharp and Pina Bausch. There were eleven categories, including such unusual ones as "Strangest Company", "Most Difficult Road Crew" and "Most Mickey Mouse Company". As a letter to the members of the RWB's road crew explained, they had "swept the Gold", winning first place in five of the most flattering categories, from "Favorite Company" to "Easiest Road Crew". Asia was to test the company's crew to the limit.

As critic Max Wyman described it at the time, the 1988 tour was "the final flamboyant feather in his artistic director's cap ... the crowning international glory of his thirty-year reign." Flamboyant feather or not, the compliment made Spohr no less nervous about what lay ahead. Advance planning for the ambitious fifty-day, seven-country, ten-city tour had been proceeding for months and involved not just the RWB's own staff but a host of local sponsors, government agencies and diplomatic missions. It was an organizational mammoth. As RWB tour manager Mark Porteous explained to a Winnipeg reporter: "It will be like going on seven different tours at once."

The framework was well set, but Spohr was not confident that his dancers had been sufficiently rehearsed. It would have taken months rather than weeks of rehearsal to prepare a repertoire as extensive and varied as the one Spohr had selected. Unusually, at the presenter's request, the RWB took its full-length *Giselle* to Japan, despite the logistical challenge of shipping so many sets and costumes and flying in professional division students from the RWB school. "We would only tour something like that if the costs were fully covered by the presenter," says Spohr. Japan wanted *Giselle* primarily because of Evelyn Hart. Through her guest appearances, Hart was already a big star in Japan.

For the rest of the tour, Spohr was determined to offer a broad sampling of the RWB's repertoire. In his inimitable way, Spohr arranged two varied programmes that were guaranteed to stretch his dancers' versatility to the limit. One programme included Kylian's *Nuages*, van Manen's *5 Tangos*, Nebrada's *Our Waltzes* and Paddy Stone's crowd-pleasing confection, *The Hands*. The other programme combined Balanchine's *Allegro Brillante* with Vesak's *Belong* pas de deux, van Dantzig's *Four Last Songs* and another crowd-pleaser, de Mille's *Rodeo*. They were classic Spohr mixed bills, designed to offer audiences the usual gamut of styles, emotions and music. By any standard the tour was a success. "Canadian Company Conquers", declared a headline in the South China Morning Post near the end of the tour. However, in Spohr's words, " it was no picnic".

The company – forty-seven dancers and staff – left Winnipeg on

January 21, en route to Taipei, via Vancouver and Hong Kong. A week earlier, the people of Taiwan had been stunned by the sudden death of seventy-year-old Chiang Ching-Kuo, the country's president since 1978. Taiwan was in deep mourning. There had even been talk of scratching Taiwan from the tour. Instead, a less dire solution was applied. The shows would go on, but the corporate receptions aimed at oiling the wheels of commerce between Canada and Taiwan would not. Two performances scheduled for the day of the president's funeral were shifted to later matinees.

In the event, all went well. Robert Kelly, head of the Canadian Trade Office in Taiwan, told the opening night audience that Chiang Ching-Kuo would have wanted the show to proceed. A moment's silence was then observed. The choice of Rudi van Dantzig's elegiac *Four Last Songs* for the first programme was deemed "very appropriate" by the China News. To judge by the laughter, it was clear that the light-hearted romance of Agnes de Mille's cowboy ballet, *Rodeo*, was just what the audience needed. An unnamed critic for one of the Chinese-language papers reserved special praise for the RWB's men and complimented their "fine line, technique and stylistic integrity". Overall attendance for the six-performance Taipei engagement exceeded eighty per cent of capacity, auguring well for the rest of the tour. Spohr's nervousness abated, but he had not reckoned on Bangkok.

The RWB was to be part of an international festival to mark the sixtieth birthday of Thailand's king, Bhumibol Adulyadej. The 2,000-seat concert hall, part of the Thailand Cultural Centre, was brand new. So was the fire retardant on the theatre curtains. Somehow it had shed a fine dust onto the stage making the surface dangerously slippery. The RWB's production manager, Jon Stettner, and his crew made many unsuccessful attempts to clean the floor. It was only minutes before curtain-up that a heavy-duty degreasing agent finally made the stage safe. Meanwhile, Mark Godden, scheduled to dance the Champion Roper in *Rodeo*, was rushed to hospital with apparent food poisoning. His understudy, Jackson McKiee, was hastily rehearsed. When Godden, still pale, appeared an hour before curtain time, Spohr told him to go back to the hotel and rest. "Jackson will do okay."

There was yet another problem threatening the opening-night gala in Bangkok. Hart had already put her ghostly, full white make-up on in preparation for the *Giselle* pas de deux when she bit into a sandwich and lost the cap from a front tooth. A Giselle with a gap in her teeth is hardly fitting for a royal gala audience, so Hart was whisked off to a dentist for emergency repairs.

As usual, the RWB managed to soar above near calamity. Hart danced serenely with a full set of teeth. McKiee rose to the occasion and danced a spirited Champion Roper. The gala audience, including among other dignitaries one Thai princess and a Canadian cabinet minister, John Crosbie, was delighted. Princess Galyani Vadhana even condescended to break precedent and attend the post-show party. Again, the reviews were glowing. Having noted that the RWB repertoire was "easy on the audience", the Bangkok Post summed up the opening gala as follows: "Ballet fiends found themselves with a choice programme that presented the best in choreography, with Canada's top dancers to show it off to perfection." The National, another English-language daily, hailed the RWB's dancing as "an emotionally powerful display".

The tour continued to Singapore, Malaysia, Japan, Hong Kong and China with the already familiar mix of narrowly averted disasters, vibrant performances, glittering receptions, occasional spare-time outings to view museums, temples and historic sites and, of course, shopping.

Almost all the reviews were laudatory. Even the Asian audiences, whom the RWB had been forewarned would be less than demonstrative in showing their appreciation, were enthusiastic. In orderly Singapore, Spohr recalls the ushers at the Kallang Theatre telling people to sit down when they tried to give the dancers a standing ovation. "Can you believe it? They told them to sit down because the show wasn't over."

Sickness was a common feature of long RWB tours. In one of the mixed programmes, Spohr actually had to cut a section from Paddy Stone's *The Hands* because Vincent Boyle had such a bad upset stomach he could not dance. In this case there was no understudy. A turbulent cocktail of anxiety and stomach flu almost took Hart out of the opening *Giselle* in Tokyo. Fortunately, the audience had no idea that the ethereal ballerina before them was also throwing up in the wings. At the end of the show, the audience brought Hart and Jurriens back for a long succession of curtain calls. Winnipeg mayor Bill Norrie was in the audience. He later told a reporter: "Certainly the ballet is our most important international ambassador."

The RWB's visit to Kuala Lumpur was one of the few times the Malaysian capital had been visited by a classical ballet company. The 3,600-seat Putra World Trade Centre was hardly the most suitable venue. It was also a challenge to mobilize local sponsors. It took a Herculean effort by Canadian diplomatic officials to make the engagement possible. A key to their success was the involvement of Ali Abu Bakar, a local rock music promoter. "Afterward he told us he was amazed we'd actually sold out," recalls Spohr. "He said even rock concerts don't always sell out there."

From a diplomatic perspective, the visit was also a dazzling success. The Malaysian Prime Minister and several of his cabinet attended. As was widely reported, after seeing the RWB, the head of Malaysia's national oil company informed Manfred van Nostitz, Canada's High Commissioner: "If you can build pipelines like you can dance, we should talk business."

When the RWB reached Hong Kong, it was joined by a specially arranged tour party from Canada made up of company friends, relatives and board members. "For a while we became like a big family," says Spohr. The group arrived in time to see the RWB skilfully negotiate the small stage of a theatre outside the centre of the city. The company's planned stop in Shanghai, March 8 and 9, had to be moved to Hangzhou because of a hepatitis epidemic. In Beijing, the RWB road crew had to do their own backstage clean-up to bring facilities at the Temple of Heaven Theatre up to Canadian standards of hygiene. The heating was also less than adequate, far below what dancers normally demand. At the opening performance in Beijing, the dancers were stunned to hear a cacophony of camera clicks and whirs coming from the audience. In Hangzhou they endured the sounds of candy wrappers, people chatting and babies crying.

And so the RWB, the artistic vanguard of a major profile-raising Canadian mission, marched on, tired but relieved, towards the conclusion of perhaps its most memorable tour ever. Joe Clark, the External Affairs Minister in Brian Mulroney's Cabinet, wrote to RWB board president Joe Wilder to express Ottawa's official satisfaction. "I would wish to congratulate you, and through you, every member of the Company, not only on the undoubted artistic success of your tour, but also on your understanding of the needs of our missions abroad, and your constant readiness to work with them."

Aptly describing the RWB as a "tight little family of cultural commandos", Max Wyman summed up the impact of the Asian tour: "The company proved once again that when it comes to making new friends and earning new recognition for Canada, it has few equals."

Spohr told a reporter that the Asian tour was "a heavenly note" on which to finish a career. "The challenge was like Mount Everest and all of us together have conquered it. We have left our distinctive Canadian mark once again."

Spohr had not finished his duties yet. When the RWB returned home to Winnipeg, the company hardly had time to rest before it launched into *Giselle* again for its March performances. Spohr also had a final bonbon to add to the repertoire in May. It was Léonide Massine's frothy, frivolous Offenbach ballet, *Gaîté Parisienne*, created half a century earlier, the same year Gweneth Lloyd and Betty Farrally had arrived in Winnipeg.

The Winnipeg performances that May were Spohr's farewell as director. He still had one last duty to perform and, naturally, it involved getting on a plane. The company's final performances under Spohr's watch were on tour, at the National Arts Centre in Ottawa. The repertoire spanned almost four decades of Spohr's association with the RWB – *Ballet Premier*, *5 Tangos* and *The Big Top*, Jacques Lemay's popular 1986 circus ballet, intended by Spohr for family audiences. Spohr had included his own first ballet because, as he put it, "it's a good show-opener and it's classical". There were hugs and tears and flowers backstage after the closing May 15 performance. And that was it. Spohr was now a grandfather.

He submitted his final report as artistic director on May 26, 1988. Spohr scaled new heights of hyperbole in an exhaustive thank-you list from which scarcely a member of the company or board was omitted. He included the fourteen board presidents under whom he had served. Spohr spoke enthusiastically about the prospect of working in the school with his "expert, devoted, loyal friend, David Moroni". Spohr heaped praise on Henny Jurriens, the successor about whom he secretly harboured reservations and, perhaps imagining that rhetoric could overcome reality, blithely ignored simmering internal tensions to offer this extraordinary assessment: "The Royal Winnipeg Ballet is a family tree, overlapping, one in the heart of the other, keeping the life blood of the company, moving together in one total stream, active and alive."

No matter that a section of the board wanted Bill Riske's scalp, or that Jurriens, if not actively scalp-hunting, was planning to drop Moroni as associate director. Spohr rose above it all to float from the job he had occupied for thirty years on a cloud of idealistic optimism. "I did not feel I was leaving the RWB. I felt I would still be connected. I just felt that my time was finished for that chapter."

Death in the Family

13

Arnold Spohr claimed to be looking forward to a break. "People think I'm a workaholic, but I'm not really. I enjoy being lazy at times." Even so, resting on his laurels under a palm tree in Florida was not quite what Spohr had in mind for his retirement.

In all likelihood, he had no real concept of retirement. Spohr is not a man of hobbies. He does not play golf or bridge. He is single. His family circle of siblings had already begun to shrink, as the memorial stones in the Spohr family plot at Winnipeg's Elmwood Cemetery testified.

Richard, the second eldest, had died in 1983. Agnes followed in 1989, as did George Jr., although his remains were laid to rest in Calgary. Wally, the brother who had sought to bring order to Arnold's chaotic financial affairs, followed the next year. Despite the eighteen-year difference in their ages, Beatrice and Erica, who shared an apartment together, died within little more than a year of each other. Beatrice, who had bossed her younger siblings around and tugged Spohr's ears, passed on in 1992 and sister Erica the following year. Spohr hid whatever grief he felt from all but his most intimate friends. Work, for him, is the ultimate anodyne and antidote to nostalgic wallowing.

Spohr had often declared his belief in the importance of continuity and his intention to remain at the service of the RWB. It is improbable, however, that he completely grasped the fact that the RWB board, for better of worse, had decided the time for real change had arrived. For Spohr, meanwhile, it was unthinkable that he would not have a continuing role in the affairs of the company. Assurances to this effect had certainly been given him. He had an impressive title and an office in the new building. But what exactly was his role to be? "There was never a clear delineation of responsibility," concedes Rod Zimmer, who followed Joe Wilder as board president in 1989. Spohr's role was an issue most people preferred to avoid and one which has never been wholly resolved.

In fairness, a solution that would have satisfied both Spohr and the RWB was probably unattainable. Spohr was not the founder of the RWB, but his unique history with the company had given him the status of a quasi-founder. It was understandable that Spohr had come to see himself as the RWB's central motivating force and that the emotional ties that bound him to the company were unbreakable.

Spohr's fellow artistic directors at Canada's other two major ballet companies, both of them founding figures, had easier transitions. When Celia Franca left the National Ballet of Canada after almost a quarter century, she joined her husband in Ottawa and began a busy new life – teaching, lecturing and serving two terms on the board of the Canada Council. Her departure from the National Ballet was not without acrimony, but Franca nevertheless kept a generally benign watch over the company from afar. For several years she continued to appear with it as a guest character artist or would visit Toronto to rehearse her production of *The Nutcracker*. At much the same time, Ludmilla Chiriaeff, a mother of five, moved from her role as founding artistic director of Les Grands Ballets Canadiens to immerse herself in the development of its associated school. Both women had a life to go to.

Henny Jurriens had no illusions about how difficult the transition would be, either for himself or for Spohr. Jurriens knew that he had been chosen over David Moroni because, in part at least, the board wanted a fresh vision and a new way of doing things. Jurriens also understood that it would be nearly impossible to establish himself as the new artistic director with Spohr still around. It would be equally impossible to expect Spohr to remain in Winnipeg and at the same time to restrain himself from coming into the new building every day. Spohr was encouraged to leave town long enough for everyone at the RWB, dancers, staff and board, to absorb the almost unfathomable reality that a new regime had begun. "We had to cut Arnold clean," says John Condra, "so we could have an idea whether the new man was half decent or not. We tried to explain this to Arnold. Perhaps we tried to ride both horses, but in the end I don't think we could have done much more."

Jurriens already had ideas about what Spohr's future role might be, but first there had to be a breathing space. "Henny was aware of the magnitude of Arnold's personal power," says Evelyn Hart. "He knew he had to wean him from being the big boss. After thirty years, Arnold had got used to that." Jurriens was worried that Spohr would interpret this as rejection.

It is hard to imagine what it must have felt like for Arnold Spohr as he began a temporary exile at his condominium in Fort Lauderdale. Spohr was used to lengthy separations from the RWB, but always knew that a rehearsal studio full of dancers would be awaiting his return. Now he had no clear idea what the future would hold. Idleness, even after thirty years of hard work, was not a virtuous point on Spohr's morality compass. Therefore, when a friend in need telephoned him, Spohr jumped to help.

The friend was Marie Hale, a ballet teacher in West Palm Beach. She and her colleague Lynda Swiadon had established a school there in the late 1960's and from the school grew a non-professional performing ensemble, Ballet Florida, in 1973.

Hale first met Spohr in 1980 when the RWB was dancing in West Palm Beach. The RWB rehearsed in Ballet Florida's studios. Hale took the opportunity to give Spohr a bundle of background material about her company. "I did it without ever imagining Arnold would actually read it all, but he did and came back to check us out." Something about Hale's ambition to create a permanent professional company appealed to Spohr's pioneering spirit. So did Stephen Hyde.

Hyde was a student at Ballet Florida, a shy late-starter who showed real promise. "Later, when Arnold was visiting his condo in Fort Lauderdale," recalls Hale, "he would often come up to see how Stephen was progressing. Arnold wanted him for his company." Hiring Hyde, however, presented problems. Spohr did not want to offend Moroni by implying that there were no suitable candidates for the male corps available in the RWB's professional division school. Hale suggested, and Spohr agreed, that Hyde should come to Winnipeg for the summer school of 1982, so that Moroni could feel he had put his thumbprint on him. Hyde was reluctant, but eventually agreed. He was unable to stay for the full summer programme, but the time he spent studying under Moroni's direction gave Spohr the confidence to offer Hyde a contract without causing offence. Spohr's friendship with Hale and Swiadon continued, as did his occasional visits to their Florida school.

By 1986, Hale felt Ballet Florida was ready to become a professional troupe, but she had not anticipated how tough it would be to keep the operation afloat. In October, 1988, she called Spohr for advice. "I'm having such a struggle," she told him. "I don't know how we can keep things going." Spohr told Hale that he had been through his share of struggles and not to worry. He would come directly and help.

Spohr largely abandoned his Fort Lauderdale condominium and took up residence in West Palm Beach in a small apartment owned by Hale. She had made clear that her problems were on the business side, just trying to meet payroll. It soon became clear that Spohr's real interest was to get into the studio and do what he loved. "I was up against the wall and Arnold kept saying he'd help me in the office, but we just couldn't keep him out of the studio. He kept himself very busy all day long and everybody loved him." Hale paid Spohr only a token stipend. "I think what Arnold really needed was to feel useful. I believe he would probably have liked to get even more involved."

Ballet Florida was preparing for its first big production beyond its obligatory Christmas *Nutcracker*, a staging of *Coppélia* that Hale had assembled from various versions she remembered. Spohr agreed to perform the character role of the Burgomaster. "I remember he was so nervous," says Hale. "He was a wreck. I had to tell him which side he entered from." Had Spohr wished it, an exit unexpectedly opened up, one of a profoundly tragic nature.

On Sunday, April 9, 1989, the RWB's forty-year-old artistic director, Henny Jurriens, was travelling south from Winnipeg on Highway 75 towards Minneapolis. Judy, his thirty-six-year-old wife, was behind the wheel of their late model Mercury Sable. Their three-year-old daughter, Isa, was in the back seat. The Jurriens' destination was the Canadian Consulate, where they intended to complete the paperwork to acquire landed immigrant status, something they were obliged to do from outside Canada. Although road conditions were generally clear, there were patches of slush-covered ice. Near Lettelier, just a few miles before the United States border, the car hit one of the ice patches and skidded out of control into an oncoming vehicle. Henny and Judy Jurriens were pronounced dead at the scene of the accident. Little Isa miraculously survived the crash with a broken leg and minor bruises.

When the news reached Spohr in Florida, Hale immediately offered to replace him with an understudy in *Coppélia* so that he could return to Winnipeg. However, having made a commitment, Spohr decided to stay for the complete run of four performances. "This is one of the saddest moments that has happened to the company," Spohr told a reporter. "Henny was the ideal person for the company – he was good and generous and considerate and full of dreams."

When Spohr did return to Winnipeg, it was to find a company in deep mourning. Not only had the dancers lost Henny Jurriens. Earlier, on the same day that the Jurriens died, the RWB's co-founder, Betty Farrally, succumbed to a brain tumour in Kelowna at the age of seventy-three. For Spohr, Farrally was a vital link to his roots, a nurturing, vivacious, forthright woman to whom he could always turn for friendly advice. Spohr, who had known she was dying, had always been much closer to Farrally than to Lloyd. The two had worked together for many summers at The Banff Centre. "She was my chum," says Spohr.

Jurriens' death hit the RWB like a thunderbolt. The company was on tour when it happened. They had started the day in Calgary and were continuing by bus for a performance that night at The Banff Centre's Eric Harvie Theatre. Some knew of Farrally's death before they boarded the bus. The performance in Banff was dedicated to her. As the evening progressed there was a growing sense backstage that something was horribly wrong. Mark Porteous, the company manager, looked tense and ashen. After the show, the entire company was asked to meet in the theatre lobby. Porteous broke the terrible news.

Jorden Morris, a young RWB dancer at the time, remembers the moment vividly. "There was that silence of death as the wave of nausea washes into you and settles with growing intensity until you can't stop shaking. Then the tears and cries of forty-five crushed people." Another dancer, Gino Di Marco, was so distraught that he picked up a chair and hurled it across the lobby, swearing. A team of crisis therapists was waiting for the dancers at the hotel, as well as a doctor.

A day later, the RWB left Banff for its next tour stop, Edmonton. The dancers were determined to carry on, but in Edmonton they began breaking down. There were tears. There was anger. Latent personal animosities broke out into yelling matches. Rudi van Dantzig's deeply emotional *Four Last Songs* was on the Edmonton programme. As the curtain came down the audience was silent. Everyone knew about the tragedy. The cast burst into tears. As the curtain rose again the audience finally erupted into applause. The dancers on stage cried even more, as did an unobserved gathering of fellow dancers, crew, wardrobe staff and others, huddled in the wings.

• • •

Much as he acknowledged the personal tragedy of Jurriens' death, Spohr's private attitude was not quite in accord with his fulsome public statements. He moved on quickly from the horror of the event to worry about its implications for the RWB. As Spohr confided, he felt that Jurriens had been moving the company too quickly in new directions and that what it needed was to stay in touch with its roots. Jurriens' decision to dispense with Moroni's services as associate artistic director had also upset Spohr. He believed he had successfully brokered a lasting truce between the rivals. Spohr may possibly have viewed Moroni's continued involvement as security for his own future with the company.

The RWB's immediate concern was who should lead the company in the interim. With the company's morale in tatters, some healing had to begin. Bill Riske had already flown out to Banff to assure the dancers that until further notice Jurriens' chosen team – André Lewis, Alla Savchenko and Cathy Taylor – would assume the artistic direction, working as a triad.

Spohr hoped to be invited back to provide stability and leadership. Rumours to that effect even found their way into print. Spohr conceived of a situation in which he could assume the kind of advisory role he had had in mind in 1978. This time, Spohr saw himself playing mentor/guide to Moroni, possibly teamed with André Lewis. Spohr was dreaming. Apart from the fact that neither man would have been likely to co-operate in such a plan, the RWB board had made the break with the Spohr era and was determined to forge a new future. "We all recognized that Arnold had done a wonderful job running the company," explains Joe Wilder, the then board president, "but everyone had agreed that it was time for him to leave. Yes, I think he would have liked to come back, but there was a feeling that his day had come and gone." At an April 13 meeting the executive committee of the board discussed the matter in some depth. It was pointed out that Jurriens had had great confidence in Lewis and intended to promote him to the position of an assistant, or even associate artistic director, in the 1989/90 season. The executive committee concluded, therefore, that for the time being the current artistic team would continue, "revolving around André Lewis as a focal point." Lewis, it was noted, "could seek the assistance of the Artistic Director Emeritus as and when necessary." Lewis had effectively been made interim director, but room was also left for Spohr to play a role.

Lewis felt confident that he and his colleagues in the artistic department were best placed to continue running affairs in accord with Jurriens' vision. Lewis did not relish potential interference. Spohr denies any intention on his part to resume full control of the company, but there was enough confusion about who was in charge for the matter to be raised at a subsequent meeting of the executive, attended by Lewis and Riske. It was finally agreed after lengthy discussion that Spohr would be appointed artistic advisor on a temporary basis, "with clearly defined parameters of involvement limited to consultation re casting changes and perhaps programming." Lewis and Riske were told to meet with Spohr to discuss the arrangements. At a May 29 executive meeting, Riske reported that the meeting with Spohr had been productive "in clarifying the role Mr. Spohr wants to play and how this fits in with the organization at this time." Spohr would be taking "a specific interest" in plans for the upcoming fiftieth anniversary gala in the fall, as well as planning alumni events scheduled for early October. Spohr had requested a $25,000 honorarium for his continuing services up to Christmas, 1989, and Riske was instructed to draft a letter of agreement to that effect. The minutes noted, in a cryptic but slightly ominous tone: "At this time, no difficulties are foreseen in having Mr. Spohr act as Artistic Advisor." Meanwhile, the search for a new, permanent director began in earnest and a further $25,000 payment was authorized for the services of a professional headhunter.

Once again, David Moroni was among the applicants and once again Spohr went to bat for him, but to no avail. The board had already ruled out Moroni as a suitable candidate and was inclined to believe that someone from outside the RWB would be best suited to carry the company forward.

Their choice was the thirty-nine-year-old Australian, John

Meehan. As a dancer Meehan had impeccable credentials, was widely liked for his genial personality and was well connected to the leading figures of the ballet world. The RWB was, however, Meehan's first artistic directorship. Before he arrived early in 1990, the RWB was struck by another family tragedy.

David Peregrine had become an enthusiastic and skilled pilot. On June 12, 1989, he was flying on a vacation trip to Alaska when his plane crashed into Mount Deborah, about ninety-five kilometres south of Fairbanks. Peregrine and his party, including Meirig, the youngest of his three brothers, all died. David Peregrine was thirty-four.

Peregrine's position within the RWB had evolved considerably since 1980 when he and Hart had returned from Varna as budding stars. Their two careers had gradually diverged. Peregrine, with his savvy business sense and independent, practical approach to life, had begun to seek opportunities elsewhere, performing with the San Francisco Ballet and Boston Ballet. He had even branched out into acting. Peregrine played the role of Smike in the Manitoba Theatre Centre's Nicholas Nickleby in the 1982/83 season. MTC's artistic director, Richard Ouzounian, created the production. He was unsure how Spohr would react to the idea of giving Peregrine a leave from his RWB duties. "I was a little nervous when I went to Arnold's office, but before I'd got all the way through explaining why I wanted David, Arnold said he thought it was a wonderful idea and would help David grow as a dancer. Arnold always had this sense that the arts organizations in Winnipeg should help each other and work together."

Peregrine was a big success as Smike. Spohr was there on opening night to lead the ovation. "He could not have been more generous and helpful," says Ouzounian. Peregrine returned to MTC and the month before his death appeared to critical acclaim in the company's production of Frankenstein: Playing with Fire. Although Peregrine's future relationship with the RWB appeared uncertain, his tragically premature death was yet another blow to the RWB's already shaken morale.

Spohr found escape from the emotional pain of all this by immersing himself in his new duties. With the company's fiftieth anniversary season approaching, he set about contacting as many former members as he could, to ensure a well-attended reunion. The task was made easier by the fact that many former dancers, even some who had left disgruntled, still felt an unbreakable attachment to the RWB because of their affection for Spohr. If they came for a reunion it would be as much for Spohr's sake as for that of the institution.

Spohr's efforts were rewarded and the gathering was so successful that it was decided to establish a formal RWB Alumni Association. Margaret Piasecki, a dancing colleague of Spohr's in the early days when she was still Margaret Hample, says the University of Manitoba's Alumni Association provided a model. A simple constitution was drawn up and Spohr's "list", a polite description of his unorthodox approach to data storage, became the basis of the first round of prospecting calls to attract members. Spohr was soon made honorary chairman of the Association. "He has always been the primary draw," says Piasecki. Spohr undertook to recruit members and would carry out this duty wherever he happened to be travelling. "You can look back," Piasecki says, "and see the membership grow or shrink according to how active Arnold has been."

The core Winnipeg membership of the Alumni Association has also become involved in preserving the company's history, trying to bring order and logic to the rather haphazard way in which the RWB archives had previously been managed. Every Monday, a group of alumni gather in a small, unventilated storage room at RWB headquarters to sort and file material, most of it destined for the Manitoba Archives. The Association also publishes a quarterly news-letter, to which Spohr contributes a regular column. His columns have become collectors' items.

Spohr's missionary work among former RWB members was often conducted during the numerous out-of-town teaching and coaching engagements he accepted after his retirement. Sometimes Spohr would complain that people asked too much of him, but he still found invitations hard to refuse and fresh challenges irresistible.

John Meehan's arrival in Winnipeg, at least officially, did not change Spohr's position within the company. From 1990 until May 1996, Spohr was billed in RWB house programmes both as Artistic Director Emeritus and as Artistic Advisor. Part of the board's original reluctance to accord Spohr a specific role beyond retirement was because it wanted to avoid placing even a perceived restraint on a new artistic director. Yet, Meehan clearly recalls being told by the board "to keep Arnold Spohr". Meehan was not given any specific directives beyond that. "It was hard for me to understand," says

Meehan, "but everyone seemed to react to Arnold in such a primal way."

Had Henny Jurriens lived to make good his intention of finding a place for Spohr, it might well have resembled what in fact transpired under his two successors. Both Meehan, who remained artistic director until 1993, and William Whitener, who occupied the post from then until 1995, were able to establish comfortable working relations with Spohr. Neither man found him intrusive.

Meehan had first met Spohr during the RWB's 1972 tour of Australia. Meehan was then a second-year corps member in The Australian Ballet. "I remember being impressed. There was an authenticity about Arnold. You felt he was the real thing. He was so filled with energy and enthusiasm in an almost childlike way." At the time, Meehan mentioned to Spohr that he was interested in choreography. Later, Spohr wrote him a short letter, something to the effect that if Meehan ever had an idea for a ballet, to let him know. As ever, Spohr was on the alert for fresh talent. After Australia, their paths scarcely crossed until Meehan arrived in Winnipeg.

Once installed as the new artistic director, Meehan was confronted with a confusing set of challenges. Unlike Jurriens, he was the first total outsider to direct the RWB since Benjamin Harkarvy in 1957. Meehan sensed that people were distrustful of him. "Winnipeg," says Meehan, "is not an easy place for outsiders." The fact that the RWB had been robbed of Henny Jurriens in such a violent, sudden way also created problems. "I found a company that was still in mourning, that felt a great deal of anger," says Meehan. In addition to his sense that the company distrusted him, Meehan had trouble getting along with André Lewis. "André had seen his future alongside Henny and could not let go of that. It was very difficult for him to accept my suggestions."

There was also the RWB board of directors to contend with. Meehan assumed that he had been hired to direct the company. He was not familiar with the unusual Winnipeg model of board involvement. "They tried to put a production committee on me, but it was short-lived." Added to this was Meehan's concern that the RWB was in the midst of an identity crisis. To Meehan it seemed as if he had been handed not one but two companies to direct. "There was the RWB that the board understood, the company that performed big full-length works with some mixed rep in Winnipeg. Then there was the RWB as the rest of the world saw us, a road company that performed mixed bills; all of it complicated and in a way compromised by the presence of Evelyn."

Meehan was also immediately caught in the middle of a difficult political situation involving Bill Riske, the general manager. "When I got to Winnipeg, I was courted by two different factions of the board. One was actively trying to get rid of Bill, the other to protect him." It did not take Meehan long to form his own opinion. He found it impossible to work with Riske. "He wouldn't communicate. It was as if he was building walls around himself." Unlike Spohr, Meehan wanted to participate in the full budget process, something Riske found hard to accept.

Spohr's nebulous role in the RWB was the least of Meehan's problems. For one thing Spohr was not a continual presence. "His schedule was erratic," says Meehan. "He always seemed to have a lot going on." Meehan took Spohr's title as Artistic Advisor literally and assumed that when advice was to be dispensed it would be at his rather than Spohr's instigation. Spohr might have liked ready access to rehearsals, but Meehan made it clear that his presence was not welcome unless by invitation. Meehan, however, would on occasion solicit Spohr's advice regarding casting and repertoire and found his comments valuable. "Arnold had a way of sneaking in his opinions, but always in a friendly and respectful way. I like to think that we had a good relationship."

Meehan had vowed to respect the RWB's tradition of presenting a varied repertoire. Dramatic ballets by Antony Tudor, Frederick Ashton and Agnes de Mille kept company with avant-garde contemporary works by company dancer Mark Godden. Meehan appointed Godden as the RWB's resident choreographer and nurtured his development. Meehan also decided to extend the RWB's repertoire of full-length ballets by staging a brand new *Don Quixote* in the 1992/93 season, a proposal that precipitated a final showdown with Riske.

The board was confronted with a choice between Riske and Meehan. It decided to hold on to Meehan. Riske, the longest-serving general manager in the company's history, was out. Reports at the time depicted Riske's departure as the dramatic finale of an epic battle of egos, but Meehan insists it was far more complex. "It had all started long before I got to Winnipeg and it was much more than a 'me or him' situation." Riske had been an honest and hard-working manager with a deep sense of loyalty to the RWB, but even Kathleen Richardson, one of his staunchest supporters, concedes that Riske often lacked diplomacy and could antagonize board members.

Looking back on her many years working with Riske, Lendre Rodgers Kearns observes: "Bill had an incredibly passionate commitment to the RWB, an unswerving dedication and loyalty. But he was socially inept. He was not a good conversationalist and he tended to isolate himself."

The battle between Meehan and Riske was played out against a rapidly worsening economic backdrop, a deepening recession that had a serious impact on many performing arts institutions across North America. As the RWB watched its accumulated deficit head towards $1 million, the plans for a *Don Quixote* were dropped and Meehan was becoming increasingly miserable. He felt personally isolated in Canada's prairie capital with its brutal winters. "Winnipeg is a lot more remote than it appears," Meehan ruefully observed.

On December 10, 1992, Meehan announced he would be quitting as soon as a replacement could be found. "It was a really complicated issue," Meehan reflects. "It wasn't just the cancellation of *Don Quixote*. It was a question of do I dig in and fight more battles, or just move on."

Meehan's last contribution to the RWB was a new staging of the full-length *Sleeping Beauty*, unveiled on October 28, 1993, with sets and costumes, rented for the sake of economy, from Ballet West in Salt Lake City. Three days after the premiere, Meehan passed the baton to his successor, William Whitener, and moved back to New York where he now directs American Ballet Theatre's young farm-team, the ABT Studio Company. In hindsight, Spohr views Meehan's departure as a major loss for the RWB. "Of all of them," he confides, "I think John was the one who could really have done something if he'd stuck at it."

The board once again had to decide whether to promote from within or entrust the direction to another outsider. André Lewis was an obvious inside contender. Moroni, twice rejected for the post, was not totally out of the running. Meehan recalls the board asking him which of the two he thought might make a better director. Meehan said that Moroni would offer a stronger artistic vision.

In appointing Bill Whitener the company made a surprising but not implausible choice. Whitener's artistic background straddled the worlds of classical ballet and contemporary dance. He had been reared at The Joffrey Ballet, a company whose repertoire and persona, particularly in its early years, were not dissimilar from the RWB's. Whitener left The Joffrey in 1979 to spend the final decade of his dancing career with modern dance choreographer Twyla Tharp. Whitener had also worked on Broadway, before becoming artistic director of Montreal's Les Ballets Jazz in the spring of 1992.

Spohr was initially alarmed by Whitener's appointment. Like many others he associated Whitener with contemporary dance and feared the consequences for the RWB's classical repertoire. Prompted by his friends, Whitener made a priority of meeting and reassuring Spohr. He understood Spohr's devotion to the RWB and respected his natural concerns for its future. It was not unlike the situation Whitener had experienced in Montreal, where Geneviève Salbaing, co-founder of Les Ballets Jazz, was still a vocal presence in the company's affairs.

As had been the case with Meehan, the board never told Whitener that Spohr was to be given specific functions. Their relationship was to be worked out on its own terms and from Whitener's perspective it worked out well. "It's almost impossible not to like Arnold. Two of his dancers, Bonnie Wyckoff and Tony Williams, were friends of mine at The Joffrey, so in a way I'd already got to know him through their eyes. I knew about the company and its wonderful repertoire."

Whitener's vision for the RWB was, in his mind, not unlike Spohr's. His goal was to build a mixed repertoire that covered a range of styles and eras and that had strong theatrical appeal. "I've always believed that it's possible to find a repertoire where the classical and contemporary can co-exist," says Whitener. "Arnold and I would talk about the face of the company at length. I think he agreed that for the RWB to make an impact, it had to do things that were bold and contemporary, just as he had done. But there was still a debate about our full-lengths and it was a fine line knowing how to balance the rep."

In many respects, Spohr reminded Whitener of Robert Joffrey, his first mentor. "I think they were cut from the same cloth. I recognized in Arnold that same insatiable curiosity about choreography. Arnold had this uncanny ability to find the heart of a ballet very quickly. He would find the essence of the work and hold on to it very strongly."

When Whitener introduced Twyla Tharp's "crossover" ballet, *Deuce Coupe*, to the repertoire Spohr was not enthusiastic. Spohr had never been a great fan of Tharp's choreography, but was still prepared to learn. Whitener brought in Rose Marie Wright, his former colleague at the Tharp company, to stage the ballet and Spohr sat in on rehearsals. "He watched so intently," Whitener recalls. "He really was making an effort to understand what Twyla is all about."

Whitener always found Spohr helpful and supportive. "I felt he was with me a hundred per cent, the whole time. I could rely on his wisdom. He loved being part of the team and he was included in the team." Whitener was happy that Spohr gave private coaching sessions to the company apprentices. "It was a project Arnold took on because he understood I didn't have enough time to spend with career entry-level dancers." Spohr never hesitated to express his opinions, but he always made sure Whitener had time to listen. "You'll tell me if I'm in the way," Spohr would say.

The only advice Spohr was unable to offer Whitener was how to save his job as artistic director. Faced with the difficult task of directing a company that was bleeding red ink, Whitener also had to contend with dancer unrest and the board's wariness of his artistic vision. Whitener was concerned that the company had lost its identity. "The RWB trademark had been very strong. If you stray too far from a formula that works, you confuse the identity of the company. The question facing us was how to grow without smudging that identity."

Spohr gave Whitener two ceramic theatre masks. "Sometimes one must wear a mask," he told the embattled director. "Arnold understood the necessity to move forward," says Whitener. "Don't show your emotions, he implied. Put the mask on and conduct your business. So I chose to ignore a lot of the backroom politics." This did not help. The knives had been out for Whitener from his first day. Jeffrey Bentley, the executive director who had succeeded Riske and who had been influential in the hiring of Whitener, was unable to save him. It took until November, 1995, for the knives to find their mark. Whitener was sent packing. Within a year, he was appointed artistic director of the State Ballet of Missouri, which he still heads under its new name, Kansas City Ballet. As in Winnipeg, Whitener inherited a resident Artistic Director Emeritus, Todd Bolender. Whitener's experience working with Arnold Spohr made it all seem very natural. Bentley soon left for Pacific Northwest Ballet in Seattle and from there rejoined Whitener at Kansas City Ballet in 1998.

Six years, three artistic directors and a crippling deficit; where would the RWB turn next? The immediate solution was easy. André Lewis knew the ropes. He had been a capable helmsman in the traumatic wake of Henny Jurriens' death. Meehan had appointed Lewis as his associate director in 1990. So, for the second time, Lewis was duly appointed interim artistic director. Spohr appeared pleased. Finally the RWB had turned to one of its own, just as it had in time of crisis almost four decades before. The moment had come to get the RWB back on course and Spohr would be standing by to help. But would the board take the next step and make Lewis the captain? If the board conducted a search for a new artistic director, it kept remarkably quiet about the fact. The board, seemingly, had also had enough of outsiders. André Lewis' appointment as artistic director was announced in March, 1996, just a couple of months after his forty-first birthday.

Lewis, from Hull, Quebec, had come to Winnipeg in 1975 to study under David Moroni in the RWB school. Lewis had danced his way up through the company ranks under Spohr's tutelage and eventually became his very able assistant. Spohr was looking forward to helping Lewis. He was therefore disappointed when, in 1996, Lewis told Spohr he felt no need of an artistic advisor. Initially the two would chat, but Lewis found it increasingly burdensome to deal with what he saw as Spohr's inability to focus his thoughts. "In practical terms there's really a limit to what I can give Arnold in the way of coaching and rehearsal," says Lewis. "It's hard to make him understand how much circumstances have changed for ballet in general and for the RWB in particular; the difficulty of arranging and financing tours, the competition from other companies."

Spohr still had his office and honorary title of Artistic Director Emeritus, but his urge to be closely involved with the RWB was now checked. However, if the RWB saw no special use for Spohr, there were others who did. There always had been.

14

The
Honorary Cajun

In the spring of 1991, Arnold Spohr's life reconnected in an unexpected way with Rachel Browne, one of his former dancers from the early days. Browne had remained with the Royal Winnipeg Ballet after Benjamin Harkarvy left in 1958. Browne danced for Spohr until 1961. She left to raise a family, but dance was still in her blood and she was soon teaching in the studio of former RWB ballet master Nenad Lhotka. By 1964, Browne had begun to choreograph and formed a small performing group, Contemporary Dancers.

Spohr was supportive of Browne's efforts. He offered advice. He sometimes watched rehearsals. With Spohr's blessing, Browne invited such RWB choreographers as Robert Moulton and James Clouser to work with her company. From Spohr's example, Browne learned important lessons about how to direct and rehearse a company. She was less successful than Spohr in learning how to keep her job.

Browne's company flourished. Winnipeg's Contemporary Dancers became fully professional in 1970 and began to tour. Browne opened an associated school in 1973. By the time things turned bad for Rachel Browne in 1982, Spohr had already gone through his crisis of leadership at the RWB. In the early 1980's, Browne's concept of a modern dance repertory company began to look outmoded and her own choreography came under fire. Just as some of Spohr's dancers had looked for a new sense of direction in 1979, Browne, too, was confronted with a palace revolt in late 1982. Spohr's board of directors had stood behind him. Browne's board fired her.

It was a traumatic experience. As Browne admits: "You have no idea how hard it is to let go." Browne, however, bounced back. She never returned to her old job, but she did manage to negotiate a not always easy agreement that allowed her to feel connected to Contemporary Dancers. In 1990, the company was again looking for an artistic director and appointed Charles Moulton, the son of choreographer Robert Moulton.

Charlie Moulton had danced with the company under Browne's direction. He was brimming over with charm and fresh ideas. The company's board of directors was confident that Moulton could put a fresh face on Contemporary Dancers. Moulton inherited a company that during the previous six years had very much been groomed and molded around the choreographic vision of artistic director Tedd Robinson. From Moulton's perspective he needed to make radical changes in order to establish his own vision.

The vehemence with which Moulton wielded his new broom astounded and alienated many of the company's dancers and supporters. He seemed bent on expunging all evidence of its past, even to the extent of attempting to sweep Browne into the trashcan of history. Before Moulton succeeded, the company itself had been pushed to the brink of financial collapse. *What Is Love?*, the show Moulton staged at Winnipeg's Walker Theatre, exhausted whatever tolerance remained for his new ideas. By the spring of 1991, Moulton was gone.

Browne was persuaded by a new group of board members to help save Contemporary Dancers. No one recalls clearly whose idea it was to invite Arnold Spohr to participate in the salvage effort. Richard Irish, who by then had become chairman of Contemporary Dancers' much-depleted board, says the government funding agencies were pressing the company to appoint a new artistic director. Spohr's name, says Irish, may have come up in discussions with the Manitoba Arts Council as someone who could help. Browne says the suggestion certainly did not come from her. In fact, she was both surprised and anxious when the "new board gang" told her that Spohr had accepted a position as interim artistic advisor.

From the outside it indeed appeared to be an odd marriage – a former ballet director working with a modern dance troupe. However, it made practical good sense to Contemporary Dancers' board. Moulton had left a poisonous legacy of public ill will, both towards the company and the cause of modern dance in Winnipeg. The ultimate ignominy had been the troupe's forced withdrawal from the Winnipeg Dance Festival that summer. Apart from having the benefit of Spohr's artistic vision, attaching his respected name to the reconstruction effort, so it was surmised, would help restore public confidence. Spohr also had rich experience in surviving crises.

As usual, Spohr was juggling several balls at the same time, personal and professional, and was not in good health. Nevertheless, he plunged into the fray with almost alarming gusto – in part out of loyalty to Browne. Although they are very different people, Spohr must have empathized with her predicament – first rudely ejected, then forced to watch her company founder from the sidelines. Despite his strong allegiance to the RWB, Spohr regarded any dance activity in Winnipeg as worth supporting. There must also have been a degree of personal gratification in being acknowledged as the man who could help put things right.

Despite Browne's original misgivings, she acknowledges that Spohr played an important and positive role in keeping Winnipeg's Contemporary Dancers alive. The process, however, was far from smooth. Irish admits that Spohr and the company's board sometimes clashed. Spohr was confident that he knew what needed to be done and proceeded to do it. "It's all part of who he is," reflects Browne, "this expansive, excitable, extremely capable person who just takes over."

Spohr consulted widely and spoke with Ruth Cansfield and Gaile Petursson-Hiley, two former members of Contemporary Dancers who had left in 1989 to form their own company, Dance Collective. "I think he wanted to unite the forces," observes Browne. Ruth Cansfield recalls her meeting with Spohr. "He has this passion for Winnipeg dance. He sees it all as connected. I think he wanted to draw me back into the fold, but Gaile and I had already moved on."

Petursson-Hiley knew Spohr from her days as a student at the RWB. She admired him greatly, cherished her memories of the times he would rehearse the school and was impressed that he would channel his energies into the rebirth of Contemporary Dancers. Spohr never made a direct offer to Cansfield and Petursson-Hiley, but it was clear to them that in his mind they would be ideal candidates to lead the company. "He has a strong sense of roots, of building from within the community, and because of our background in Contemporary Dancers he probably saw us as providing continuity." Petursson-

Hiley remembers board members inquiring if Spohr had made an offer to her and Cansfield.

For Spohr, it was also essential to keep the colours flying in order to reassure everyone that Contemporary Dancers was still in business. While the board undertook the difficult tasks of raising funds and finding a new artistic director, Spohr did what he knows best. He put on a show. He reserved the RWB's 150-seat performance space, the Founders' Studio, for three evenings in October, 1991. He hired dancers and programmed an evening under the title "Synergy" that was to include an eclectic mix of choreography.

While Spohr was moving ahead, someone suggested that Tom Stroud might also be able to assist the reconstruction efforts. Hamilton-born Stroud, then thirty-seven, had been a latecomer to dance, but by 1991 he had accumulated broad experience as a dancer with several Canadian contemporary troupes. He was also a choreographer. Stroud was in New York when he got a call from Spohr asking if he might be able "to do a ballet" for the October performances. Stroud told Spohr he did not "do ballets", to which Spohr's quick response was, "Who cares? It's all dance." Stroud was eventually persuaded to come to Winnipeg, his first visit, in a vaguely defined, consultative role. The board may have already targeted Stroud as the most promising candidate for the directorship, but that was not his understanding.

Spohr met Stroud at the airport and brought him to his office at the RWB for a meeting with Cansfield and Petursson-Hiley, part of his effort to rally the Winnipeg dance community behind the cause of Contemporary Dancers. Stroud soon discovered that the company's financial situation was even worse than expected. He urged the board to appoint a new director as soon as possible and even gave Irish a list of eligible candidates. Somehow, his name kept bouncing back. Both Browne and Spohr were included in the selection process. Browne's recollection is that it took time before Spohr was convinced that Stroud was the right candidate. The offer was finally made and Stroud agreed to take the job, effective September 1, 1991.

Contemporary Dancers now had a new artistic director with his own vision of the future, as well as an artistic advisor who already had the bit between his teeth and was running fast. It was an inherently problematic situation, but Stroud says Spohr worked through it with considerable grace and sensitivity. "As soon as I was in place, he completely turned the company over to me, deferred to my decisions and was very supportive."

The October performances that Spohr produced went ahead as planned. The first night was a benefit event, attended by many of his friends and admirers. Before it took place, Spohr had suffered a mild heart attack and was in hospital. "I remember Arnold wanted it all kept quiet," says Stroud. "He didn't want people to worry. I was so busy I didn't even get a chance to visit him, but I heard he was on the phone all day from his hospital bed, trying to sell tickets to the show."

Spohr's telemarketing assault paid off. The programme was a classic Spohr mix that incorporated works by two of Contemporary Dancers' former directors, Browne and Robinson, as well as work by Stroud. There was also a contemporary ballet by the Montreal-based Argentinean choreographer, Mauricio Wainrot, along with a work by former company dancer Bruce Mitchell and a pas de deux performed by two RWB dancers. The performances sold out. They did not solve Contemporary Dancers' financial problems, but did confirm that the company was not about to vanish.

Spohr may have expected a longer involvement with Contemporary Dancers. Those close to him suggest he emerged from the experience with a faint sense of having been used. "Arnold was putting his heart and soul into it, and it had been really stressful for him," says Petursson-Hiley. "He had so many ideas for the company and then he was somehow cut out of it." As far as Stroud recalls, Spohr receded gracefully from the scene but still showed his continuing interest by attending performances and offering encouragement. "He would stay in touch, send cards and little gifts just to show he was thinking of us."

Spohr's health problems took an alarming turn the following summer in South Carolina. William Starrett, one of Spohr's dancers from the mid-1970's, had become artistic director of Columbia City Ballet in 1985. The two had stayed in touch through the years and Starrett still remembers the advice Spohr gave. "He told me my job as artistic director was to inspire everyone – dancers, staff, board, patrons. It's only when I had to do it myself that I understood much better what Mr. Spohr had achieved."

When Starrett launched an intensive training programme called The South Carolina Summer Dance Institute, he began inviting Spohr to teach and coach. "As usual, Mr. Spohr was overdoing it," Starrett recalls. "It was hot and we just could not slow him down. Finally we had to ban him from the studio." It was too much for Spohr. Suffering from chest pains and shortness of breath, he was taken to hospital. He had had a mild heart attack and required an angioplasty to correct the coronary blockage. "He gave us a very big scare," says Starrett. Spohr refused to let his heart condition slow him down and in 1993 took on the biggest commitment of his post-RWB career. He became associate director of Ballet Jörgen in Toronto.

Ballet Jörgen's founder and artistic director, Bengt Jörgen, was born in Stockholm in 1963. He trained at the Royal Swedish Ballet School and later at the National Ballet School in Toronto. In 1982, Jörgen auditioned for the RWB, a company he found more interesting than the National Ballet. Spohr declined to give him a contract. "I think he was very loyal to the RWB school," says Jörgen, "and wanted to hire from his own sphere." Jörgen stayed in Toronto but only lasted long enough in the National Ballet to create two promising pieces for company choreographic workshops. He quit in 1986 and the following year took the bold step of founding his own company. It was Jörgen's practical solution to the problem of finding an outlet for his work. Initially, the new company appeared to be little more than a platform for Jörgen's ballets. Soon, however, he developed the troupe into a showcase for other emerging choreographers.

His initial meeting with Spohr in 1982 had impressed Jörgen. "I just had this good feeling about him." In 1988, Jörgen asked Spohr if he would act as artistic advisor to the company on an ad hoc basis. Spohr accepted and attended Ballet Jörgen performances when he was in Toronto. In 1992, Ballet Jörgen appeared at the Gas Station Theatre in Winnipeg. It was the company's first performance outside Ontario. As usual Spohr was there and offered Jörgen encouraging comments. Spohr said he was very enthusiastic about the young company's progress, he saw it going places and said he would be interested in becoming more closely involved. Jörgen and his wife, the former dancer Susan Bodie, were delighted by Spohr's proposal. "We never thought of the idea," says Bodie, "because we assumed Arnold had retired."

The problem was how to finance a new position. Jörgen and Bodie put in a grant application for seed money to a Winnipeg philanthropic foundation. Those who receive grants from the foundation are specifically required not to acknowledge the fact publicly. In 1993, the foundation gave Ballet Jörgen a three-year grant, enough to create the position of associate director for Spohr and to hire the company's first administrative assistant. Until then Bodie had carried the administrative burden alone.

Spohr has always enjoyed Toronto and has many friends there. The prospects of spending more time in the city and of having a ballet company to nurture held strong appeal. In his initial years as associate director, Spohr spent three months a year with Ballet Jörgen. By the late 1990's he scaled back his annual visits to three or four weeks.

When Spohr's appointment was first announced, some people assumed it was merely titular, a smart move on Ballet Jörgen's part to enhance its credibility and image. In fact, from the start the relationship was very much a hands-on arrangement. "He brought a sense of stability in helping us believe in ourselves when times were tough," says Jörgen. "He made us feel comfortable about our roots and his emphasis was always on quality."

The results of Spohr's involvement were quick to show. By the end of his first year with Ballet Jörgen the company's dancing was notably sharper, more musical and communicative. The performances were altogether more stylish and polished. Once again, "the Spohr touch" had worked its magic.

"As he told us," says Jörgen, "you do it right or you don't do it at all. There's an intuitive creativeness he brings to coaching my own choreography that I've never felt interfered. He works from the interpretive side. When you're creating something, he'll sit through rehearsals for hours and hours when most people would fall asleep. And he remembers it all. He gets to know the feeling you want and then he'll keep drilling it into the dancers. It can be frustrating for them at times. Dancers are impatient. You have to learn to work with Arnold. It's a skill, but he'll get you there if you participate fully and in the end you'll feel really good about it."

Although Spohr's major activity was in the studio coaching dancers, he also served as a mentor to Jörgen. "He worked very hard with me on the concept of programming and other aspects of artistic direction, drawing from his own experience." Despite the almost forty-year age difference, Spohr was also sensitive to Jörgen's position as artistic director. "It has all seemed very natural," says Jörgen. "I think at times we may have taken him a bit for granted. Arnold is easily hurt. He needs and deserves appreciation; just little things done for him, little caring things."

As Spohr's visits became shorter and less frequent, Bengt Jörgen felt the need to introduce another experienced outside eye, Linda Stearns. Stearns spent most of her career with Les Grands Ballets Canadiens as dancer, ballet mistress and finally artistic director. In 2000, Stearns worked alongside Spohr at Ballet Jörgen and was astonished. "I've worked with many of the greatest but with Arnold it's like sitting at the feet of a master. What he sees in a dancer, what he brings out, his eye for detail – it's utterly extraordinary."

Spohr's outside activities did not replace his urge to remain connected to the RWB. If anything they increased it. The revival of his private teaching career made him all the more eager to contribute to the development of the RWB school. By his retirement, Spohr believed that he had reached a pedagogical point where he had finally assembled the knowledge gained from a lifetime of study into an understanding of the fundamental bedrocks of classical technique. Like Audrey de Vos, among the earliest guest teachers he brought to the RWB, Spohr believes in getting the fundamentals right. Body placement is for him the key, which, if not instilled correctly, will always prevent dancers from achieving their full potential.

In Spohr's mind everything can be improved and the doors to new ideas should always be open. He felt a need to pass on his own insights and believed these could benefit the RWB school. Spohr thought the instruction in the school needed rethinking and believed he had the knowledge to help. David Moroni had become very protective of the school and did not welcome potentially disruptive encroachments, particularly from someone who is unused to accepting a subordinate position and thinks he alone knows the right way. "David told me I'd demoralize his teachers," says Spohr.

Moroni had a rather different viewpoint. He sympathized with Spohr's personal need to feel involved, but saw no effective way to integrate him into the RWB school. "It just would not have worked," says Moroni. "I adore Arnold. He's been like a dad to me, but the fact is he's not a good teacher in the conventional sense." Moroni did find some classes for Spohr to teach in the general school. However, Moroni says that Spohr, with the many distractions in his life and his recurrent health problems, became unreliable. Spohr's relations with Moroni, once so close and warm, became cool enough to make a polar bear shiver.

Despite feeling "shut out" from the RWB school, Spohr has continued to find enormous gratification in helping dancers, both inside and outside the RWB, whenever the need and opportunity presents itself. Over the years, company dancers have come to him on an informal basis for intensive help on points of technique and interpretation. Spohr has also happily taken on many aspiring young professional dancers who need special attention, often using his vast list of contacts to direct them towards career opportunities.

Spohr considers Brandon Downs, an RWB member from 1994 to 1998, one of his earliest "special projects" and also a guinea pig. He effectively took Downs apart and put him back together again. Downs' subsequent emergence as an elegant, naturally expressive dancer confirmed Spohr's confidence in his own ability to unlock previously hidden talent.

Once Spohr knew he had the key, he was willing to share his knowledge with whomever needed it. In the summer of 1996, for example, he was introduced to David Zurak, a very late starter in dance with a degree in engineering from Hamilton's McMaster University. Zurak explained that after intensive study at the National Ballet School, he still had a number of unresolved technical problems. Zurak had no great urge to become a ballet dancer and had also been training for three years in modern dance at the School of Toronto Dance Theatre. What Zurak wanted was a sufficient classical foundation to equip him to become a versatile contemporary dancer. That was enough for Spohr. He immediately offered to help and invited Zurak to come that fall to study with him in Winnipeg. Spohr even found him a place to stay.

With the forgivable arrogance of youth, Zurak expected Spohr to be locked into the teaching theories of an earlier generation. Instead, to his surprise, he discovered that Spohr was knowledgeable about contemporary approaches to the training and conditioning of the dancer's body. "His private coaching provided a nourishing, supportive atmosphere," says Zurak, who went on to a successful career as a modern dancer in Montreal and then New York. Even in the mid-1990's, Spohr was still a poker and a prodder. "He'd keep telling me that my sternum was my jewel and so I must show it," says Zurak. "I think he'd heard it way back from Erik Bruhn or someone. Then he'd hit you to make his point and it really hurt. He just gets so carried away."

Only in rare moments will Spohr admit to a sense of being shunted aside and forgotten. While pretending to make light of the fact, he takes great pride in his awards and honours. It mildly irks him that many other senior figures in Canadian dance, including Evelyn Hart, have been promoted to the exclusive top rank of Companion of the Order of Canada. Like Brian Macdonald, another important contributor to the RWB's success in the 1960's and beyond, Spohr had been among the early crop of artists appointed to the Order of Canada after it was inaugurated in 1967. It took until January, 2002, before Macdonald was promoted to Companion. To Spohr, the fact that he has been neglected is as if all his accomplishments since being appointed to the Order in 1970, and all the achievements of the RWB under his leadership, have passed unacknowledged.

Spohr's sensitivity in this regard was partially remedied in 1998 when he was named among the six winners of that year's Governor General's Performing Arts Awards. Gweneth Lloyd had been among the first group of recipients when the awards were launched in 1992. Once again Spohr was following in Lloyd's footsteps, and proudly so.

Although the organizers of the awards do not pay for recipients to travel to the advance media announcements in Toronto and Montreal, they are urged to be in attendance if possible. Spohr was determined to oblige. He was already booked to fly to Toronto to work with Ballet Jörgen, but not quite in time for the media announcement. So, ever frugal when it involves his own comfort, Spohr boarded a Greyhound bus in Winnipeg on a Saturday morning and headed for Toronto. By the time he had reached Sault St. Marie he was feeling seriously feverish, but decided to keep going. When he reached Toronto on the Sunday afternoon he was feeling even worse and went straight to bed. Even so, still running a temperature, Spohr dutifully appeared smartly dressed at the media announcement the next morning, along with such other recipients as tenor Jon Vickers and the entire cast of The Royal Canadian Air Farce. After that, Spohr returned to bed for the next three days.

The official awards ceremony in Ottawa was a glamorous affair, or rather a series of affairs. The recipients were trooped into the gallery of the House of Commons to be "recognized" by members. On the Friday night, November 20, there was the actual presentation of medals at Government House, followed by dinner. Then, on the Saturday, there was a star-studded gala at the National Arts Centre, televised for later coast-to-coast broadcast on CBC. Spohr is never comfortable seeing himself on screen and was not happy with the video tribute included in the gala. Still, Evelyn Hart was there to dance for him and David Moroni appeared on stage to offer a personal tribute. Spohr had especially invited him in an effort to heal old wounds. In addition to his medal, Spohr returned home with a welcome cheque for $10,000.

Spohr proudly added yet another medal to his collection on July 13, 2000, when he was invested as a member of the newly launched Order of Manitoba. Sol Kanee, the former RWB board president who had played a major role in advancing the company's fortunes, was also among the twenty-seven inaugural recipients.

Soon after, Spohr set off on a new assignment, to work with former RWB dancer Sally Ann Mulcahy. She has a school in Helena, Montana, and directs a small company called Artisan Dance Theatre. Each summer, Mulcahy heads an intensive programme for young professional dancers from across the United States and abroad that culminates in a series of performances. Spohr loved the positive atmosphere engendered by Mulcahy and the enthusiasm of the students.

One of the students was Peter Quanz, an ambitious twenty-one-year-old from Ontario. Quanz had studied at The Banff Centre summer dance programme in 1996 after graduating from high school. From there he moved on for three years of training at the RWB's professional school. Quanz had already set his sights on becoming a choreographer. Spohr was impressed by Quanz' determination and, as he had for so many young dancers before, became a mentor. "He was so supportive," says Quanz. "He gave me a wall to grow up against. I'm impatient but Mr. Spohr was always taking the longer view. He'd say 'Rome wasn't built in a day. Why do you think you will be?' He always had my best long-range interest in mind."

From his own experience, Spohr knew Quanz had to get out of Winnipeg and expand his artistic horizons. In the summer of 1999 he helped Quanz secure a choreographic fellowship from the RWB named in memory of Judy and Henny Jurriens. Spohr gave Quanz introductions to an A-list of European choreographers and directors.

The following summer it was Spohr who arranged for Quanz to come to Mulcahy's programme in Helena. Spohr gave Quanz special private classes, usually late in the evening after a full day rehearsing.

"As a teacher," says Quanz, "it's the simplicity and directness of his approach that's so fantastic. In two weeks he'd corrected things about my body placement that I'd never learned in three years at the school."

Spohr was invited to return to Helena in 2001. Early in July, he set off from Winnipeg in his little car, headed along the Trans-Canada Highway towards Calgary, 1,300 kilometres away. His plan was to visit his widowed sister-in-law, Lynda Spohr. Then he was to get a ride south to Helena. Spohr had intended to break the journey to Calgary but the drive was progressing so smoothly that he decided to push on. Spohr almost ran out of gas and lost his way, but finally arrived at his sister-in-law's home, totally exhausted.

Two days later he was in Helena, working a busy schedule and relishing every minute of it. Mulcahy was delighted to have him there again. As she told a reporter from Helena's Independent Record, "Dr. Arnold Spohr is a world master. There is nobody in the world better than this man. To have him here and for him to be on the same page with me is pretty darn cool."

All was going well until Friday, August 3, the day after Artisan Dance Theatre's opening performance. Spohr began to experience chest pains and shortness of breath. He took his heart pills, re-scheduled a rehearsal and lay down to rest. Later the same day he was admitted to hospital where tests revealed that he had suffered a heart attack. "For a while we really worried that we were going to lose him," Mulcahy recalls.

The doctors informed Spohr that he was at imminent risk of a massive attack and would require heart surgery as soon as possible. As various treatment options were considered, Spohr lay worrying in his hospital bed. Quanz came to visit and was astounded when Spohr said he wanted to teach him a class right there in his large hospital room. Finally, not knowing how soon he could be treated in Canada, even if he managed to make it back alive, Spohr agreed to enter Saint Vincent Hospital and Health Center in Billings, Montana. He was flown there by air-ambulance on August 9 and underwent quadruple bypass surgery the next day.

In Canada, news of Spohr's condition spread quickly. He was inundated with messages and two days after surgery was beginning to accept calls. "Well, it seems there are some people who still want me around a bit longer," he dryly observed.

Less than a month later Spohr was back in his apartment in Winnipeg, weak in body but determined in spirit. Stephanie Ballard, a former member of Contemporary Dancers and a longtime friend of Spohr, helped nurse him back to health. Former RWB colleagues Rod Zimmer and Carol Reznick also rallied to assist. It was a long recovery but by January, 2002, Spohr was feeling fit enough to travel to Ontario to visit friends and was back there again in May to see Ballet Jörgen perform. Spohr felt much happier when he was able to start driving himself around again. His relations with André Lewis also improved.

Although Spohr understood the challenges confronitng Lewis and sympathized with his plight, he had nevertheless become critical of Lewis' artistic leadership. Spohr was alarmed by what he saw as a decline in the standard of dancing and by the inferior quality of Lewis' audience-courting programming. Alumni members Ted Patterson and Margaret Piasecki recall how Spohr would come to Association meetings full of strategies "to set things right". Spohr was by no means alone. Evelyn Hart, nearing the close of her dancing career, made no secret of her frustrations with Lewis. Just as Spohr had endured crises, disaffection among the dancers and wavering confidence from his board, so too Lewis found himself under siege. But as Spohr could have told him, storms have a way of blowing over.

By the spring of 2002, Spohr had become more sympathetic to Lewis and Lewis more open to him. In what seemed almost like a peace offering, Lewis scheduled an "Arnold Spohr Retrospective" programme for the May, 2003 Winnipeg performances, including a typical Spohr mix touching on the major phases of his directorship – Vesak's *Ecstasy of Rita Joe*, the gold medal-winning pas de deux *Belong*, Balanchine's *Allegro Brillante* and Kylian's *Symphony in D*.

• • •

Arnold Spohr will always be driven by the urge to pass on what he has learned, to help dancers achieve their dreams, to find ways to restore the RWB to what he recalls proudly as its glory days, the days when everyone stuck together, no matter what. He craves anything that can connect him productively to the company and to the art of dance. "For Arnold," says his friend and former partner Eva von Gencsy, "dance is life and death. It's a total commitment."

Spohr's commitment has been rewarded internationally with a

constellation of prizes, awards and honours throughout his career. One of the more curious is a signed proclamation from the mayor of Lafayette, Louisiana. It declares him to be an Honorary Cajun, "with all the rights and privileges and the joie de vivre thereby accruing."

The word Cajun is a corruption of "Acadiens". In the late eighteenth century, these hardy French colonists fled what are now the Canadian provinces of Nova Scotia and New Brunswick in the face of British religious persecution. Some of them finally settled in the French-held territory of Louisiana. The proclamation presented to Spohr includes a vivid description of the Cajun character. It had been written twelve years earlier by historian Bob Hamm.

The Cajun, wrote Hamm, "is a man of great friendliness who will give you the crawfish off his table, the Sac-au-Lait off his hook or the shirt off his back … If he likes you, he'll give you his whole world. If he doesn't, he'll give you a wide berth. A Cajun is a complex person, with as many ingredients in his makeup as there are in the gumbo Mama makes for special company. He has tolerance for those who earn it … charity for those who need it … a smile for those who will return it … and love for all who will share it. BUT … a Cajun can be as stubborn as a mule and as ornery as an alligator. If he sets his head on something, he'll fight a circle saw before he'll yield to your opinions. You'd as well argue with a fence post as try to change the mind of a Cajun."

Few who know Arnold Spohr could describe him better.

Author's Acknowledgements

In researching this biography I have incurred many debts of gratitude, particularly to the members of the RWB Alumni Association who, since 1989, have laboured hard to ensure that the documentary record of the RWB is preserved. For service beyond the call of duty, I am especially grateful to Association members Barbara Cook, Marilyn (Young) Marshall, Ted Patterson and Margaret (Hample) Piasecki. Alumni member Richard Rutherford has also endured my constant pestering for information with grace and patience. It goes without saying that my conversations with Kathleen Richardson, the RWB's Honorary President and tireless supporter, were crucial to my research. The RWB itself has always made me a welcome guest at its Winnipeg headquarters and my thanks especially go to staff members Greg Klassen and Arlette Anderson who repeatedly allowed me to invade their office space.

In 1977, long before the work of the Alumni Association began, a large quantity of the RWB's records was transferred to the Provincial Archives of Manitoba and there have been similar transfers in the years since. The Provincial Archives are now housed in

Winnipeg's former Civic Auditorium where many notable ballet companies, including the RWB, once performed. My thanks go to the Archives' helpful staff for their assistance in guiding me to a treasure trove of RWB history that includes official minutes of the board of directors and its various committees, correspondence files, press clippings, programmes, photographs and audio/video records. My thanks also go to the RWB for authorizing access to certain restricted files in the Archives. Jane Parkinson, Archivist of the Banff Centre, went to considerable trouble to help fill in some of the details of Arnold Spohr's long involvement with the Centre's summer dance programme. Former Banff Centre President David Leighton and his wife, Peggy Leighton, and former Banff Vice-President Ken Madsen also helped greatly in this regard. Choreographer John Neumeier was most helpful in providing his insights and in sending copies of documents from his personal collection relating to his work with the RWB. Sharon Vanderlinde, Manager of Education, Publications and Archives at the National Ballet of Canada, was quick to respond to my requests for information.

It would be difficult and invidious to try to enumerate the particular contributions of all the many people who have given of their time and knowledge to help me piece together a complicated and sometimes undocumented story. They include: Carol Anderson, Annette av Paul, Lynne Axworthy, Stephanie Ballard, Susan Bodie, Frank Bourman, Amy Bowring, Rachel Browne, Jim Cameron, Ruth Cansfield, Hilary Cartwright, Jim Clouser, Irena Cohen, John Condra, Kate Cornell, Brandon Downs, Marina Eglevsky, Dick Foose and Shirley (New) Foose, Sandra Foster, Celia Franca, Peter Garrick, Eva von Gencsy, Brian Glow, Mark Godden, John Graham, Laura Graham, Marie Hale, the late Benjamin Harkarvy, Evelyn Hart, Tom Hendry, Linde Howe-Beck, Richard Irish, Bengt Jörgen, Lendre Rodgers Kearns, the Honourable Richard Kroft, Bill Lark, Barbara Laskin, André Lewis, David Y.H. Lui, Brian Macdonald, Sheila Mackinnon, Dame Alicia Markova, Grant Marshall, Justice Deborah McCawley, Anna McGowan, John Meehan, Susan Mertens, Monique Michaud, David Moroni, Jorden Morris, Sally Ann Mulcahy, Sandra Neels, Christopher Newton, Jean (Stoneham) Orr, Richard and Pamela Ouzounian, Joost Pelt and Marilyn (Lewis) Pelt, Gaile Petursson-Hiley, Peter Quanz, Craig Ramsay, Carol Reznik, Geneviève Salbaing, Sergei Sawchyn, Jerry Shore, Maggie Morris

Smolensky, Lynda Spohr, William Starrett, Linda Stearns, Gailene Stock, Leonard Stone, Grant Strate, Tom Stroud, Lynda Swiadon, Sonia Taverner, Gérard Theoret, Eddy Toussaint, Gail Thomas, Rudi van Dantzig, William Whitener, Joseph Wilder, Anthony Williams, Ken Winters, Gordon Wright, Bonnie Wyckoff, Max Wyman, Rod Zimmer and David Zurak. If I have inadvertently omitted any names, my apologies are abject. Each person in this list has contributed in a significant way.

Although I never imagined that I would one day be writing a biography of Arnold Spohr, I am now grateful that my curiosity about the RWB and its past prompted me to keep notes of conversations with such important and now departed company figures as Salvatore Aiello, Agnes de Mille, Betty Farrally, Henny Jurriens, Gweneth Lloyd, David Peregrine, Norbert Vesak and David Yeddeau. Arnold Spohr has suffered me with unswerving patience. Whatever conclusions I have drawn in this book are naturally my responsibility alone.

A number of books and references have been invaluable to me in preparing this biography. I would especially refer those who wish to learn more about the RWB to Max Wyman's important volumes: *The Royal Winnipeg Ballet: The First Forty Years* (Toronto, Doubleday Canada, 1978); *Dance Canada: An Illustrated History* (Vancouver, Douglas & McIntyre, 1989); and *Evelyn Hart: An Intimate Portrait* (Toronto, McClelland & Stewart, 1991). Also valuable are Christopher Dafoe's *Dancing Through Time: The First Fifty Years of Canada's Royal Winnipeg Ballet* (Winnipeg, Portage & Main Press, 1990); James Neufeld's *Power to Rise: The Story of the National Ballet of Canada* (Toronto, University of Toronto Press, 1996); Celia Franca and photographer Ken Bell's *The National Ballet of Canada: A Celebration* (Toronto, University of Toronto Press, 1978); Carol Anderson's *Rachel Browne: Dancing Toward the Light* (Winnipeg, J. Gordon Shillingford Publishing, 1999); and *Grant Strate: A Memoir* (Toronto, Dance Collection Danse Press/es, 2002). The *Encyclopedia of Theatre Dance in Canada/Encyclopédie de la danse théâtrale au Canada* (Toronto, Dance Collection Danse Press/es, 2000) is an indispensable source of factual information.

A grant from the Dance Section of the Canada Council for the Arts helped underwrite the costs of my research in Winnipeg and several other cities. Lawrence and Miriam Adams, my publishers at

Dance Collection Danse, have been a constant source of guidance, encouragement and necessary goading. The friendly and efficient staff at Place Louis Riel All-Suite Hotel in Winnipeg made my many research trips to the city pleasant and affordable.

My special friends, Leonard Genore and Bramwell Pemberton, have stood by me throughout and countered my occasional spells of writer's despair with love, good humour and practical help.

Publisher's Acknowledgements

We gratefully acknowledge the people whose labours and generosity have allowed this book to happen:

The Laidlaw Foundation, Donald K. Johnson, and the Royal Winnipeg Ballet Alumni Association, whose financial contributions put this project on the rails; Margaret Piasecki for her time, undivided attention, advice and wisdom; Stephanie Ballard whose energy, enthusiasm and humour gave us confidence; the text editors and readers – Carol Anderson, Amy Bowring, Kaija Pepper and Teresa Spanjer – whose extraordinarily quick work must have kept them up late into the night/s; the University of Manitoba Archives for their co-operation in finding research materials; Reg Skene for his knowledge of correct spellings; Evelyn Hart and Kathleen Richardson for kindly assembling their thoughts and words with which to paint the Preface and Foreword for this book; Michael Crabb for his valiant research efforts and skills, and his insightful, intriguing and entertaining manuscript – which we hope will inspire a new generation of dance writers to produce more work; and, of course, Arnold Spohr for being ARNOLD SPOHR!

Lawrence and Miriam Adams
Co-Directors, Dance Collection Danse